A Hundred Years in
Tardebigge

A *Hundred Years in* Tardebigge

The Parish in the Twentieth Century

The Revd Alan White, M.Sc., M.A., M.Ed.

BREWIN BOOKS

BREWIN BOOKS
56 Alcester Road,
Studley,
Warwickshire,
B80 7LG

www.brewinbooks.com

Published by Brewin Books 2011

A CIP catalogue record for this book is available
from the British Library.

ISBN: 978-1-85858-487-4

Printed by
Cambrian Printers.

Contents

List of Illustrations

The cover photograph of Tardebigge Church is by Dave Besley

The source, where known, of each illustration has been added in brackets following the caption

Introduction

IN 1931 the book "A Thousand Years in Tardebigge" was published. It had been researched and written by Margaret Dickins, A.R.C.O., a daughter of Canon Allan Dickins, Vicar of Tardebigge from 1855 to 1917. It contains a wealth of information about the history of the Parish of Tardebigge from the tenth up to and including the nineteenth century. The book ends with an account of her father's life and ministry. The aim of this book is to continue the history of the parish by recording many of the changes and events which have since taken place in the parish during the twentieth century. In so doing it has been necessary to refer back to earlier events which set the scene in various parts of the parish at the beginning of the 1900s.

Until 1855 the Parish of Tardebigge extended over a large area. It covered, in addition to its present extent, the centre of Redditch and an area to the north of the town, including the remains and grounds of Bordesley Abbey, and it also included Batchley and Webheath. In 1855 the growing town of Redditch became a separate parish, so that at the beginning of the twentieth century Tardebigge Parish consisted of its present area, including Brockhill, together with Webheath. It was not until 1981 that the Parish of Webheath was created, mostly out of the Parish of Tardebigge, but including a small part of the Parish of Headless Cross, to become a constituant part of the Ridge Team of parishes. Hence this history covers Webheath, including the Foxlydiate area.

The twentieth century, with its many technological discoveries and advances and the two world wars, saw great changes in the way of life of the population of this country in general. Many of these changes, mentioned in the first chapter of this book, had an impact upon the landscape, the employment, and the domestic life of people living in the Parish of Tardebigge. Particular to Tardebigge and Bentley were the changes which came about when, immediately following the second world war, the Windsor-Clive family sold Hewell Grange and their extensive Tardebigge Estates and severed their ties with Tardebigge, and the Gray-Cheape family abandoned their former residence, Bentley Manor, and made the decision that it should be demolished.

Although the Brockhill housing development within the boundary of the Redditch New Town has meant the loss of farm land, including that of Birchensale Farm, nevertheless the Parish of Tardebigge remains predominantly rural, and farming continues to extend over most of the land. The history of many of the farms is contained in chapter 10, but some of the farms are covered in chapters 7 and 8 in the history of the locality in which they are situated.

The story of these and other changes and events which took place in the parish is told in the following pages. Information has been culled from parish magazines, local newspapers, local almanacs and county directories, parish registers, personal scrapbooks and, not least, the memories of many older people, some of which are recorded in the final chapter of this book.

I am very grateful to many people for the loan by them of diaries, documents and photographs, and to all who, in interviews and general conversation, have supplied information. My thanks especially to the following people: Michael Ainge, Sue Anfilogoff, Rosemary Ashwin, Elizabeth Atkins, Sue Atkinson, Joan Badger, Robert Barnett, Eileen Beale, Roger and Peggy Boss, Peter Burman, Linda Butler (grand-daughter of Alf Westover), Jo Casey, Rosalind Chambers, Ken Clarke, Gladys Eaborn, Kate Eades, Molly Edwards, Rhona Farrin, Andrew Frisby, Peter Frowley, Diana Gibbs, Sheila Gibbs, David Goulbourne, Madge Guise, Philip Guise (for the loan of Tardebigge Village Hall Committee minute book, 1911-14), Ruth Harper, Martin Harris (for the history of Webheath Baptist Church), Tim Hill, Roy Hims, Pat Hutchings, Martin Kealy, Brian Kimberley, Ray King,

Olga Lane, Andrew Mason, Tony May, Jennie McGregor-Smith, Bobbie Matulja, Mary Mitchell, Michael Morgan, Mary Morris, Norman Neasom, Mavis Pardoe, Mary Peers, The Earl of Plymouth, Michael and Elisabeth Price, Anthony Scott Warren, Fred Shrimpton, Audrey Stubbings, Connie Swann, Keith Tolley, Lionel Tongue, Ron Tongue, Doreen Underhill, George Underhill, Malcolm Ward, Peter Whitaker, Stephen Wood, Marion Wormington.

I also thankfully acknowledge the assistance received from the staff of Worcester Record Office and History Centre, the Local History Department of Birmingham Central Library, and Bromsgrove Library.

Last, but not least, I am very grateful to my daughter, Helen Chant, and my friend, Rosemary Troth, for carefully monitoring and correcting the original text and for proof reading.

Alan White
March 2011

Map of the Ecclesiastical Parish of Tardebigge c. 1950.

CHAPTER 1

A Century of
Great Changes

URING THE twentieth century the inhabitants of the Parish of Tardebigge were subject to the many great changes which affected the lives
of people in the country as a whole. Many of these changes are therefore
an integral part of the local history and need to be recorded along with the
particular changes which took place in the parish.

Of the many changes for the better which affected the lives of people
countrywide during the century, perhaps the most beneficial were the
improvements in hygiene, including the installation of indoor sanitation
and the supply to households of piped drinking water, also the supply of
gas, and electricity. In the more rural and isolated parts of Tardebigge
Parish some of these benefits were slow to arrive, and in some parts there
is still no gas and no piped sewage disposal. Domestic appliances, cookers,
vacuum cleaners, refrigerators and freezers have also transformed household management. The installation of central heating has also added to
life's comforts, but many people living in the older houses in the countryside still enjoy the pleasures of coal or log fires, as well as enduring the
draughts from ill-fitting doors and windows.

Amongst material changes affecting things in everyday use was the introduction of plastic materials, used widely in the manufacture of furniture, window frames, liquid containers, and very many other items and gadgets in daily use. Another development was the use of synthetic materials as an alternative to natural materials such as wool and cotton, in the manufacture of clothing and furnishings. Yet another invention which has come into almost universal use, and which we take for granted, is the zip fastener which has transformed the manufacture of clothing and many other items and has proved to be a great convenience.

In the early part of the century, as was usual in earlier times, most women, following marriage, used to stay at home to look after the home and care for their young children as well as their husbands on their return from work. Families with as many as ten or more children were not uncommon in the early 1900s, and there were many such large families in Tardebigge Parish. By the end of the century families had been reduced in size through birth control to mostly one, two or three children, and many women were pursuing a career or other employment to augment the family income. Most men, for their part, learnt to share in the household chores and shopping, as well as gardening and caring for the almost universal family car or cars.

One casualty over the years has been the institution of marriage together with the preliminary procedures, chaperones, courtship, engagement and parental consent. Previously frowned on, the cohabitation of men and women outside of marriage has become common and there are now many one-parent families for various reasons, including sexual promiscuity, a decline in marital fidelity and the availability of easy divorce.

Other social changes followed the introduction of secondary education in 1902, the gradual raising of the school leaving age from 13 to 15, then 16, and the increase in sixth form and university and college education. In the early 1900s many children used to leave school as soon as possible, girls to become household servants, shop assistants or shorthand typists, boys to be trained as apprentices in local industry or to go into farming. Today most children stay on into the sixth form and go on to higher education, looking for a business or professional career, often, in the process moving away from the family home to live and work elsewhere.

Another change, affecting us all, has been in medicine, where the family doctor, who used to be available at all times and charged his patients for his services, has, following the introduction of the National Health Service in 1948, become a partner in a joint practice of several doctors working limited hours, with out-of-hours coverage. The health of people in general has improved; diseases such as tuberculosis, diphtheria and poliomyelitis have been practically eradicated, and others such as pneumonia and influenza more successfully treatable. However there have been setbacks including the spread of AIDS and the continuing health hazards of drink and tobacco and, in more recent years, drugs.

The twentieth century also saw the establishment of the Welfare State and a welcome reduction in dire poverty. In the early years, before its inception, the poor, many unable to subsist, were admitted as paupers to the local workhouse (the one in Bromsgrove served the destitute of Tardebigge); others begged on the streets or from door to door. The Welfare State has, over the years, seen the closure of workhouses, helped the poor and needy with allowances and introduced the old-age pension. In earlier years many needy people received help from their local church. At Tardebigge there were, until recent years, four charities: the 1631 Whitbread Charity of Endimion Canning for the distribution of bread to the poor after Sunday Services; the 1859 James Holyoake Charity for the provision of blankets, sheets etc to the needy; the 1897 Queen Victoria Jubilee Convalescent Homes Fund, and the 1936 John Johnson Fund. In the 1990s the Charity Commissioners approved the amalgamation of these charities into two, one for relief of need and the other for relief in sickness, both administered by one trust consisting of the parish priests and lay representatives from the areas of the parish as it was in 1859, including part of Webheath and part of St Stephen's, Redditch. Now individuals and groups, such as schools, can apply to the combined charity for modest grants for special needs.

Another social change, especially affecting those in the countryside has been the breakdown of class distinctions. In the early 1900s, and persisting in some places well into the century, the landed gentry and professional people were treated by their tenants and other ordinary folk with due deference, the doffed cap or raised hat, the bow or curtsy, and addressed as Sir or Madam. In Tardebigge the Earl of Plymouth and his family, and in Bentley Pauncefoot the Squire of Bentley, were thus respected, as well as the Vicar and senior members of the Dixon farming family.

Following WW2 the growth of supermarkets led to the inevitable decline and closure of many small shops. In rural Tardebigge in the early part of the century there were several small shops, not as we know them with a plate glass window and display, but just the front room of a private house with, for sale, foodstuffs, sweets and tobacco, candles, paraffin, and other requirements. Until WW2 there was little inflation and prices were stable. Since then prices have increased dramatically. For instance, milk used to be only 2d a pint and a small loaf of bread cost 3d. Before decimalisation in 1971 there were 240d (old pence) to the pound (twelve pence to the shilling and 20 shillings to the pound), and coinage included the threepenny bit, the sixpence (or "tanner"), the shilling (or "bob"), the florin (2 shillings) and the half-crown (two shillings and sixpence). Until decimalisation we had a ten-shilling note and a pound note.

During the century advances in food hygiene meant that, in shops, whereas many items of grocery such as butter, bacon, sugar and biscuits used to be weighed or counted and put into the shopping basket in paper bags, in the latter part of the century most were pre-packed and, as a result, packaging added significantly to the increasing problem of refuse disposal. Milk, now pasteurised and delivered to the door in bottles or purchased from shops and supermarkets in plastic containers, used to be delivered by many small farmers, who had a local milk round, in churns, straight from the cow and measured out in pints and gills into the jugs of householders on the doorstep. A number of farmers in Tardebigge Parish had local milk rounds extending to parts of Bromsgrove and Redditch.

Dress, especially that of women, changed over the century, partly due to the wars in which they took on many traditionally male occupations. The ankle-length skirt worn by women in the early 1900s gave way to skirt lengths which changed from year to year in accordance with the trend in fashion; but by the end of the century, it was "wear what you please", and for the younger generation, sadly, colourful skirts and dresses have been widely replaced by drab jeans or trouser suits. Men's clothing, however, has changed little apart from being, mainly outside of business and

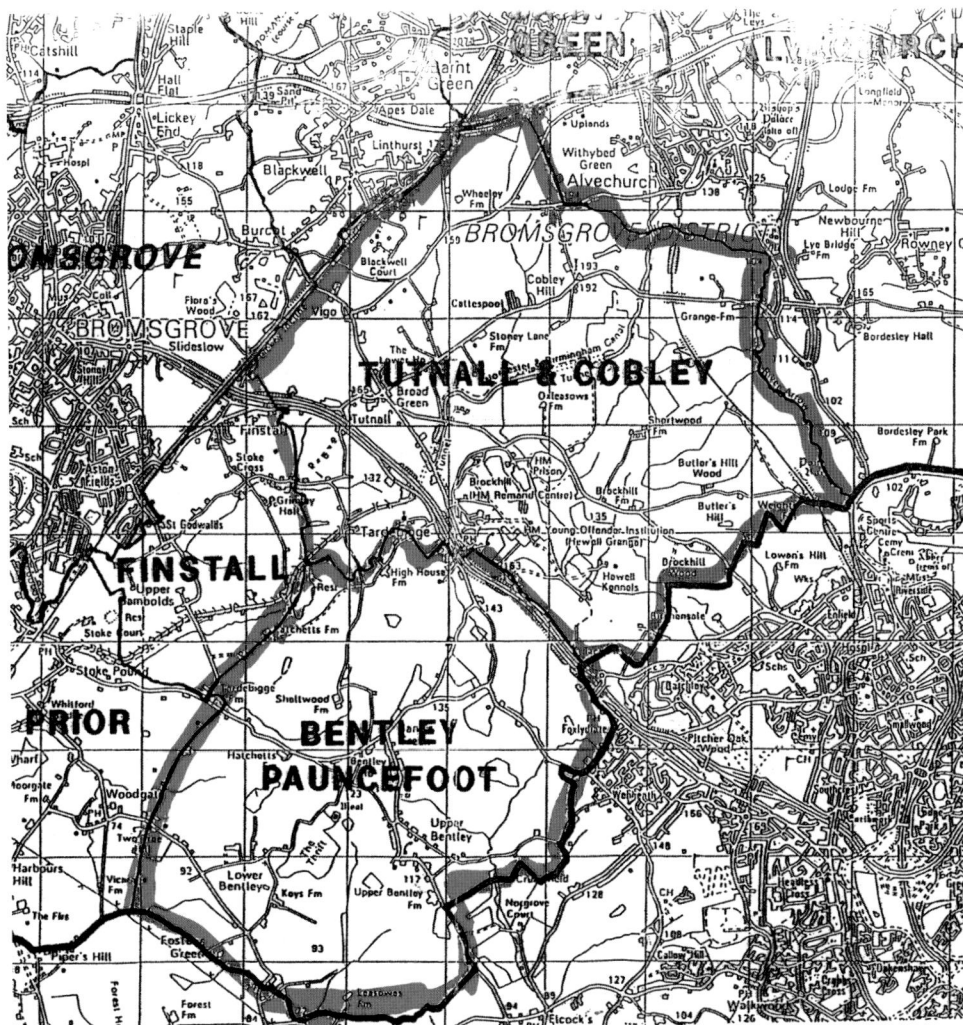

Map of the Civil Parishes of Tutnall and Cobley and Bentley Pauncefoot.

professional wear, more casual. Between the wars there was the "plus-four" phase, and, in more recent times, the wearing of shorts in the summer.

During the century, road transport was revolutionised by the advent of motor cars and lorries. Roads and lanes, formerly adequate for the use of horses and carts, had to be widened and their surfaces firmed and strengthened with concrete or tarmacadam. Locally the narrow main road between Bromsgrove and Redditch became quite inadequate for the growing traffic of the mid-century, and so the A448 dual carriageway was constructed in the 1970s, and this necessitated changes to the local road system along its length, especially in the Parish of Tardebigge at Tutnall, Hewell and Foxlydiate.

It is not always realised that Tardebigge Parish has a section of railway across it, but no station, between Alvechurch and Redditch. The railway used to extend beyond Redditch to Alcester and Evesham, but the section Alcester to Evesham closed to passenger traffic in October 1962, passenger traffic between Redditch and Alcester ceased in June 1963, and freight was finally withdrawn in July 1964. Thereafter the tunnel beyond the station in Redditch was closed and the redundant track lifted. Following the end of steam traction in 1968, diesels took over until the line from Barnt Green to Redditch was electrified in the late summer and autumn of 1993.

Some of the most significant advances made in the last hundred years have been in the realms of personal and general communications, the inventions of radio and television, the almost universal extension of the telephone system to private homes as well as to businesses, and now the extensive use of computers and the internet, of email, and ultimately the ubiquitous mobile phone. The telegram disappeared mid-century, together with the telegraph boy on his bicycle. At Tardebigge, as elsewhere, the rural post office, for many years located at the New Wharf, then at the Old Wharf, and finally at Broad Green, closed for business well before the more recent spate of closures of post offices across the country.

Many people in the parish of Tardebigge were, as mentioned in the Introduction, closely affected by the sale of the Plymouth Estate in 1946, the consequent loss of the presence and influence of the Plymouth family locally, and the loss, by many, of their employment in the Windsor household and on the estate. To a lesser extent many estate workers at Bentley also lost their jobs following the departure of the Gray-Cheape family from their Manor House, which was demolished soon after WW2.

A major factor which began to affect the Parish of Tardebigge directly in the 1990s by greatly increasing its population was the creation, in 1964, of the Redditch Development Corporation. As in the case of other post-war developments such as Welwyn Garden City, Milton Keynes and Telford, designed to house overspill families from the cities, the function of the Corporation was to plan and monitor the expansion of Redditch to house overspill families chiefly from the Birmingham area. Because the

Birchensale Farm area of Tardebigge Parish lay within the boundaries of the newly created Redditch Council, it was earmarked for housing, and the building of new homes began in 1996 alongside Salters Lane, opposite Batchley. Because of the proximity of the Brockhill Woods, the area, with its spine road from the Foxlydiate roundabout to Brockhill Lane, was designated "Brockhill". It is estimated that the new development has added around three thousand to the pre-existing population of around one thousand people in the parish of Tardebigge. It was the Development Corporation which was responsible for the above-mentioned planning and construction of the A448 dual carriageway between Bromsgrove and Redditch.

In the mainly rural parts of the parish farming has continued to dominate the scene. Apart from the introduction of new crops, such as oil seed rape, and the loss of the elm trees due to disease, there has been little visible change in the landscape but, as detailed in chapter 10, farming has been concentrated mainly into larger businesses, using machinery and minimum manpower. Fortunately the rural character of the present parish, apart from the Brockhill housing development, has been protected from the invasion of large industrial firms and housing estates by green belt legislation and because it lies mostly within the Bromsgrove District Council area.

CHAPTER 2

Hewell Grange – From Stately Home to Prison

ॐ

SOME BACKGROUND HISTORY

For 400 years, from 1542 until World War 2, Hewell Grange remained the residence of many generations of the Windsor family. It was following the dissolution of the monasteries in 1539 that King Henry VIII offered the large estate, which had belonged to the Cistercian monks of Bordesley Abbey, to the Windsor family in exchange for their estate at Stanwell, near Staines, which he himself wanted. Having little or no option but to agree to this, Lord Andrew Windsor took possession of his new domain in the Parish of Tardebigge in 1542. By this time the Abbey buildings had been badly plundered and damaged and were uninhabitable, so he chose to make his home at Hewell Grange, which was evidently the most suitable of the farm houses on the estate. In the following year he died and his son William took over the house and the estate. The house was very likely modified and extended in the early years.

In addition to acquiring the monastic lands and property, the Windsors also gained the manorial rights of the manors of Tardebigge and Bordesley, which had originally been granted to the Abbey when it was founded by

Hewell Grange, rear view of the house and gardens.

the Empress Maude in 1138. This brought in, from the tenant farmers and others, income from the tithes and from the court fees and fines.

In 1682 Lord Thomas Windsor, having served his Sovereign, King Charles II, well as Lord Lieutenant of Worcestershire, as Governor of the new colony of Jamaica, and as naval Admiral, inflicting a defeat upon the Spaniards, was created the first Earl of Plymouth. It was he who purchased from the Crown the Lordship of the Manor of Bromsgrove, thus extending his estate and increasing its income. In 1687 Thomas's young grandson, Other, the third Earl of Plymouth, married Elizabeth Lewis, heiress to St Fagan's Castle, a Tudor mansion in extensive grounds near Cardiff, together with the estate on which now stands Penarth. Subsequently, for many years, the Windsors made little use of St Fagan's, especially after the replacement of the old Hewell Grange by a new impressive stone mansion completed in 1712. Remains of this Palladian style house, built round a courtyard, still stand.

In 1833, on the death of Other Archer, the 6th Earl of Plymouth, his sister Harriet inherited the whole of the Hewell Estate. Back in 1819 Harriet had married Robert Clive, a grandson of Clive of India and they had been living at Oakly Park, Bromfield, near Ludlow. From 1833 the couple spent much of their time also living at Hewell. It was thus, through their marriage, that Oakly Park was added to the Hewell and St Fagan's estates.

Another consequence was that the family surname was changed to Windsor-Clive. From 1833 the Earldom passed to Harriet's two childless brothers, Andrews and Henry, in turn. When Henry died in 1843 the Earldom lapsed.

Lady Harriet was granted the title of Baroness Windsor in 1844. Her husband died in 1854, but she lived on until 1869, during which time she took a great interest in the welfare of the people on her estates, in the growth of Redditch and its industries, and in the churches and schools. She and her husband had three children, all boys. The eldest son, Robert Windsor-Clive, who married Lady Mary Bridgeman, went to live at St Fagan's in 1852. There he was interested in overseeing the development of Penarth on the estate as a seaport. He died in 1859. It was his son, Robert Windsor-Clive, Harriet's grandson, who succeeded her when she died in 1869. He was only twelve years old at the time. It was his mother, Lady Mary, who was then responsible for his upbringing. He went to school at Eton and then on to St John's College, Cambridge. When, in 1878, he came of age, there were traditional large-scale celebrations on each of his three properties. In Hewell Park a great marquee was erected and there was feasting and many speeches were made in praise of his upbringing and expressing hopes for his future happiness and the well-being of his estates, his workpeople and tenants.

In 1883 he married 18-year-old Alberta Paget, daughter of Sir Augustus Paget, formerly British Ambassador in Rome, and they had four children, three sons and a daughter.

Soon after their marriage Lord Windsor surprised the neighbourhood by embarking upon a major enterprise, the building of a new impressive Elizabethan-style mansion to replace the one built in 1712 which was in poor repair and suffering from damp and insecure foundations due to being built too close to the Hewell lake. He had an artistic temperament and he travelled quite frequently to Italy where some of the buildings he saw had an influence on the design and furnishings of his new mansion which took seven years (1884-91) to complete. The dark red sandstone used in its construction came from Runcorn in Cheshire, being transported by canal to the Old Wharf and then by a temporary horse tram-road up to the building site. No expense was spared in its construction and in furnishing the magnificent lofty hall, the chapel within the house, and other rooms. The finished building and its gardens and grounds were Lord Windsor-Clive's pride and joy and the reason why Hewell remained his principal residence throughout the rest of his life.

TWENTIETH CENTURY HEWELL UNDER TWO EARLS OF PLYMOUTH

By the beginning of the new century, Hewell Grange was a bustling place for much of the time with, besides Lord and Lady Windsor-Clive and their four teenage children, servants and gardeners, also, at times, relatives and distinguished visitors. By this time Lord Windsor-Clive had taken on various posts and responsibilities in public life, including those of Lord Lieutenant of the County of Glamorgan, Deputy-Lieutenant of the Counties of Worcestershire and Shropshire, Lieutenant-Colonel of the Worcester Imperial Yeomanry, Paymaster-General to the Forces (1891/2) and Mayor of Cardiff (1895/6).

In 1905, as he continued to serve the community in some of these and other ways, including the Government post of First Commissioner of Works (1902-5), Vice-president of Bromsgrove Cottage Hospital and a trustee of Bromsgrove School, he was made Earl of Plymouth, thus recreating the Earldom which had lapsed in 1843.

On Wednesday 3 January 1906 a great banquet was held at Hewell, in a special banqueting room erected within the ruins of the old mansion, to celebrate the coming of age (actually on 23 October 1905) of the Hon. Other Robert Windsor-Clive, eldest son of the Earl. The large gathering included guests from the nobility and gentry, the Worcester Imperial Yeomanry, farm tenants, and residents from Tardebigge, Redditch, Bromsgrove, Barnt Green and Alvechurch. There were many loyal addresses and presentations and hopes expressed for the young man's future well-being. The celebrations continued with a Ball on the Thursday and a meeting of the Worcestershire Hounds and a Servants' Ball on the Friday.

There was great sadness at Hewell when, in 1908, Other Robert died in Agra, India, whilst serving as Assistant District Commissioner to Lord Minto, the Viceroy of India. In 1911 Tardebigge Village Hall was built in his memory, by the Earl, to serve the people living locally on his estate. A

Robert Windsor Clive, first Earl of Plymouth, and his family c.1910. L to r: Hon Archer Windsor Clive, Lady Phyllis, The Earl, Ivor Viscount Windsor, Alberta Countess of Plymouth (Lord Plymouth).

further bitter blow to the Earl and his family was the death of his youngest son, Archer, an officer in the Coldstream Guards, killed in action in France at the beginning of the War in August 1914 in the battle of Landrecies during the retreat from Mons. On the day following the receipt of this news, the Earl, characteristically, fulfilled his engagement to preside over a forces recruiting meeting in Cardiff.

Besides fulfilling his many public duties, the Earl found time to indulge his artistic talents. He produced sketches and plans, and he designed furniture and stained glass windows, including the East window in Tardebigge Church. He collected many works of art, ornaments and paintings, and he encouraged various crafts to be practised in his Village Hall. He became the chairman of both the Tate Gallery and the National Trust. When the Crystal Palace in London was threatened with being sold and demolished in 1911, he opened a fund to buy it for the nation and contributed £35,000 himself to complete the purchase.

A special table, a present for the Viceroy of India, with Henry Tremlett, the estate carpenter who made it, and young Alf Westover who carved it, c. 1900 (Linda Butler).

Whilst in residence at Hewell Grange the Earl and Countess took a great interest in the church and local affairs, and in the welfare of the tenants on their estates. Hewell Park was often the venue for social events, one of which was the annual Flower Show organised by the Hewell and Foxlydiate Horticultural Society and held on the first Monday in August which used to be a Bank Holiday.

In March 1923 the Earl died suddenly at his London residence, Great Cumberland Place. His funeral took place at St Bartholomew's Church, Tardebigge, being conducted by the vicar, the Revd F G Ellerton. Besides his family, estate workers and local people, there were many high-ranking persons present, including statesmen and representatives of the many organisations which had benefited from the Earl's interest and active support.

Ivor Miles, second Earl of Plymouth, and his family. L to r: Other Robert (later the third Earl), Lady Plymouth, Lord Plymouth, Gillian, Richard, and (in front) David, Rosula, Clarissa (Linda Butler).

The second Earl of Plymouth who, at the age of 43, succeeded his father in 1923 was his only remaining son, Ivor Miles. Following the outbreak of war in 1914 Ivor had served with the Worcester Yeomanry in France, then in Malta, and finally, back in France in the Intelligence Corps. In 1921 he had married Lady Irene Corona Charteris, and they had three sons and three daughters. He inherited his father's sense of duty and followed him in the posts of Lord Lieutenant of Glamorganshire and Deputy Lieutenant of Worcestershire and of Shropshire. He had been M.P. for Ludlow for only a year when, following his father's death, he became a member of the House of Lords where, over the years, he took on various important government posts.

Apart from his official duties, he was happy to pursue his sporting interests. He had played cricket and tennis during his time at Eton and at Trinity College, Cambridge, and he played tennis for Cambridge University in 1909/10. Locally he often played in the Hewell cricket team. He also became a playing member of the Hewell Bowling Club and arranged matches between the Hewell and St Fagan's clubs. He was president of Bromsgrove and Hewell Cricket Clubs and of Worcestershire Bowling Association.

Unlike his father, Ivor Miles, though spending some months each year at Hewell, spent more of his time at St Fagan's. When, after the start of World War 2 in 1939, Hewell and its grounds were taken over for military use by the Royal Army Ordinance Corps, the Earl and his family had to live elsewhere, mainly at St Fagan's. There, after a spell of ill health, he died in 1943. His eldest son, Other Robert Ivor, the third Earl, must have realised as the war continued that Hewell had become a liability and was no longer really needed by his family.

Back in the mid-nineteenth century, the family's wealth had greatly increased due to the Bordesley area of their estate being developed for use by industry, factories, warehouses and dwellings. Some of this wealth was wisely invested in land at Cofton Hackett and Barnt Green, then sparseley populated. Later, to help meet the cost of building the new mansion, money was raised by the sale, in 1889, of desirable building plots on some of this land in the Lickey Hills area. In 1919, to raise further income, there was a major sale of further land in the Barnt Green and Cofton Hackett areas. Death duties, following the death of his father in 1943, together with other taxes and the increasing cost of maintaining a superfluous property, led to the third Earl's decision, in 1945, to sell

Hewell Grange and the whole of the Hewell estate. In August of that year he wrote to all the tenants:-

> I know the tenants, for whom my father and his family have always had so friendly regard during the many years that Hewell has been our home, will know, without my telling them, my very great regret at having to write this letter. The very large death duties which have to be paid make it inevitable that I should sell the estate, and the moment has come when the matter must be carried through. In coming to this, to us, very sad conclusion, I am making every effort to ensure that the estate is sold as a whole, hoping in these circumstances that the tenants will be more likely to be left undisturbed. I shall hope at the first opportunity to see you and, furthermore, never to lose touch with the friends who will always be associated with days of great happiness and goodwill.

In 1946 Hewell Grange and its surrounding parkland, extending to 231 acres, at first suggested as suitable for a girls' school, was purchased by the Home Office, and in the following year it opened as a Young Offenders Institution, or Borstal. The rest of the large estate was bought by a consortium of four local people, comprising: Joseph Beckett, farmer of Shortwood; Howard Bird, company director of Redditch; Dr Herbert Houfton, medical practitioner of Redditch, and John Coney of High House Farm, Tardebigge. In the face of competition they were given, by the executors of the Estate, 48 hours in which to agree the purchase. Their decision to do so was made at a lengthy meeting, chaired by Joe Beckett, which went on into the early hours of the following morning. Following the purchase, estate agents Guy Bigwood of Birmingham acted for the syndicate in selling by auction on 8 July 1946 many of the properties. These included Lowans Hill Farm, Stoney Lane Farm, Hollow Tree Farm, Birchensale Farm, building land on the top of the Lickey Hills, manufacturing premises "Windsor Mills" and "Forge Mills", houses, cottages, woodland, and fishing rights on the Worcester and Birmingham Canal between Alvechurch and Stoke Prior and on Tardebigge Reservoir. Other properties omitted from the sale were divided by agreement between the four. Joe Beckett and his wife Janie took up residence at Hewell House, the farm house previously occupied by the Earl of Plymouth's estate manager.

Following the end of the War, the Third Earl decided to make his home permanently at Oakly Park, near Ludlow, and in 1946 he gave St Fagan's, the house, gardens and estate of some 18 acres to the Welsh nation. Since then it has been developed as the National History Museum of Wales with, besides the house and gardens, a rural area with a scattered collection of over forty interesting old farms, industrial, community and domestic buildings moved from various locations all over Wales.

MEMORIES OF LIFE AT THE STATELY HOME

Especially when the family was in residence at Hewell, but also at other times, many people were employed in the house and the grounds. There was the home farm with its dairy herd, stables for shire horses used on the farm for ploughing and transport, hunting horses, polo ponies and children's ponies. Besides farm workers and grooms, other people were employed in the timberyard, in the carpenters' shop, in the dairy, the kennels, in the walled vegetable garden beyond the village hall, and as gamekeepers. In addition there were individuals employed as laundry workers, electricians, plumbers, blacksmiths and gardeners.

Amongst senior officials there was the Estate Manager, for many years Lionel Foley Lambert, J.P., living at Greenhill but with his office at Hewell. Also holding office for many years were Henry Bate, Land Surveyor; Henry Spiers, Estate Bailiff living at Hewell Lodge; Andrew Pettigrew and, following him in 1915, Frank Molyneux, head gardener, living in the house next to the Hewell gardens in Holyoake's Lane; Emmanuel Phillips and later Joseph Carey, Head Gamekeepers; Sir Mortimer Margesson, private secretary to the 2nd Earl; and John Wilson, electrician to the Earl. Other lesser mortals who were involved are mentioned in the following extract from the recorded memories of Marion Tongue who, before her marriage to Ernest Reeve, worked from 1930 to 1938 as a housemaid at the Grange:

Hewell Grange was a little town all on its own. As well as the housekeeper, Mrs Gates, and housemaids, there was the butler, two footmen, the cook, three kitchen maids, a daily woman, three odd-job men and four laundry maids. I don't know how many gardeners there were, I know there were three in the kitchen gardens, they were a long way off from the house. The gardeners used to grow all the food for the family's house in Hyde Park in London; they sent it every day by rail. We had nurses and nursery maids and governesses and a schoolroom maid. The Earl and Countess of Plymouth had six children. They used the same pram that the Countess had when she was a baby. The gentry never throw anything out.

We used to have to be downstairs at half-past six. That meant half-past six and not 25 minutes to seven. It could be a bit earlier but never a minute later. They were all very punctual as regards time. My first job was lighting fires, first was the housekeeper's room, the second was the business room and the third was the dining room. The family often had guests staying overnight, and at seven we had to call the gentry with a cup of tea if they hadn't got a ladies' maid. We used to have to go to the butler's to get the tray then go to the kitchen for the water for the tea. Sometimes the footmen would carry the tray upstairs for us but, of course, they were busy first thing in the morning. We used to have important guests; Anthony Eden stayed there and the Prime Minister, Stanley Baldwin.

At eight o'clock there would be breakfast, then from twelve until one o'clock was our lunch. We always had our own meal before the gentry; we never had what was left. Ours was cooked specially for us and there was always ample. At a quarter past one the gentry had lunch and as soon as they went into the dining room we used to go to the drawing room and fluff up the cushions and tidy up. We finished work at two o'clock and had two hours off until four o'clock. Often we had to put water in each room in a can and put a towel over it for the gentry to wash their hands before they went downstairs.

The dinner was at about a quarter to eight. We would go and look round the bedrooms to see they were alright, turn the beds down and put the hot water bottles in. Then we had finished for the day. We would be in bed long before ten o'clock.

We had half a day off each week, which started at two o'clock. On my half day I would sometimes go home. From October to February the shooting season was on, there were shooting parties and we were much too busy to have our half days. We never had them made up. We forgot about the outside world, we were so happily engaged with our work.

In the summer the family were away and we used to spring-clean. We had fifteen shillings a week for food, one pint of milk a day, and the gardeners used to bring us vegetables on a Saturday morning; they had to last a week.

Her ladyship was very good-looking, tall and smart. We didn't see much of his Lordship. He was the Under Secretary for Foreign Affairs, and he was often in London. They were a very nice family. If any of the village people were ill, food used to be sent to them.

His Lordship and her Ladyship didn't give money, they gave presents. I remember when the butler had a cruet and the housemaids had brooches, never any money. At Christmas there were such a lot of us for presents that we had to queue up in the linen room in a long line. His Lordship would hand the present to her Ladyship and she would give it. I remember I once had an umbrella and another time I had a nice nightdress with lace on the top.

I loved every inch of Hewell Grange. It was a beautiful place. There was a notice in the house telling you how long it had taken to build – seven years. The dining room had hand-painted silk on the walls. One of the bedrooms had hand-painted leather on the walls. There was an electric lift and the whole house was rewired in the 1930s.

In the summer time we used to play tennis in the ruins of the old house. His Lordship had a tennis court made there with a bathroom attached. He had a tennis pro., Ernie James, to teach him. Ernie played with him regularly.

We had the foxhounds meet there, outside in the ruins. Drinks were provided and all the staff had drinks. There was always beer for the men.

UNDER THE HOME OFFICE

Hewell Grange Borstal opened in October 1946. It was run on Public School lines, and the young offenders, known as trainees, were subject to strict discipline. Up at 6.30 am, they had 15 minutes of physical exercise and, after breakfast, were out and about working from 8.00 am to 4.30 pm. They had evening classes and at 8.45 pm house prayers. The aim was to train them in various skills and personal and social responsibility. They were allowed, under supervision, to assist in the local community at, for example, the Adult Training Centre at Redditch, the Saltways Cheshire Home in Webheath, the meals-on-wheels centres and the children's wards at Lea Hospital in Bromsgrove. They worked in the Hewell grounds and nurseries and, on Sundays, some went to the morning service at Tardebigge Church. Contacts with the local community were encouraged, and many elderly folk were invited into Hewell Grange for a Christmas lunch and party, and were served and entertained by the trainees.

The Governor of the Borstal during its first eight years was Mr D G Hewlings. He and his wife and family were active church members, and he was happy for church social events to take place in the grounds of Hewell and in the Officers' Recreation Club. Staff involved in the maintenance of the house and grounds of Hewell included several former employees of the Earl of Plymouth. Frank Molyneux was retained as farm manager. Jack Wilson continued to serve as electrician. Alfred Chellingsworth, who had been one of the Earl of Plymouth's gamekeepers, became an officer in charge of the plant. He lived in the North Lodge of Hewell Park (just off Brockhill Lane) which was demolished when Blakenhurst Prison was built. Most of the staff who were qualified to supervise and train the Borstal inmates were newcomers to the area and they were soon accommodated in houses on The Park, which were built using the labour of the Borstal lads.

In 1986 Hewell changed from being a Borstal Institution into a Youth Custody Centre, i.e. a prison for young people, and it was soon renamed a Young Offenders Institution. It could accommodate up to 193 inmates. By 1991 it held only 117 youths and employed a staff of around 100. Following a report that year by the prison authorities criticising its "appalling conditions" which included poor sanitation, it was threatened with closure. In 1992 this happened and Hewell Grange was converted into a category D men's prison. Here prisoners convicted of less serious offences live under strict discipline, sleeping in dormitories, not cells, and they are mostly employed by day on the prison farm or in the gardens, or in the outside community under supervision. Tardebigge Church has been fortunate in often being able to employ one of the prisoners to assist Martin Kealy, a former officer of the Borstal, who for many years has done an excellent job in maintaining the churchyard.

In 1965 a specially-built remand centre, H.M. Brockhill, was opened in the Hewell grounds to cater for young male and female prisoners on remand awaiting trial or, if convicted, their sentence. Due to increasing numbers it was soon restricted to male prisoners aged 14-21 years. Intended for 177 inmates, it held some 250 by 1983. The welfare of its occupants was promoted by educational and physical activities. The Vicar of Tardebigge was one of three chaplains to the remand centre.

In 1991 H.M. Brockhill underwent a change of use, becoming a women's prison. Its fortunes were mixed and it experienced a number of suicides each year as it housed many mentally disturbed women prisoners. Eventually, in 2006 there was another change of use as the women were replaced by Category C men prisoners.

Early in 1992 a third large Category B prison, named "Blakenhurst", was completed in the Hewell Park grounds close to Brockhill Lane. It was built to house securely just over 600 male prisoners, but it has had to hold many more. After a period when it was run by a private firm, it has, in recent years, reverted to being under Home Office control.

In 2008 the three prisons, Hewell, Brockhill and Blakenhurst, were united to become constituent parts of H.M.P. Hewell, holding altogether over 1,400 prisoners.

CHAPTER 3

Bentley Pauncefoot

THE MANOR OF BENTLEY

That part of the Parish of Tardebigge known as Bentley Pauncefoot takes its name from being a lea, or clearing, in the Royal Forest of Feckenham, and from the fact that in the 13th, 14th, 15th and 16th centuries, until about

Bentley Manor (E A Hodges Post Card).

1560, the Pauncefoot family held the Manor of Bentley with some 300 acres of farm land and 30 acres of woodland. Margaret Dickins in "A Thousand Years in Tardebigge" notes that on the tithe map of around 1840 the moated ground near the Thrift at Bentley is marked "The Banquiting Orchard", and Bentley House Farm is marked as Bentley Manor House, so it seems that the moated orchard was a pleasure ground, not far away from the residence of the Pauncefoots, to which they could resort on a summer afternoon.

In 1630 Henry Cookes acquired Bentley Manor through his marriage to Ann Northgrove of Norgrove Court, and the Cookes family remained in possession of the estate for the next two hundred years, their manor house being Norgrove. Best known of this family is Sir Thomas Cookes who, in 1792, at the age of 24, married 14 year old Mary Windsor, the daughter of Thomas Windsor, first Earl of Plymouth. The monument to them both in St Bartholomew's Church was commissioned in the lifetime of Sir Thomas after the death of his wife at the age of 35. It was first located in a specially built small chapel north of the chancel of the old church at Tardebigge, and so it escaped the damage done to the chancel and Windsor monuments by the collapse of the tower in 1775 and was re-erected in the new church. In 1793 Sir Thomas Cookes, in a trust deed, arranged for trustees to donate annually fifty pounds of the income from lands he owned in Bromsgrove for the re-endowment of King Edward VI Grammar School, Bromsgrove, (now Bromsgrove School). Sir Thomas died in 1801. In his will he left £10,000 to provide scholarships and fellowships at university for scholars from Bromsgrove and Feckenham Schools and for the establishment of Worcester College, Oxford.

In 1830 John Cookes, then with financial problems and no heir, sold the Manor of Bentley to William Hemming, a wealthy needle manufacturer of the Forge Mills, Redditch. In the early eighteenth century William's father, Richard Hemming, Lord of the Manor of Great Alne, near Alcester, had encouraged many of his estate workers and their families to earn extra money by making needles at home. The success of this cottage industry led to him and later his son William developing the business in Redditch. William invested part of his growing wealth in the purchase of the Foxlydiate Estate in 1790, also land at Beoley and Inkberrow, and then in

1830 the Manor of Bentley. He had additions and improvements made to the old gatehouse or lodge on Bentley Heath and transformed it into the Manor House. Norgrove Court now became the Home Farm.

When William Hemming died in 1848, his estates, including the Bentley Estate, passed to his son Richard who, with his wife Catherine whom he had married in 1846, soon moved into the Manor House. He it was who opposed and prevented the removal of his family pew in St Bartholomew's Church in 1877. Though still continuing his needle business in Redditch, Richard Hemming lived the life of a country squire, firm yet respected for his interest in and kindness to his tenants. He was involved in community affairs as a magistrate and in 1863 as High Sheriff for the County of Worcester. In his early years he served as Captain in the Worcester Yeomanry, he was interested in farming and in country pursuits, riding and hunting, and he was a keen art collector. He had one son and five daughters. In 1873 his eldest daughter, Maude Mary, married Captain George Cheape of Wellfield, Fife, Scotland, and when her father died in October 1891, she immediately inherited the Bentley Estate, now of some 6,000 acres, together with many other properties, including the Haselor Estate, which had been purchased many years earlier by her father. Apart from other properties left by her father to his widow, the needle business in Redditch went to her youngest sister Favoretta (Mrs Ingram).

It was back on 21 December 1853 that Maude Mary Hemming had been born at Bentley Manor, and she had grown up there. Attached to the Manor was a stable block with horses and ponies, and young Maude soon learnt to ride a pony. She helped to look after the animals and she enjoyed accompanying the hunt. In her teens she became an accomplished horse rider. She also loved farming and fishing and used to spend time at the Home Farm at Norgrove with its fishing pool. Following her marriage, her home for some eighteen years was at Wemyss Hall in Fife where, besides bringing up her young family, three sons and three daughters, she indulged her love of riding and hunting, her husband being an M.F.H. (Master of the Foxhounds). She also had a pack of beagles and became Master of the Wellfield Beagles. When, in 1891, the family moved from Scotland to Bentley Manor, she arranged for her beagles to be brought to Bentley to occupy the kennels there.

Maude Mary Cheape, the "Squire", in her younger days (from "The Squire of Bentley").

The reason why Richard Hemming left his Bentley Estate to his eldest daughter Maude and not to his son Frank was that he knew she was best fitted to continue to look after it as he had done, and when she inherited it she was determined to follow in her father's footsteps. Soon after settling in at the Manor, one of the estate workmen inadvertently addressed her as "Squire". She was happy to accept this title, by which her father had been addressed, and from henceforth she was known and addressed by her estate tenants and local people as "The Squire".

In the running of the Bentley and other estates, Captain George Cheape, husband of "The Squire", seems to have taken little direct part. He needed to spend time at his family home and estate at Wellfield and to travel on business. He was some years older than his wife, and he died in September 1900 after a period of ill health. So from the beginning of the century and until her death in 1919, the management of her properties was ultimately the sole responsibility of "The Squire". But she had the services and assistance of many trusted servants. These included house-keepers, cooks, maids and gardeners at the Manor, estate managers, kennels huntsmen who lived at "The Kennels" opposite to the timberyard and looked after the hounds (beagles or harriers), and estate workmen based at the timberyard who kept the estate property, farms and cottages, in repair.

The "Squire" at Bentley Manor in 1919 (from "The Squire of Bentley").

One of the longest in the service of "The Squire", for 43 years, was Thomas Harding, who was her huntsman in Scotland from 1876, and came with her to Bentley in 1891 to be her stud-groom from 1891 until her death. In Bentley he lived with his family at first at the Upper Bentley Farm house and then from 1907 at The Kennels black-and-white house, remaining there until 1946. His four daughters all attended Bentley School and a grandson, Richard Cozens, was organist at Bentley Church and then at St Bartholomew's, Tardebigge, during WW2.

Besides having the responsibility of seeing to the management of her estates at Bentley, Haselor and other smaller properties in Warwickshire and Gloucestershire, "The Squire" also owned two large estates in Scotland, Carsaig and Timoran, each with coastline, on the south side of the Island of Mull. These had been purchased after the sale of another Scottish estate by her husband in 1893. Most summers she spent some weeks on Mull where, with members of her family and friends, she enjoyed entertaining and outdoor sports, sailing, fishing and riding. It was during one of these holidays in 1896 that her daughter, Daisy, aged only twelve, was drowned in Loch Scredian off Mull when the sailing boat she was on foundered in squally weather. This was the first of the tragic losses of four of her children, as well as of her husband. In May 1914 her married daughter Katie died with other passengers on the ship "Empress of Ireland" which was rammed and sank in the St Lawrence River, Canada. Then, during the 1914-18 War two of her sons, both in the Warwickshire Yeomanry, died, Captain Leslie Cheape in a military operation in Egypt in 1916 and Colonel Hugh Gray-Cheape in 1918 when the ship "Leasowes Castle", which was carrying his regiment, was torpedoed and sank in the Mediterranean.

Whilst living at Bentley Manor, "The Squire" enjoyed her interest in horses and her hounds, in riding, hare-hunting, and hunting with the Worcestershire Fox Hounds. She also loved socialising and entertaining and visiting her tenants, especially those retired from her service. During the 1914-18 War she continued, to a lesser degree, to pursue these interests and she travelled each summer to Mull. The death, in July 1918, of her son Hugh who, in her husband's will was named as heir of Bentley, was the final blow from which she never really recovered, and she died in November 1919.

Following the death of "The Squire" the Bentley Manor and estate were in the care of trustees and managed by Mr W H Hall of Dodderhill, since Hugh's young son, Leslie Gray-Cheape, was only two years old when his father died and could not inherit until he came of age. However, in 1927, Mrs Maudie Ellis, remaining daughter of "The Squire", came down from Scotland to live at the Manor with her two daughters, Sheila and Patsy, and her son Lindsay. She had a very high regard for her mother, and perhaps the writing of her mother's biography had helped to kindle in her a desire to follow in her footsteps. Mrs Ellis made it her business to carry on, as her mother had done, in looking after the Manor, the Estate and tenants, and in taking an interest in Bentley Church and Bentley School. She continued her mother's gener-osity in giving each household on the estate a joint of beef at Christ-mas.

Soon after the outbreak of World War 2 in 1939, the Govern-ment commandeered most of the Manor and its grounds to be the headquarters of the local Field Battery of the Royal Artillery. Later the Essex Regiment took over and as many as 3,000 troops were billeted in and around the Manor. The Royal Engineers fol-lowed them, and next the Manor housed U.S. troops, white and coloured units in turn. Towards the end of the war the Manor was used as a prisoner of war camp,

Mrs Maudie Ellis and her three children at Bentley Manor, 1925. (from "The Squire of Bentley")

with Germans and Italians interned there. Finally it accommodated displaced European nationals.

During the early part of the war, Mrs Ellis continued to live in part of the Manor House, but early in 1942 she died. In May 1942 the furniture and other contents of the house, altogether 978 items, were put on sale by Messrs Luce and Silvers of Bromsgrove. The cleared building was then wholly occupied by the military.

Following the war, Lt.-Col. Leslie Gray-Cheape, having inherited the Bentley Estate, found the Manor, when it was returned to him, in a very bad condition and with dry rot in the timbers. Restoration would have been excessively costly, so the decision was made to have it demolished. Demolition of the house, a rambling edifice of no great architectural merit and with 35 rooms, took place in the early summer of 1950. The stables,

The demolition of Bentley Manor, May 1950. ("The Bromsgrove Messenger")

which could accommodate 25 horses, were removed later, leaving few remains of what had been an extensive residence. Lt.-Col. Gray-Cheape, after a short period living at Hallow, came in 1947 to settle at Sillins on the edge of his Estate. When Bentley Manor was demolished he had the gates to the main drive moved to Sillins.

The new Squire of Bentley continued to live at the Sillins as his main abode until around 1966, when he returned to Scotland. During his twenty years or so residence on the outskirts of Bentley he and his wife Dorothy took an interest in the Bentley community. He attended St Bartholomew's Church, where he exercised his right to sit in the Bentley box pew. He visited the local farms and joined in the local hunt. For some time he was Master of the Worcestershire Hunt. He was chairman for several years of the annual church fete held in the grounds of Hewell Grange. Since his death in 1990, his two sons Hamish, who lives at Haselor between Alcester and Stratford-on-Avon, and Hugh, based in Edinburgh, have retained much of the former Bentley Estate, some farms and property having been sold, and administration of it is now in the hands of Estate Agents.

ST MARY'S CHURCH, LOWER BENTLEY

The little church of St Mary, Lower Bentley, was not the first place of worship to exist in the Manor of Bentley. In the 13th and 14th centuries there was a chapel situated on what has long been known as Chapel Meadow some way below Hatchett's Farm. It was dedicated to St Stephen and it was an outpost of Bordesley Abbey. Remains of the chapel, some stones, pottery and other items, have been unearthed on the site.

St Mary's was built in 1874-5 on a field called Parson's Piece which, as its name suggests, was a piece of glebe land belonging to the Church. It received its licence from the then Bishop of Worcester on 1 October 1875. The licence states that it was approved "for the performance therein of Divine Service for the Convenience of the Inhabitants residing at a distance from the Parish Church of Tardebigge". It was not licensed for weddings, but baptisms were allowed on condition that "every Baptism shall at the time of its celebration be registered in the Registry of Baptisms belonging to the said Parish Church".

A copy of the bill for erecting the church, made out to Lord Windsor, reads:-

	£	s	d
Willm. Buckley Builder Contractor & Extras	305	16	3
W. Blew and Son for Bell	20	13	6
Labourers Levelling Ground & Fencing &c.	4	16	3
Evans for Gravel for Entrance		10	6
Team Work Drawing Gravel & Cinders	4	10	0
	336	6	6

The cost of 100 chairs with rush bottoms was about £18. Other furniture, including the altar table and wooden prayer desk, were probably paid for by local parishioners whose subscriptions, according to the Bromsgrove Almanac of 1876, "largely aided by Lord Windsor", raised the money to build the church.

Details of other church embellishments were given by Mr Edward (Teddy) Taylor in an address he gave to the congregation at a service held to mark the 100th anniversary of the church on 1 October 1975 : "The main window, an Annunciation, was dedicated in 1924 to the memory of Mrs Cheape, the Squire of Bentley, and we are told that subscriptions for this came from all over the world. The two side windows, in memory of her

St Mary's Church, Lower Bentley. (Rosemary Troth)

The interior of St Mary's Church, Lower Bentley, showing the three memorial windows, to the "Squire" (central) and her two daughters, Catherine (left) and Daisy (right). (AW)

two daughters, were dedicated at the same time. The one on the right is in memory of Daisy, drowned in a sailing accident off the Island of Mull in 1896, and shows St Margaret with a stag. This is the Bentley boxed stag; I am told the stag was taken to the meet in its box and released to lay a trail for the hounds – happily for the stag it was put back in its box at the end of its run before the hounds caught up with it. The left hand window was dedicated to Catherine who was drowned in May 1914 when the ship "Empress of Ireland" was rammed in the Hudson River; it shows St Catherine and her wheel and a black-headed gull, which I take to be a symbol to show that she died 'over the water'. At the back of the church are two inscriptions, one to her son Leslie who was killed in action in Egypt in 1916, the other to her son Hugh who was killed when the troop ship bringing him home from Egypt in 1918 was torpedoed. The front pew is in memory of Mr Samuel Jagger, trustee and agent for the Bentley Estate, and is made from Bentley Oak, probably from the Thrift, certainly from the Estate. The organ stool was given in memory of Patsy Ellis, the Squire's granddaughter; and the little font at the back of the church is in memory

Kneelers made by church members for St Mary's Church.

of Mrs Harvey, who lived at Grasmere, close to the church, and used to play the harmonium."

It is evident that the family at Bentley Manor took an interest in the church and that, over the years, it has meant a lot to local people, many of whose funeral services have taken place there, one being that of Mrs Maudie Ellis, daughter of "The Squire" in 1942.

For many years after the church was built a service was held each Sunday at 3.00 pm. Canon Dickins travelled over on Sunday afternoons, usually by pony and trap, and likewise his successor, the Revd F G Ellerton. The Revd. Scott Warren usually rode his bicycle. In 1967, the first year of the Revd. David Copley's incumbency, it was reported in the October Parish Magazine that he would be taking the first service at St Mary's to be held there "for quite a long time". There had been suggestions that the little church might close, but local people rallied round and early in 1968 a meeting hosted by Mr and Mrs John Gibbs at Lower Bentley Farm decided that services should be held at 9 am on the first Sunday of each month, Holy Communion on two Sundays and a family service on one Sunday, every three months.

Latterly Sunday services have usually been held on the second Sunday in the month at 9.30 am, alternating between Holy Communion and a Family Service. There have also been occasional services of Evensong in the summer months. In the 1990s a mid-week Evensong in June each year was organised by Tardebigge Churchmen's Group at which men's groups from other parishes in the Black Country and Astwood Bank, together with their families, were invited.

In the summer of 1993 a group of ladies of the congregation met to plan the making of sixty kneelers for the church. The idea for the kneelers came from Mrs Hilary Corbett. Mrs Eileen Beale suggested that they should depict wild flowers. Mrs Louise Burn created the nine designs used, and Mrs Jean Harper undertook the organisation of the project. Many people were involved in the sponsoring and making of the kneelers, and on Sunday 4 June 1995, at a special evening service, they were dedicated by the Revd Alan White, Priest-in-Charge. Souvenir brochures, produced by Michael and Michelle Stafford, were given out, and Mrs Beale gave a short account of the history of the church.

Over the years, although the PCC has been responsible for the finances and upkeep of the building, its loving care and amenities have been in the hands of local individuals, members of its congregation. From the 1920s until after WW2 Ernest Twitty acted as sexton, he opened up and rang the bell, and he kept the grass cut around the church. Later Richard and Elizabeth Debenham spent much time looking after the church. Richard, a consultant surgeon at the Queen Elizabeth Hospital in Birmingham, had operated on Martin Gibbs of Upper Bentley Farm, and they had struck up a friendship which resulted in Martin arranging for Robert, newly married in 1956, to rent Grasmere from Colonel Gray-Cheape and for Robert to exercise Martin's beloved horse which he could not ride himself for some time after his operation. Following the Debenhams' move to Stoke Pound in 1961, they still continued to look after St Mary's, Bentley, for many years.

There have been in the church, over the years, several harmoniums and, more recently, electronic keyboards donated by various people. The alms dish of oak was donated by Mrs Hilary Corbett in the late 1990s in memory of her husband.

Little Bentley Church is well loved, supported and cared for by local people. Long may it remain so.

BENTLEY SCHOOL

In her book "The Squire of Bentley" Mrs Ellis states that Bentley School was founded by her grandfather Richard Hemming to save local children the long walk to Tardebigge School. Initially "it was a dame school, and a little black-and-white half-timbered cottage on the estate was set aside for the old lady who taught the few children round her in the parlour. But the number soon outgrew the parlour, so the old Squire built a small school close by, the cottage becoming the schoolmaster's house, as it is today." To the left of the entrance to the school building, now the village hall, there is a stone in the brickwork with the date 1882, the year when it was built, originally to take up to 60 children.

In 1898 "The Squire" enlarged the school, which continued to be owned and maintained by the estate. It now consisted of three classrooms, the largest one where the village hall bar now is, a smaller one where the entrance hall and toilets now are, and the smallest one where the kitchen

Teachers and children at Bentley School 1904/5. Top right, the schoolmaster, Mr John Hopkins. The photograph, in the possession of Peggy Boss, shows her mother Elsie Wormington (in front of the lady teacher), and her brothers Thomas (in front of her) and Arthur (fourth from left in front row).

area was until recently. The toilets were in a separate building outside at the back of the school, where the hall extension was later built. They were of the primitive two-seater non-flushing bench variety.

Up to around 1900 the school seems to have had a sequence of head-mistresses including, in the 1890s, Miss G Hilliat, Miss Lorton and Miss Ann Gelder. These were followed by three headmasters, Mr John Henry Hopkins from about 1900 until around 1925, then Mr Morton Rowles until 1948, and finally Mr Alfred Kidd from 1948 to 1958. For most of the time there were lady assistant teachers, not necessarily qualified, to teach the younger children. The last of these was Miss Phipps who, when the school closed in 1958, joined the staff of Tardebigge School.

Until the second world war the ladies of the Manor, first Mrs Hemming, then Mrs Cheape, and later Mrs Ellis, took a great interest in their village school. Besides visiting the school, they provided annual treats for the children at events held in the summer and just before Christmas. On 6 June 1914, for instance, the children and their mothers marched from the school in procession, headed by Redditch Town Band, to the Manor, where "a sumptuous tea awaited them". There was a Punch and Judy show, and school prizes were presented, including: BOYS: 1st prize Alfred Goulbourne and Albert Wormington (tied); 2nd Frank Hutchinson; 3rd Percy Hopkins; 4th Edwin Boulton; GIRLS: 1st Phyllis Broome and Annie Dodd (tied); 2nd Beatrice Berry; 3rd Nellie Gardiner; 4th Alice Day. The master, J H Hopkins, thanked the Squire and also Mr and Mrs Carwardine who had helped.

During the earlier years of the Headship of Morton Rowles the school caretaker was Mrs Frances Thompson. She lived with her husband, who was lumber-jack and hedger on the Bentley Estate, in separate accommodation at the rear of the School House. Their son Walter, who was a pupil at the school until he left in 1936 at the age of fourteen, recalls helping his mother by fetching coal from the coal-house at the back of the school and lighting the coal-fired heating stoves in the three classrooms at 7 am each school morning. His mother, who cleaned the school at the end of each school day, was paid 25 shillings a month.

Several people who attended the village school in the 1930s have spoken of their happy memories of attending the annual Christmas Party provided by Mrs Ellis at the Manor, usually on 21 December, the birthday of her late mother "The Squire", at which the school children were entertained and came home with a tied large white-spotted red handkerchief containing various "goodies", cake, mince pies, nuts and sweets.

Over the years special events in the life of the school have included the celebration of the Diamond Jubilee of Queen Victoria in 1897, when the children received Jubilee medals; the unveiling by the headmaster, Mr J H Hopkins, in 1920 of the wooden War Memorial tablet listing six men, William Henry Austin, Harold Morgan Bowen, Harry Fisher, Alfred Hunt, Ernest Morris and Alfred Smout, who gave their lives in the 1914-18 War; and the day when, in 1933, the head, Martin Rowles, and a deputation of children from the school brought presents for Sheila and Patsy, daughters of Mrs Ellis, on the occasion of Patsy's 21st birthday.

As with many elementary schools until the 1950s, children could stay on at Bentley School until the school leaving age of thirteen, later fourteen, but when all children had to move to secondary education at the age of eleven, and also, due to smaller families and easier transport, there were fewer and fewer pupils, it became inevitable that the school should close, and this came about in 1958.

Already, some years earlier, a fund had been started by villagers to build a village hall. This became unnecessary when, soon after the closure of the school, Lt. Col. Gray-Cheape decided to donate the building to a trust for it to be maintained and managed as a village hall. It was "sold" by him for a legal token £1, and money raised by local people enabled the spacious meeting room to be added at the rear of the building and the conversion of the school rooms into the bar area, the kitchen, and the cloakrooms and toilets. The converted building was officially opened by its donor on 3 November 1962.

The Village Hall has proved to be a great asset to the local community. It is used by organisations including the W.I. and play groups, for social gatherings, whist drives, harvest suppers, game shoot lunches and family parties. As mentioned later, it was for some years the venue of the local football and cricket teams, matches being played on Sundays on the field behind. In recent years its caretakers have been Mrs Joan Badger, followed by Mrs June Brazier, who have also been on hand to provide catering services when needed.

BENTLEY VILLAGE

According to Mrs Ellis in her book "The Squire of Bentley", the central area of Upper Bentley, known as The Common, is surrounded by little lanes, none of which could be called a street. Strange it is then that for the past fifty years or so one of them has been known as "Angel Street". Today the scattered communities, farms and cottages, of Upper and Lower Bentley have no local shop, post office or public house. In days gone by, when there was no public transport, apart from one bus to and from Redditch on Saturday, and few folk had cars, some local people provided a service and made themselves a small income by stocking and selling items of food and other necessities from a room of their dwelling. In Lower Bentley, one such shop was run by Mrs Elizabeth Berry, during and after WW1. Before and during WW2 Mrs Gorton sold sweets, lemonade and cigarettes from a cottage (since demolished and replaced by the bungalow "Kestrels") along

Fosters Green Lane. Her husband Horace Gorton was a painter for the Bentley Estates and during the war he was the local Air Raid Warden. Another shop was kept later in the 1940s by Ernest Twitty. He worked at the Austin motor works and lived in the second of two cottages (since demolished and a house built on the site) along Woodgate Road from its junction with Lower Bentley Lane. He and his wife Mabel sold tobacco, cigarettes, sweets, pop and other items at the door, and he was the local men's hairdresser. He charged 2d for a haircut and he was "ticked off" by the local bobby, Harold Kidwell, for working for money on a Sunday. As already mentioned, he served as sexton at St Mary's Church. He is remembered as "a lovely old man".

In Upper Bentley there was a shop at Rose Cottage (now Lychgates) in Angel Street, the home of Sidney and Elsie Bowen, where groceries, sweets and cigarettes were sold through a window of the cottage. This could be reached by a convenient footpath across the common from the school.

The old forge in Manor Road, where the village blacksmith used to live and work, shoeing horses and attending to the machinery and equipment of local farmers, still stands, but in recent years it has been a private residence. The blacksmith from around 1876 until 1917 was James Tongue. He was succeeded by Ernest Barrett who came from Feckenham and continued to run the business for fifty years until it closed, following his death, in 1968. Of him it is recorded, in the Parish Magazine of June 1968, that "he was a first class shoeing smith and to him a set of shoes on a shire horse was a work of art; as also was the making of hoops for the local school children who placed their orders with him and received in return a perfect circle of metal in which it was impossible to detect where the two ends of metal met, so smoothly was the welded union made. A visit to the village smithy in Mr Barrett's day was a rewarding experience for he had a keen sense of humour and, as likely as not, one came away not only admiring his skill as a blacksmith but also tickled to death at some story he had told or some remark he had let drop." With his wife Kate and five children, Ernest was involved in the life of the village, and he served on the local parish council for some years. Although rented from the Bentley Estate, the forge was run independently of the Manor where, in the time of "The Squire", David Hutchinson from Scotland was both electrician and blacksmith.

At Bentley Forge, the blacksmith Ernest Barrett and, on horseback, farmer Martin Gibbs (Diana Gibbs).

The black and white house, formerly The Kennels and home to the keeper of the hounds, is now a private house. Opposite to it was the timberyard, where for many years timber from the Thrift and other woods on the Estate was sawn and stacked for use. Local children used to love to play there. The two semi-detached houses at the far end of the timberyard were, between the wars, the homes of Tom Morris, the head carpenter, and Arthur Farmer, the head gardener.

On the bend of Manor Road, between the village hall and the old forge, is Upper Bentley House, formerly Nursery Cottage. Here lived for many years Harold Coombes, the Bentley Estate Manager, and his family. He was a manager of the village school and he did much to raise the money, some £4,000, for its transformation into the village hall. The meeting room extension is named after him.

Of the various organisations using the village hall, the Women's Institute has been a most outstanding success. Soon after the hall came into

Employees and tenants of the Bentley Estate about to depart on two coaches to attend the wedding of Hamish Gray-Cheape at the Guards Chapel, Wellington Barracks, London, on 8 October 1965 (Diana Gibbs).

use, Mrs Rhona Cash challenged Mrs Joan Badger to start a W.I. to meet there. With the help of Mrs Diana Gibbs and others the branch was formed and at the inaugural meeting on 9 June 1963 Mrs Badger was elected its first president. The branch has continued to be well supported and to have an enthusiastic membership.

In spite of having a scattered and relatively small population, the Bentley area has maintained a strong community spirit, with people supporting community activities, such as social events, including harvest suppers in the village hall, and pancake races organised at times by the W.I. In the late 1960s and until the early 1980s a generation of the younger men were members of a Bentley football team and a Bentley cricket team, managed by John Hyde and Michael Morgan. They played at home against visiting teams on Sunday mornings behind the village hall before retiring inside to the bar for sustenance. The teams travelled as far as the Channel Islands for away matches.

One activity which has survived is the annual winter pheasant shoot. Pheasants used to be bred locally, but in recent times around 2,500 seven-

The start of the WI pancake race in 1976. In the background is the old timber-framed school house, at one time a dame's school. From l to r: Marjorie Weaver, Eileen Beale, Sue Deben-ham, Elizabeth Debenham, Diana Gibbs, Wendy Harber, Mary Vine, Vera Tatlow (in back-ground), Peggy Boss, Audrey Badger, Molly Hill (in background), Ros Brookes, Marion Talbot with children in pushchair, Mrs Bennett, and PC Ron Taylor who started the race (Peggy Boss).

weeks-old birds have been purchased from game farms each July, kept and released for the shoots held every week or so in the months from November until 1 February, each followed by refreshments in the village hall. From the 1920s until the 1950s the estate game-keeper, living with his wife in an old brick and timber-framed keepers cottage opposite the Thrift, was Walter Miles. It is said that when his wife at times was provoked and threatened to throw herself down the well, he just took no notice. Since they retired to the cottage down the lane, as their old cottage was demolished, and Colonel Gray-Cheape went to live in Scotland, the shoot has been carried on by a consortium of around twelve people. Part-time gamekeepers have included Edgar Empson, Frank Jenkins, Steve Talbot and, since 1974, Graham Badger.

Since the creation of civil parishes in 1894, Bentley Pauncefoot has had its own Parish Council consisting of seven elected councillors and an appointed part-time parish clerk. Councillors' term of office is four years and they must live in the parish or reside within three miles of the parish boundary. The existence of the council and its powers to deal with local affairs, over the years, has helped to maintain community cohesion.

CHAPTER 4

St Bartholomew's Parish Church

THE REVD.CANON CHARLES ALLAN DICKINS, VICAR 1855-1917

The beginning of the twentieth century saw the Vicar of Tardebigge, Canon Charles Dickins, after 45 years in office, still, at the age of 70, actively involved in the life of the parish. He was supported by his wife, Frances, their marriage having taken place ten days after his induction as Vicar. Their two unmarried daughters, Margaret and Barbara, were, like their mother, musically talented and played the organ and trained the choir. Canon Dickins was well liked and respected by his parishioners. His aim was to visit them in their homes twice a year. Weather permitting, on Sunday afternoons, if enough boats were moored at the New Wharf below the church, he would often conduct an open air service for the boat people. Apart from his church duties, Canon Dickins played a leading part in the life of the local community. He was a sportsman, having rowed for his Oxford college, and having played cricket for Bromsgrove and Hewell Cricket Clubs. He was examiner in theology at Bromsgrove School, an Assistant Diocesan Inspector of Schools, and he was a manager of Saltley

Teacher Training College. In 1895, in recognition of his services to the Diocese, he was made an Honorary Canon of Worcester.

It was during his incumbency that, during 1877-9, the chancel was built, the organ was removed from the gallery to its present position in the chancel, side galleries extending eastwards across the first two windows each side of the nave were removed, and the nave was transformed by the removal of all but one of the box pews and their replacement by the present pews. In 1902 the 135 feet high church spire was subject to major repair, being practically rebuilt. This was when the topmost stone dated December 1777 was removed, and it has since rested in the sanctuary beside the altar.

In July 1905, to mark the completion by Canon Dickins of fifty years as Vicar and his and his wife's Golden Wedding, a garden party was held at the vicarage, attended by over 400 people, at which Lady Windsor and Colonel Dixon on behalf of the parishioners, the head teacher of the church school, Mr A C Dilks, on behalf of the teachers and scholars, and other representatives presented gifts and spoke in praise of Canon and Mrs Dickins for their unselfish love and care for the people of the parish. To commemorate this achievement, in May 1907 the vicar's stall with its canopy and the choir stalls in the chancel, which had been made by a Mr Bridgman of Lichfield and were a gift from the parishioners, were dedicated by the Bishop of Worcester at a special service. Before the service the Earl of Plymouth,

The creeper-covered parish church in the early 1900s (Victoria County History).

Canon Charles Allan Dickins and his wife Frances (Hugh Dixon's Scrap Book).

who had donated the other seating in the chancel behind the choir stalls, presented a purse of gold to Canon and Mrs Dickins and spoke of the deep regard and affection in which they were held by all. Traditionally the local Lord of the Manor was responsible for the upkeep of the chancel and he and his family sat in the chancel during services. The Earl and Countess of Plymouth followed this practice and made use of the adjacent chancel door.

It was also in 1907 that the unique metal lectern, designed by Amy Walford and made in the workshops of the Bromsgrove Guild, was placed in the church and dedicated by the Archdeacon of Worcester on 30 October. Amy was the eighth daughter of the Walfords of Tack Farm, Tardebigge. Her father Walter, who died when she was only three, had been a church warden at St Bartholomew's in 1850 and 1851. Following training at the Royal College of Art, South Kensington, London, and the School of Art, Bushey, Herts., she was appointed to the staff of the Bromsgrove School of Art in New Road, Bromsgrove, in September 1900 and succeeded Walter Gilbert in December of that year as Principal until 1905. The lectern is of bronze, enriched with copper and with silver decoration. Amy Walford was also the designer of the memorial stained glass window in the church,

The interior of the church in the early 1900s. This post-card picture shows the Bentley pew still in its original position extending to the centre aisle, the Chantrey memorial before its removal to the chancel to make way for the War Memorial, the use of oil lamps, and the small altar table now situated under the War Memorial (Phillip Coventry).

in memory of the two wives of Thomas Dixon, which was made in the Guild's workshop.

In February 1908 Canon Dickins suffered the sad loss of his wife. Besides being a caring and supportive spouse, she had made her own mark in various ways, as organist and choir mistress in the early years of his ministry, as a founder and secretary of the Hewell Nursing Association, as branch secretary of the Girls Friendly Society, and as a member of other women's organisations.

In 1914, at the start of World War 1, Canon Dickins' health began to fail, and to prevent his resignation, the churchwardens, Messrs H W Dixon and E Cash, arranged for an additional curate to be appointed. In 1915, on completing sixty years as Vicar, Canon Dickins was presented with a beautifully bound "Tardebigge Address ", signed by 543 parishioners. Two years later, in July 1917, he was taken ill and he died the following October, aged 87. There must be few clergymen who have remained as the incumbent of one parish as long as the sixty-two years Canon Charles Allan Dickins served at Tardebigge.

In May 1918, in recognition of their services to the parish, as organists, Margaret and Barbara Dickins were presented with a Broadwood piano plus £280, and their brother Herbert received a bicycle. In a letter of thanks from Bridge House, Hook Norton, Banbury, the sisters wrote "We shall never forget the happy years in which we had the great privilege of being organists of Tardebigge (more than forty), nor are we unmindful that in all that time we never heard an unkind criticism of the music, but that everybody was always ready to help to make the church music better in any way they could."

THE REVD FRANCIS GEORGE ELLERTON, VICAR 1918-1930

Son of the Revd John Ellerton, writer of the well-known hymns "Saviour, again to thy dear name we raise" and "The day thou gavest, Lord, is ended", the Revd F G Ellerton began his ministry at Tardebigge in 1918, towards the end of World War 1, having served previously as Vicar of Ellesmere in Shropshire and Rector of Warmingham in Cheshire. Three years later, in 1921, he was appointed Rural Dean of Bromsgrove, and he continued in this post, maintaining his oversight of the parishes in the Bromsgrove and Redditch areas and their priests, until his retirement.

It was in 1921 that the 1914 -18 War Memorial was erected in the place of the Chantrey memorial to Other Archer, Lord Plymouth, which was moved into its present position in the chancel. At the same time two pews immediately below the war memorial were removed, thus making space for the present platform and table, believed to be the original altar before the new chancel was built, to be placed there.

On Christmas day 1922 the new East Window, which had been made in the glass workshop behind the Village Hall, was dedicated. The top part, depicting the Ascension of Jesus, was designed by the Earl of Plymouth; the bottom part by the creator of the window, Alfred Pike. The window was the gift of Lord Plymouth and was an added memorial to Canon Dickins.

In 1926 faculties were obtained for the placing of the large memorial slab in the centre of the chancel floor in memory of Robert, Earl of Plymouth, who had died in 1923, also for the new gilded oak reredos, new altar rails, and alterations to the Bentley Pew. The reredos was the gift of the Dowager Lady Plymouth in memory of her husband. The Bentley Pew was reconstructed so that it no longer protruded into the church.

Further additions to the furniture of the church were made in 1926. These included the Bishop's Chair, the Litany Desk, the credence table, the pair of candlesticks on the side table, and the creation of the Children's Corner. The Bishop's Chair was the work of Bromsgrove artist and craftsman Mr Pancheri and it was donated by the daughter of Willoughby Montgomerie Mullins in her father's memory. The Children's Corner at the back of the church was the idea of the Vicar. He was very interested in the young people of the church and school, and he encouraged them to say their prayers in the Children's Corner.

Another innovation in the Revd F G Ellerton's time was the Free Will Offering Scheme which was launched in 1926, with 125 names on the list of participants. This, like the present weekly offering envelopes, helped to provide a steady regular income for the church.

At the end of 1930, after 44 years service in parochial ministry, Mr Ellerton retired from the living of Tardebigge due to ill health. As reported in the Bromsgrove Messenger, he and his wife "have won the esteem and affection of all with whom they have come into contact during the past 12 years."

THE REVD PERCIVAL SCOTT WARREN, VICAR 1931-49

The Revd Percival Scott Warren came to Tardebigge with a wealth of experience in ministry and in local government. A native of Worcester, ordained in 1906, he spent four years in between two curacies as a missionary in Basutoland. During WW1 he worked with the YMCA in Belgium serving the troops. Whilst Rector of Tilston, Cheshire, in the 1920s, he was a local councillor 1925-29. In 1929, through an exchange of livings, he became Vicar of St Godwald's, Finstall. Two years later he moved with his wife Ione and his three young sons to Tardebigge as Vicar.

During Scott Warren's 18 years of ministry at Tardebigge the lives of many people were deeply affected by significant events in the life of the nation and the locality. The early 1930s saw the great depression with strikes and mass unemployment. Then came the threat of war and the war years, 1939-45, and following the war the continuation of austerity and food rationing which, in the case of most foods, finished in 1948, but did not finally end until 1954 when meat was derationed. In the Tardebigge area a major consequence of the war was the decision of the Earl of Plymouth to abandon and sell off his Hewell Estate in 1946, which meant the job losses of estate employees, the loss of the facilities enjoyed by many Tardebigge people as the Village Hall closed and was sold, but, not least, the loss of the benevolent involvement of the Plymouth family in the affairs of the parish, the church and school, and social and sporting events.

In the depression of the early 1930s the church, like many families, suffered financially. To help raise funds, Scott Warren wrote, and produced in January 1933 in the Village Hall, a pantomime "Robinson Crusoe", drawing from the local community the actors including himself, musicians and the makers of scenery, costumes and refreshments. Tickets cost just 2d (old pence) and the pantomime raised £87.6.8d for the church. The success of this first production was followed by that of five others, in 1934 "Bluebeard", in 1935 "Dick Whittington", in 1937 "Babes in the Wood", in

The Revd Percival Scott Warren (Michael Scott Warren).

1938 "The Sleeping Beauty", and in 1939 "Cinderella". These pantomimes were long remembered by many local people including those who, as adults or children, took part, or who were members of the audiences.

Events in the life of the church before the war included the installation of electricity for lighting in 1932. Lord Plymouth generously bore the cost. In the parish magazine the vicar wrote that there was now no excuse for folk to avoid Evensong because it was difficult to read the books, as it had been before. In September 1933 Tardebigge Choral Society came into being and probably helped with the pantomimes. In 1936 Mr Liddell, the church organist, and Mr Horace Lott, the choirmaster, both resigned, and in place of both Mr A Davies was appointed at a salary of £30 per year. Mr Davies was musical director of the 1937 and 1938 pantomimes. St Mary's, Bentley, seems to have been well attended at this time, a service being held there every Sunday, on the second Sunday Holy Communion at 9.30, on other Sundays Evensong at 3.00 pm.

Soon after the declaration of war on 3 September 1939 the parish registers were put in a safe place after they had been microfilmed by the Geneological Society.

In support of the vicar during the war and for most of his ministry were churchwardens William (Bill) Thompson and Major Llewelyn Ryland. Major Ryland, promoted from his previously retired rank of Captain, was, together with Major Holt, who was a member of the PCC Standing Committee, an officer in command of the local Home Guard during the war. For a time the rifles belonging to the Home Guard were stored in the vicarage.

It was during the war, in 1941, that Scott Warren's wife died. His three sons, Michael, David and Richard, had attended Finstall Park Preparatory School and went on to public school. Scott Warren always expressed his deep gratitude to his parishioners for their generous Easter Offerings which, as was the custom in those days, he received, and which helped to pay for his sons' education.

From time to time during the war came the sad news of the deaths of servicemen from the parish. One of the last of these was Major Peter Dixon of the T & M Dixon farming family. He had earlier been awarded the Military Cross for the brave rescue of his commanding officer and seven other wounded comrades from an enemy-occupied French village using a commandeered lorry. He died in March 1945, one of nine men in a glider hit by enemy flak during an airborne crossing of the Rhine. The simple stained glass window overlooking the war memorial was installed in his memory in 1947.

Following the war it was no longer possible to stage pantomimes, as the village hall was no longer available. Instead the main money raiser was the fete and show held annually from 1947 in the grounds of Hewell Grange Borstal with the cooperation of the governor.

During his time at Tardebigge Scott Warren served from 1934 to1946 on the Bromsgrove Rural District Council representing Bentley Pauncefoot, and he was also chairman for many years of Tutnall and Cobley Parish Council.

During the last three years of his ministry at Tardebigge Scott Warren suffered from heart trouble, and he died suddenly in Bromsgrove Cottage Hospital in June 1949. He had been a prominent Freemason, being an honorary member of three Lodges and Provincial Chaplain for Worcestershire. At his funeral at Tardebigge, the address by a Masonic Chaplain highlighted this aspect of his service in addition to his parochial ministry. In the "Bromsgrove Messenger" newspaper there were glowing tributes by other people to his tireless work as a parish priest and his service as a local councillor.

THE REVD REGINALD WILLIAM UNDERHILL, VICAR 1950-66

On Friday 20 January 1950 the Revd Reginald Underhill was instituted by the Bishop of Worcester, the Rt Revd W W Cash, to the living of Tardebigge. Mr Underhill had begun his church work as a Church Army Captain in

Redditch and, after ordination, had served three curacies, the last being from 1946 in the Parish of Alvechurch, where he had special responsibility for Hopwood, and where he had been very popular. At his institution the church was packed to overflowing; members of Hopwood choir supplemented those of Tardebigge and Webheath; and there were many clergy present. The new Vicar, his wife Doreen, and children, were welcomed and introduced to parishioners at a social evening in Hewell Recreation Club arranged by the churchwardens, Robert Goodman and Major Ryland.

During his first year the new vicar was involved, together with the Church Council, with the decision which had to be made concerning the future status of the church school. It had been handed over to the church by Lord Windsor in 1946 when the Hewell Estates were disposed of, and the church was now responsible for funding the upkeep of the buildings. There were two options, either for it to remain as an "Aided School", with the managers continuing to appoint the head teacher and staff and safeguard the religious teaching, but having financial responsibility for the repair and maintenance of the buildings, or for it to become a "Controlled School", having managers with less church control but with the LEA responsible for the upkeep of the buildings. Despite the financial liability, the Parochial Church Council decided that the school should retain its "Aided" status, and this has remained so.

The following year, 1951, was quite eventful. It was designated by the Diocese of Worcester as a year of mission, in which special efforts were expected to be made by the parishes to increase church membership. At Tardebigge the Revd Christopher Ludlow, Precentor of Canterbury Cathedral and a friend of the Vicar, came for a fortnight as Missioner, and a team of church members went round the parish visiting especially those married and those whose children had been baptised at Tardebigge.

On Wednesday 25 April there was a large congregation at a Service of Thanksgiving as the church reopened for worship after four weeks closure for the redecoration of the interior following several months of repairs to the outside walls and the retiling of the roof, the building having been surrounded by scaffolding. Painting of the walls and ceiling a cream colour was undertaken by a party of a dozen boys from Hewell Borstal, with the support of the Governor, Mr D G Hewlings. Whilst the church was closed, the 8.00 am Holy Communion Service and 11.00 am Mattins were held in the chapel of Hewell Grange and the 6.30 pm Evensong took place in the Hewell Recreation Hall, erected the previous year. The repairs and redecoration had been done at a cost of just over £3,000 as a memorial to the late Vicar, the Revd P Scott Warren.

Also this year the organ, the bellows of which had previously been pumped by hand, had an electrical blower installed, thus ending a task performed by generations of mostly young people. A different duty, usually entrusted to a choir member, was the carrying of the processional cross which was the gift, this year, of Mr and Mrs A H Cooke of Redditch.

The most memorable event of the year 1951, reported at length in local newspapers, was a Pageant of the History of Tardebigge performed in the grounds of Hewell Grange in front of the impressive ruins of the former stately home. It was held on Saturday 1 September, with afternoon and evening performances, the latter floodlit. Some 140 players enacted scenes from "A Thousand Years in Tardebigge", as the story was narrated over a loudspeaker. The script was written by Maurice Elvey, Deputy Governor of the Hewell Borstal, and the performers included parishioners, dancers from Redditch, and Hewell inmates. Money raised by the pageant went towards the expenses of the now "Aided" church school.

Whilst Hewell Grange remained a Borstal, with the Vicar of Tardebigge as its Chaplain, there was a happy and useful relationship between it and St Bartholomew's Church. Lads from Hewell attended morning service under supervision, and in the early years Hewell Park was available for church

The Revd Reginald William Underhill and his wife Doreen. (Bromsgrove Messenger)

events, one of which was the annual Fete and Show. This fund-raising event took place usually on the first Saturday of August in the grounds beside the Grange, and included stalls and sideshows, a flower and vegetable show run by the C of E Men's Society, a children's fancy dress competition, and a pony gymkhana. Inside the Grange there was usually an exhibition of arts and crafts created by the inmates. The sixth and last Fete and Show to be held in the grounds of the Borstal was in 1952 when local newspapers were keen to report on the capture of the Vicar and the Governor of Hewell by a gang of pirates (lads of Hewell). To obtain the release of the two hostages, ransom money had to be raised by the folk present – an unusual money-raising ploy!

In 1953 a garden party was held on Wednesday 29 July in the grounds of the Vicarage, and a flower and vegetable show, organised by the C of E Men's Society, was held in the school three days later on Saturday 1 August. In the following year the two events were combined, and this arrangement, Vicarage Garden Party, with side shows, refreshments, entertainment and the flower and vegetable show, continued as an annual event throughout the remainder of Reginald Underhill's time at Tarde-bigge, being held usually on the first Saturday in August.

One of two noteworthy events in 1953 was the installation of new oak west doors to the church, the gift of Major and Mrs B G Holt of Blackwell. The other notable event was the farewell to Major Llewelyn Ryland as, in the autumn, he and his wife Muriel moved to Sidmouth after many years of service to the church and church school, as well as to the local community. He had been church warden for fifteen years, 1938-53, and chairman of the managers of the church school, having fought vigorously for the retention of its aided status. In the wider community he had been president of the Tardebigge and District Branch of the British Legion and, for the young people of Bromsgrove, he had raised money, acquired land and built the Youth Centre on New Road, with its extensive playing field. His home had been at Walnut Cottage, Finstall. He a was a J P, and he had served in local government and taken an active part in village life.

In February 1955 there was a BBC radio broadcast of Morning Service from St Bartholomew's, and letters of appreciation were received from people world-wide. This year Cyril Wilson who had been church organist since before 1949 retired and in his place Cyril Moseley was appointed. During the year a room in the Vicarage was adapted by the Men's Society into a Parish Room for meetings.

1959 saw the retirements of two friends who had played active parts in the local community, Mr A T Knight, Headmaster of Tardebigge School for more than 25 years, and Mr Frank Molyneux who had come to the village in 1922 as head gardener to the Earl of Plymouth and in later years had been the farm manager at Hewell Grange. Together, at a presentation ceremony, they were thanked for their service to the community. Both, with their families, were moving to live as next-door neighbours in Studley.

In January 1960, at a special service in St Bartholomew's Church, the Vicar, the Revd R W Underhill, was installed as Rural Dean of Bromsgrove by the Bishop of Worcester, the Right Revd L M Charles-Edwards. Many of the Deanery clergy were present and, following the service, there was a gathering in the school to celebrate the completion by the Vicar of his ten years in office. Almost £300 had been subscribed by parishioners in appreciation of his caring ministry. He was presented with a television set and a cheque, Mrs Underhill received a bowl of pot plants, and there were many congratulatory speeches on his new appointment and on his achievements as Vicar.

As Rural Dean the Revd Reginald Underhill's workload extended to oversight of the churches and clergy in the Bromsgrove and Redditch areas, officiating at deanery events such as those of the Mothers' Union, and liaising with the diocese and with parishes. These tasks he undertook conscientiously in addition to his parish ministry. An extra duty was added in 1965, when he became chaplain of the newly opened Brockhill Remand Centre for prisoners awaiting trial.

In 1962, to mark the 300th anniversary of the 1662 Book of Common Prayer, the parish church was floodlit for a period after Easter. March 1962 saw the completion of work on the Vicarage. The house, built in 1815 to replace a previous one which had been on the site for about 700 years, had been enlarged in 1868 by the addition of a large Victorian kitchen. This had now been demolished and the space had become a car park. During the alterations and refurbishment of the Vicarage the Underhills had chosen, despite the upheaval, to remain in residence.

In 1965, the old pulpit, which was out of keeping with the other furnishings of the chancel, was replaced by a new one, the gift of Mr W P Beck, made by Robert Pancheri. The old one found a new home in the Roman Catholic Chapel at Severn Stoke, south of Worcester.

Unfortunately in 1965 Mr Underhill was seriously injured in a motor accident on the M6 Motorway, and this may have contributed to the illness in the summer of 1966 which culminated in his death in the Queen Elizabeth Hospital in Birmingham on 3 September. At his crowded funeral in St Bartholomew's Church, the Bishop of Worcester, Dr Charles-Edwards, included these words in his tribute:

"His brother-clergymen knew him as a leader and a friend, who used his office as Rural Dean to serve all in this area. The people of this parish regarded him as a friend and a priest, who shared in their joys and sorrows, and who taught them through his own life the truths of the Christian faith. He and his family had given the people of the parish a wonderful example of what a Christian family and home should be."

In subsequent months the parish rallied round and contributed generously towards the purchase by Mrs Underhill of "Church Cottage" in High House Lane for herself and her teenage children, Prudence and George.

THE REVD DAVID JUDD COPLEY, VICAR 1967-81

David Copley was a Londoner. On leaving school he had worked in a London bank. During WW2 he served in the Royal Naval Volunteer Reserve at the shore base in Singapore until it fell to the Japanese. He was then a prisoner-of-war of the Japanese for three and a half years. After the war he trained for the ministry at Lincoln College, Oxford, and Wycliffe Hall, and following his ordination he served two curacies at Old Swinford and Norton, Stourbridge, before becoming Rector of St Kenelm's, Romsley, from 1956 to 1967. He became Vicar of Tardebigge on 10 March 1967 and his duties extended to being also chaplain of the Hewell Grange Borstal and also Brockhill Remand Centre. He arrived at the Vicarage with his Dutch wife Margaretha and their daughter Ruth. One of the highlights of his time at Tardebigge was the wedding at St Bartholomew's on 14 July 1973 of Ruth to Stuart Harper.

From the outset people were made welcome at the vicarage, meetings continued to be held there and the vicarage garden remained the location of the annual fair and show held on the first Saturday in August. One of the most memorable of these was the 1974 fair when Bob Goodman made a balloon ascent, and as he did so shouted down "I'm nearer heaven than you are Vicar". He landed safely near Bromyard. David Copley was keen on social events, and he organised a Barn Dance in the vicarage garden in the evening following each fair and show. A Parish Dinner Dance was held in November at the Foxlydiate Hotel in 1967 and 1968, and a Halloween Party took place there in 1969, but this may not have been too well supported, for there is no mention of further such events in subsequent parish magazines, apart from a Parish Social which took place at Blackwell Court on 1 December 1972. However, Harvest Suppers were regularly held in Bentley Village Hall.

One of David Copley's first actions was to take over the editorship of the Parish Magazine. This was a task he evidently enjoyed and which he continued to undertake throughout his ministry. He wrote a mostly long, but interesting, letter each month, and sometimes included copies of his lengthy sermons for those who had been absent, or perhaps asleep, during their delivery. He seems to have had no difficulty in filling the magazine with informative and often humorous articles and news, and sympathetic obituaries. One regular contributor, with interesting nature notes, was Jim Hutchings, Head Teacher of the Church School, who lived in the School House. Another was George Bate, retired foreman carpenter of the Canal Company, who contributed thirteen instalments of his memoirs, since reproduced as a booklet available at the church.

Two years into David Copley's ministry, in 1969, a parish drama group was started. Besides the Vicar and his daughter Ruth, there were a number of parishioners involved including Jane Boyer, proprietress of the Mount School in Bromsgrove, Cyril Billington and his son Simon, Madge Guise, Bert Gateley and Fred Shrimpton. The first performance of the Mount Players, as they were called, was in March 1971 with two plays "The Bathroom Door" and "Unto the End". They were produced by Mrs Boyer and staged at the Mount School, as were many other plays in subsequent years.

When David Copley arrived at Tardebigge in 1967 there had been no services held at St Mary's, Bentley, "for quite a long time". Monthly services were started again in November of that year, at first on a trial basis, then held again regularly, as they have been since, usually on the second Sunday in the month. At St Bartholomew's a new idea was the taking of some family services by young church members. This first happened in 1970 and those who took part included Frank Head who played the organ, Diane, Jennie and Marion Archer, Ruth Copley, Bridget Kidwell, David Goulbourne, Mick Nye, Ian Robinson, David Taylor, George Underhill and Chris Newbon (guitar). Another innovation in 1970 was the monthly prayer service in which, alternately at Matins and Evensong, special prayers compiled by some members of the congregation were included. These prayer services continued for the next 30 years until the year 2000, the prayers being prepared over many years by Pamela Atkins and Kate Thomson.

Prior to the publication of the Alternative Service Book in 1980, new modern language services had been tried out in use in most C of E churches. Here at Tardebigge the Series II Service, a modern language version of the BCP Communion Service, was introduced in 1971 rather than the restructured Series III service which foreshadowed the present Common Worship form of Holy Communion service.

1977 was an eventful year. Besides celebrating the Queen's Silver Jubilee in June, the parish also celebrated the bicentenary of the completion of the building of the present church with a number of special events. The first of these was a dramatic performance which took place in church on Thursday, Friday and Saturday, 26, 27 and 28 May, entitled "TARDEBIGGE TIMES – an Evening of Scenes and Poems relating to Local Life through the Years". The writer of the script was Simon Billington, the producer was Jane Boyer, music was provided by Mary Goulbourne, the narrator was John Hedley, presenters were David Copley and Karl Hearne, and poetry readers were Bob and Peggy Goodman. The actors were drawn from church members and children from Tardebigge School. Scenes covered the history of the parish, Bordesley Abbey, the Gunpowder connection, the fall of the tower which necessitated the rebuilding of the church, the cutting of the canal, and the beginnings of the school.

At the Harvest Supper in Bentley Village Hall, 1970. The hymn books on the table were needed for the short Thanksgiving Service before the meal. L to r: Rhona Cash, Peggy Boss (serving), Ted Cash, Margaretha Copley, Audrey Badger (serving), Revd David Copley, Joan Badger, Eric Badger, Janie Beckett, Joe Beckett (Peggy Boss).

On 10 and 11 June an exhibition was held in the church of local arts and crafts and also items connected with the history of the Worcester and Birmingham Canal. The annual diocesan service of the Church of England Men's Society, usually held in Worcester Cathedral, was this year held at Tardebigge on 21 June. There was a concert in church of music of the 17th and 18th centuries. The annual fair and show was specially honoured by the presence of the Earl and Countess of Plymouth. Unfortunately and exceptionally, it rained heavily and some of the stalls and the entertainment had to be located in the church school. The final commemorative event was a thanksgiving service on 11 September at which the Bishop of Worcester preached.

In 1980 the Diocese of Worcester celebrated 1300 years of its existence. Highlights were the Queen's visit to the Cathedral on Maundy Thursday, the open air Eucharist on the County Cricket Ground with the Archbishop of Canterbury in May, and Cardinal Hume's visit to the Cathedral in September. Celebrations at Tardebigge included a combined bonfire, barbecue and barndance held on Ascension Day, and a pageant which took place in church on Thursday, Friday and Saturday, 2, 3 and 4 October. Again the script was by Simon Billington and the producer was Jane Boyer. About 35 people, adults and children, were involved in the acting and organisation. A blending of serious and humorous scenes related to events in the Diocese over thirteen centuries.

Towards the end of 1980 David Copley announced his intention to retire in the following Autumn after over 14 years as Vicar. His last Sunday Services on 27 September 1981 were followed by a farewell Harvest Supper at the Foxlydiate Hotel on the following Wednesday. He and his wife Margaretha moved to Hunnington in his former Parish of Romsley, and after a long and happy retirement he died in 2009.

THE MINISTRY OF PETER FROWLEY, FROM READER TO PRIEST, 1981-1988

In the middle of October 1981, only two weeks after the retirement of the Revd David Copley, came the good news that by an agreement between the Diocese and the Home Office, the Revd Charles Birtles, who had been chaplain of H M Prison, Leicester, was about to be appointed as Vicar of Tardebigge and Chaplain of Brockhill Prison. However, before he was able to meet the Tardebigge churchwardens, Roger Farley and David Taylor, Charles Birtles died suddenly, and the parish was left in sequestration and its future under review by the Diocesan authorities. The Home Office decided to appoint its own Prison Chaplain. The Diocese, through the Rural Dean, the Revd John Gathercole, considered the possibility of creating a United Benefice of Tardebigge with a neighbouring parish, St Stephen's, Redditch, or St Godwald's, Finstall. Meanwhile communion services were being taken by local priests, and other services, matins, evensong and family services, by Peter Frowley who had been Reader serving both Webheath and Tardebigge churches since his licensing in 1969.

In January 1982 the head Teacher of Tardebigge School, Jim Hutchings, and his wife Pat moved out of the School House to live at Finstall, prior to his retirement later in the year in July. In June Peter Frowley announced that he had been accepted for training as a non-stipendiary minister (NSM). In August he and his wife Maureen moved into the School House, and he began his theological training, part-time, at the Queen's College, Birmingham, in October. In the following July of 1983 Peter retired from his secular job and took on the pastoral ministry of the parish.

During the early years of the interregnum the supervision of the parish was in the hands of the Rural Dean. In February 1984, in anticipation of Peter's ordination as deacon in June, the Revd David Salt, Vicar of St Stephen's, Redditch, was appointed Priest-in-Charge of the Parish of Tardebigge, so that Peter could "serve his title" legally as curate under a parish priest. David Salt officiated as Chairman of the PCC and took an interest in the parish and the Church School, but Peter continued his pastoral ministry and the taking of church services as deacon and then, from June 1985, as priest.

Some years earlier the Bishop had suggested that parishes should try and produce their own NSMs to serve in their own parish. It was in

The Revd Peter Frowley and his grand-daughter, Sarah, whom he baptised in Tardebigge Church (Peter Frowley).

accordance with this idea that Peter, with the support of church members, had gone forward for ordination. When, following his ordination as priest, the hope was expressed to the Bishop that Peter could be appointed sole Priest-in-Charge of the independent parish, this idea was dismissed in a letter, received from the Bishop in January 1987, as being against the current practice of the Church of England. There followed many meetings of the churchwardens and the PCC with the Bishop and church officials and in the Deanery Synod. Eventually the Bishop was persuaded to agree to the licensing of Peter as Priest-in-Charge of the parish, but for a limited period of three years, and the parish was to be linked to the Bromsgrove Anglican Group of parishes. The licensing service took place on 3 December 1987, and at this point David Salt ceased to be Priest-in-Charge.

It had been, as far as relationships with the diocese were concerned, a traumatic time. But the parish had been well and happily looked after by Peter. Much had been achieved, and the attendances at church services had grown steadily. Great credit was due to the churchwardens, David Taylor and Roger Farley, who were in office together from the conclusion of David Copley's ministry until 1986 when Noel Kenchington succeeded Roger Farley for two years, Bert Gateley took over from David Taylor in 1987, and Fred Shrimpton followed Noel Kenchington in 1988.

1982 was an eventful year. On Easter Sunday there was the dedication by the Revd David Copley of the new altar frontal made by Janet Angell in memory of her late husband Hal. The white frontal, used on festal occasions, depicts the rays of the sun and it carries the words "I bring tidings of great joy". Some of the material came from her daughter Fiona's wedding dress; sons John and Nicholas helped with the lettering and design, and son Colin built the frame on which the frontal hangs in the chancel when not in use. This year, for the first time the annual Fair was held in the churchyard. It had previously been held in the Vicarage Garden. In October the diocesan Bishop, Philip Goodrich, came on a wet and windy Saturday to consecrate, in the presence of a large congregation, an extension to the graveyard on land which had been donated by the late Mr and Mrs John Green in 1958. During the year the former infants school building, which had been in use as a dining hall and kitchen, became available for church use, following the discontinuation of school meals. Plans were drawn up by the PCC for the installation of curtains and improvements for its use as a parish room or church hall.

1983 began with the creation of the Stonework Fund by the gift of £1,000 from an anonymous donor "in appreciation of so many years of happiness and friendship within the four walls of Saint Bartholomew's Church". The donor's aim was to stimulate the raising of many thousands of pounds which would soon be needed to restore much of the church's stonework. In July the PCC resolved to apply for a Faculty to remove two pews from the back of the church and convert them into bookshelves for hymn books and prayer books, and also provide extra space. This was granted and the work was done.

The year 1983 also saw the start of two new societies. On 13 January there was the inaugural meeting of the Gardening Club which was to exist for many years with a nucleus of enthusiastic members including Maureen Frowley whose idea it was. The Club met monthly with talks in the winter months and outings to gardens in the summer. It eventually came to an end in June 1995 when the chairman, Jean Honeybourne, and the secretary, Diana Scott, stepped down and no-one volunteered to take over. Towards the end of 1983 Peter Frowley started a youth club for 12 to 16 year olds to meet in the Church Hall on Wednesday evenings from 6.30 pm to 9.00 pm. The leader initially was Gordon Barton, and an appeal was made for equipment for indoor games, darts and table tennis. The club later met in the summer on Saturday afternoons. It remained in existence, two of its most active members being Rachel and Rebecca Farley, until May 1988 when, through lack of numbers, it closed. Another innovation in 1983 was the Pets Service held by Peter, most of it outdoors, on a Sunday morning in July, and later repeated in other years.

From the beginning of June 1984 the time of Evensong was changed from its long-standing 6.30 pm to 6.00 pm, as it has been since. On 13 May 1984 George Underhill ran in the London Marathon and raised over £400 for improvements to the Church Hall. This, together with other fund-raising efforts, helped to pay for the porch to the Hall which was completed in the Autumn. The bricklaying, tiling and the wooden frames were done by Len Cave with the help of his wife Pauline, the glass was procured and fitted by Sid Wall, and Peter Frowley acted as general labourer, chief digger and sweeper-up. In January 1984 the chancel of the church was decorated by J & A Brazier of Bromsgrove, the cost being covered by an anonymous donor. Later in the year Mrs Barbara Gibson initiated a successful fund-raising effort to pay for the redecoration of the nave, and this work was carried out in January 1985.

During 1985 the Gardening Club undertook the creation of the small garden in the churchyard on the site of an old pit, together with a small paved area and a seat. People responded generously to an appeal by Maureen Frowley and Barbara Gibson for shrubs and small trees to be planted in memory of loved ones. This garden of remembrance with its bird bath has since been a place to relax and enjoy the wonderful view over the Worcestershire countryside. During the year the windows of the Church Hall were curtained by Mrs Dorothy Knight and seat cushions were made by Mrs Pat Hutchings. For a great many years the field at the side of the Church Hall had been a jungle, full of briars, nettles and elderberry trees. During the summer farmer Tony May and his sons William and Martin, assisted by a working party of boys from Hewell Grange Borstal, cleared the ground and it was ploughed, rotovated and seeded to make the grassy area since used annually for the church fair, plant sale and other outdoor events.

In January 1986 the nationwide Church of England Men's Society was closed down. The Tardebigge Branch had been in existence for about 35 years, providing Christian fellowship and service to the church in many ways, including the organisation of the flower, fruit, vegetable and produce show at the annual Church Fair. In April it was decided at a men's meeting to form a Tardebigge Churchmen's Group to continue independently, and the officials elected were Chairman Ron Barnett, Secretary John Smith, Treasurer Tim Powell, Chaplain Revd Peter Frowley and Committee Members Roger Farley, Ken Knight and George Waite. Over the years since, the Group has continued to serve as before, with a programme of devotional meetings, social events open to all, the annual New Year's Day Walk and a mid-week midsummer service of Evensong followed by refreshments, held for many years at St Mary's, Bentley, with visitors from other parishes possessing a men's group.

It was also in 1986 that the Evergreens Club for elderly people was started and it had its first meeting in May with about 40 people attending. Since then the Evergreens have continued to meet at 4.00 pm on the third Monday, most months, in the Church Hall for afternoon tea and a chat and sometimes entertainment, free of charge. Transport for those needing it has been provided by church members, and there has usually been a Christmas party and a summer outing. The first club leader was Mrs Pam Shaw, and the first arranger of transport was Mrs Doreen Underhill. Over the years many church members have been involved in the organisation and the provision of the refreshments, and many people, especially those living on their own or in the two nursing homes in our parish, have enjoyed the meetings.

At the annual Parochial Church Meeting in March 1988 there was general satisfaction expressed that the parish now had its own Priest-in-Charge and had not been united with another parish; also that new enterprises such as the Evergreens and a Mums and Tots Group had been started and much else had been achieved by Peter Frowley and church leaders. It must have come as a "bombshell" when, only four months later, in July, Peter announced that he would be leaving Tardebigge in the Autumn and moving to Hong Kong to join the pastoral staff of the Cathedral Parish Church there on a four year contract. In the event, parishioners were understanding of the reasons for Peter's move to a new and challenging post, and he and Maureen left in November with the thanks and good wishes of the people of Tardebigge and Bentley. It was a blessing that earlier in the year at Easter, John Bonaker had been licensed as a Reader to serve the parish as it faced an uncertain future.

THE REVD ALAN WHITE, ACTING PRIEST-IN-CHARGE 1989-2000

In the autumn of 1988, following the departure of the Revd Peter Frowley to Hong Kong, one of the churchwardens, Bert Gateley, happened to meet the Revd Alan White in Bromsgrove High Street and enquired if he would be willing to help out at Tardebigge. Within a few weeks it was arranged with the Archdeacon, the Revd John Gathercole, that he should act as Priest-in-Charge and look after the parish for two years, spending one and a half days a week, taking Sunday services and visiting. This temporary ministry commenced at the beginning of January 1989. Actually, taking into account the various other duties involved, attending PCC and other meetings, monthly services in the two nursing homes, Plymouth House and Tutnall Hall, taking weekly school assemblies, baptisms, weddings, funerals, and the preparation involved, preparing sermons and writing parish magazine letters, around three days per week of time was involved. But, after serving for many years on the staffs of Leeds Grammar School and then Bromsgrove School as Chaplain, parish work came as an enjoyable and happy change of ministry.

Following the agreed two years, the Diocese seemed happy to let well alone, and as the years rolled by the two years eventually stretched to eleven. During ten of those years, Alan was assisted by John Bonaker, Reader, who had transferred to Tardebigge from Headless Cross Parish at Easter in 1988 and whose ministry over the years, sharing the taking of services and preaching, was greatly appreciated by church members. He was much missed when, in 1999, he retired from business in Redditch and moved to the Isle of Wight, where he has continued to serve as Reader at the old church in Shanklin.

In the summer of 1989 there was major upheaval in St Bartholomew's church as pews were moved to allow the oak floorboards in the nave to be lifted and treated against infestation by woodworm. For several weeks services were held in the church hall. By the autumn the work was finished and on 29 October there was a special thanksgiving service at which new carpeting along the centre aisle and new pew cushions were dedicated. The lovely pew cushions, or runners, depicting canal boats, lock gates and many religious symbols, had been designed by church members Sandra Bugden, Kate Thomson and Janet Angell. Janet was the guiding light throughout their creation by a devoted band of volunteers from the congregation.

In 1990 the PCC decided it was time to consider restoration work on the exterior stonework of the church. By November 1991 a stonework appeal had been launched to raise money towards the restoration work. One fund-raising effort on the part of Barbara Kenchington was the design and ordering of tea-towels depicting St Bartholomew's and St Mary's churches, the canal and local places of interest, and these were much sought after.

There was an approach to English Heritage for financial assistance but, as acceptance of such help would have meant a limitation on the powers of the PCC to undertake further structural work, the PCC decided not to accept it. From the spring of 1993 to the spring of 1994 many of the sandstone blocks in the north, east and south walls of the church were replaced by the contractors, Ben Davis of Worcester. Scaffolding was retained until June 1994 for the completion of stonework and other repairs to the tower, but not the spire. In May 1994 a survey of the spire revealed that the vane rod which runs from the top to the bottom of the spire and holds it together was corroded to half its diameter in places, so it was decided to replace it with one made of stainless steel. Repairs to the spire and weather vane were carried out using a steeplejack early in 1995, and during these repairs several intrepid church members were permitted to climb the steeplejack's ladders to test their nerve and gain extensive views of the surrounding countryside from on high. The cost of the stonework and steeple repairs amounted to around £77,000, much of which was raised by appeals, events and bequests. Repairs to the west end of the church were put on hold and eventually carried out in 2004/5.

Hardly had all this extensive restoration work been finished when it became necessary to have the east window removed and the surrounding stonework rebuilt. This was due to cracks in the wall just above and around the window. Whilst these repairs, undertaken by Ben Sinclair of Norgrove Court, were in hand in the autumn of 1995, the chancel was partitioned off and services were confined to the nave of the church, accompanied by a small electronic organ. Fortunately the cost of this work, amounting to around £4,000, was covered by a generous legacy from the estate of Mrs Jessie Houfton.

On 18 August 1995 there was a disastrous fire, almost certainly deliberately started, which destroyed the fuel-oil tank and gutted the boilerhouse, which were situated outside the main building of the church alongside the choir vestry. Fortunately the fire brigade arrived promptly and saved the church from all but minor damage. However the fire was a blessing in disguise for, with the help of insurance money, a gas supply was piped to the church the following spring and much more efficient gas central heating was installed.

Of great benefit to both church and school was the creation, in the autumn of 1994, of the car park just before the entrance to the churchyard. This was made possible by the purchase of the land when the field below Church Lane and alongside the canal was acquired by British Waterways. The fencing and surfacing of the car park was organised by Councillor Peter Whittaker of Stoney Lane Farm, using manpower and plant from Hewell Grange.

Whilst all the above mentioned work on the fabric of the church had been going on, the worship and other activities of church members had continued. The 1990s had been declared a nationwide "Decade of Evangelism". Accordingly, in the autumn of 1995 the PCC undertook a congregational survey in the form of a questionnaire seeking views mainly on the times and forms of service. January saw the launch of "Challenge 96", a Parish Mission involving the visitation by pairs of volunteer church members to the homes of non-church members in the parish. The leader of the mission was David Taylor, and the paperwork administration was efficiently done by Bert Bugden. Sister Joan Hudspeth of the Church Army

Tardebigge Church Choir, 1991. Back row l to r: Ron Barnett, Robert Barnett, John Bonaker (Reader), Ray Hopkins, Gareth Chambers, Noel Kenchington, Geoffrey Troth. Next to back row l to r: Margaret Barnett, Marianne Chambers, Rosalind Chambers, Barbara Kenchington. Next to front row l to r: Rosemary Troth, Joanne Stephens, Revd Alan White, Vi Empson, Mary Goulbourne (Organist). Front l to r: Bert Gateley (Churchwarden), Lisa Waring, Gill Walford, Fred Shrimpton (Churchwarden). (Margaret Barnett's Scrap Book).

met the parish visitors at preliminary meetings to give advice and encouragement. A special information pamphlet and parish magazines were distributed during the visitation. Those involved in the door to door mission were generally well received, but the mission was interrupted by the following events.

In May 1996 the future of the parish became an issue following the departure of the Vicar of Finstall. Archdeacon John Gathercole and the Diocesan Pastoral Committee were very much in favour of the appointment of an incumbent to serve a union of Tardebigge and Finstall Parishes. At the same time, if this were to happen, it meant Tardebigge losing, to St Stephen's, Redditch, the Brockhill area of the parish which was due for housing development, starting in the autumn of 1996. Following meetings of the PCC and church members at which the issue was hotly debated, there was a meeting of the PCC in July at which the Archdeacon was present to press his case, but the PCC voted to reject the proposals. This was by no means the end of the matter, for the DPC (Diocesan Pastoral Committee), despite the opposition of our PCC, persuaded the Church Commissioners to proceed with the plan to transfer the Brockhill area of our parish to St Stephen's. Following representations to the DPC and a visit to Tardebigge by a subcommittee of the Church Commissioners in January 1998, the DPC, with the sympathetic approval of the new Diocesan Bishop, Dr Peter Selby, changed its mind, and withdrew the change of parish boundary proposal. Thus ended two years of deep concern and of action to retain the integrity of the parish.

Meanwhile, early in 1996 houses began to be built on what had been Birchensale Farm land and later in the year the first residents moved into their new homes. As the development continued on both sides of the spine road of the Brockhill development in the next few years, people moving into new homes were welcomed with a clergy visit and given an information leaflet about Tardebigge Church and School, the church services, organisations and events. To keep the people of Brockhill and other parts of the parish informed about the church and school, a thrice-yearly news-sheet was delivered throughout by church members. It is estimated that by the year 2000 around 2,000 extra parishioners had moved into the area and at least another thousand were soon to come. As one would expect, with a large influx of population reflecting the secular trend and mix of society as a whole, and with the parish church being some distance away from the centre of Brockhill, there has been only a modest impact upon the church at Tardebigge. However, there has been an encouraging attendance of young people at family services and a steady stream of baptisms and weddings from Brockhill. The church school, fortunately saved from the threat of closure in the winter of 1998/9, has benefitted from many pupils attending from the catchment area of Brockhill.

For some time the need for a sound amplifying system in St Bartholomew's, including a loop system for the hard of hearing, had been felt. As a result of the examination of sound systems in several other

Churchwardens, verger and choir, 1955. Lhs: Churchwarden Teddy Cash and verger Percy Carr. Rhs: Churchwarden Les Boffey. Back row l to r: Roger Wilson, David Wright, Les Thompson, Mr Wilson, Edgar Hughes, Malcolm Cook, Tim Cash, Mr Cook. Middle row l to r: Sheila Scargill, Mrs Scargill, Mr Wilson (organist), Revd Reg Underbill (vicar), Kathleen Hood, Susan Mason, Vi Empson, Alma Mason, Mr Sandilands. Front row l to r: David Mann, Sam Mann, John Thompson, ?, Tim Petford, Andrew Mason, Robert Barnett. This was before ladies who sang with the choir were allowed to be robed (Margaret Barnett's Scrap Book).

churches, by the vicar and churchwarden Jean Honeybourne in the autumn of 1997, the present system was chosen and it was installed in January 1998 at a cost of £6,000, most of the money being donated by interested parties.

In February 2000 the Revd Alan White retired from acting as the parish priest. He and his wife Fran were thanked at a special service on Sunday 27 February. Fran had not been well for some time and it was with the Bishop of Worcester's permission that they were allowed to continue to worship at St Bartholomew's where they had made so many friends. Fran died in 2001. Alan has continued to take some services as Assistant Priest under his successors, the Ven Frederick Hazell (2000-3), the Revd Glyn Dew (2004-5), the Revd Derek Taylor (acting, 2005-6) and, from 2007, the Revd Pete Worrall.

CHURCH OFFICERS

Over the century many people gave good service in various offices, as churchwardens, secretaries and treasurers of the church. As can be seen from the list of churchwardens, some served in that capacity for many years. Of a long list of PCC secretaries, which includes A T Knight, headmaster of the church school, Harry Guise, Harold Kidwell and Barbara Kenchington, one of the longest serving was Alma Westwood, from 1989 to 2005. Two treasurers who gave long and devoted service were Keith Milligan who served from 1953-65 and 1979-91, twenty-four years in all, and Vic Sadler who also did two spells, 1966-78 and from 1991 until his death on holiday in October 1998, a total of nineteen years.

THE CHURCH CHOIR

Unlike many parish churches, which do not now have a choir, Tardebigge Church has been fortunate in having retained its choir to lead the singing at the regular Sunday services, Morning Service at 11.00 am and Choral Evensong at 6.00 pm. Also, besides singing at weddings when required, members of the choir attend, on a voluntary basis, all the funerals which take place in church, and this is appreciated.

Over the years the composition of the choir has changed. In the early part of the twentieth century the robed choir, as in most other churches, consisted of men and boys only. There was often a waiting list of lads

Mary Goulbourne at the organ in Tardebigge Church. Mary, the daughter of Walker and Mabel Bray, was born and lived for many years at Holly Cottage, Upper Bentley. She attended Bentley School and was taught to play the piano by her aunt who lived nearby and who had played the piano at the memorial service in Bentley Manor for Mrs Cheape ("The Squire") before her funeral in Scotland in 1919. For over twenty years, after WW2, Mary played the organ for the services at St Mary's, Bentley. There she met her husband Dick Goulbourne to whom she was married in 1951. Dick, who died in 1975, was treasurer at Bentley Church and later churchwarden at Tardebigge. In 1968 Mary succeeded Alfred Drew as organist at Tardebigge, and she continued to play for the services there for over thirty years until a few months before she died in 2002. No mean achievement on her part was, in her seventies, accompanying the choir for Stainer's "Crucifixion" in 1994 and 1996, and for Maunder's "Olivet to Calvary" in 1995 and 1997. (David Goulbourne)

hoping to join, and, if accepted, they would spend some time as probationers before becoming full members. Due to various factors, including the two world wars, when the younger men were away on active service, and the gradual proliferation of secular Sunday activities, attendance on

TARDEBIGGE CHURCHWARDENS

From 1893 to 2010

Vicar's Warden		People's Warden	
1893	E Kemp	1893	T Cash
1904	H Walford Dixon		
		1907	E Cash
1920	L Lambert		
1927	E Cash	1927	R Thompson
		1928	F Buckley
1930	W Thompson		
		1935	J Mellor
		1938	L Ryland
1948	R Goodman		
1951	E Cash		
		1954	L Boffey
		1959	A W Fletcher
1964	F D Goulbourne		
		1965	P Beck
1970	P Beck	1970	F H Gateley

In 1974 designation as either
Vicar's or People's Warden ceased

1974	P Beck	1974	F H Gateley
1975	J Hedley		
		1978	D G Taylor
1979	A W Fletcher		
1981	R L Farley		
1986	N S Kenchington		
		1987	F H Gateley
1988	F N Shrimpton		
1993	D C Daniels		
1995	K A Hearne	1995	H H Bugden
1997	Mrs J B Honeybourne	1997	F N Shrimpton
		2001	R Powell
2004	M Price		
		2005	D Stubbings
		2007	C Lee

the part of men and boys steadily declined and, since the 1950s, the ladies have been welcomed as additional choir members.

Since, and including, the time of Margaret and Barbara Dickins, most organists have also acted as choir masters/mistresses. However, in the latter years of Mary Goulbourne's long spell as organist (1968-2001), choir member Ray Hopkins has served as choir master, commencing in 1990 and continuing on until 2004, since when he has trained as a Reader, being licensed in June 2009. Ray and his wife Pat (who has served as sidesmen's secretary and helped to run the Evergreens for many years) are one of many families who, over the years, have contributed so much to the life of the church community.

ORGANISATIONS

HEWELL NURSING ASSOCIATION was founded in 1894 by Lady Windsor, who was its first president and treasurer, and Mrs Dickins, wife of the Vicar of Tardebigge, who was its first secretary. Its purpose was to provide nursing care to families, parents and children, in time of need, in return for a weekly subscription of 2d, which was collected by volunteers. Starting with one district nurse, it gradually extended its services over a wide area, including The Lickey, Rubery, Stoke Prior and Wychbold, as well as Tardebigge, and employed as many as sixteen nurses.

TARDEBIGGE NURSING ASSOCIATION was created in January 1930 following a public meeting held in the Tardebigge Village Hall on 12 December 1929. It was a smaller organisation for the local people, with the same aims, service and subscription as the Hewell Association. Lady Irene, Countess of Plymouth, became its president in the late 1930s. Its one nurse was supplied with a cottage on the Hewell Estate and an upright lady's bicycle, and she was a familiar figure as she rode around. Both of these nursing associations, and many others nationwide, became unnecessary and were disbanded when the National Health Service with its own provision of district nurses came into being in 1948. The district nurse covering Tardebigge from 1948 and through the 1950s was Nurse Price, and her name was included in the Parish Magazine each month together with the list of church officials.

The TARDEBIGGE WOMEN'S INSTITUTE was started in 1917 during WW1 by the Countess of Plymouth. Between the wars, in the 1920s and 1930s, it met at the Village Hall where, in addition to its usual "Jam and Jerusalem" meetings, it organised Christmas lunches at the hall for the old folks of the parish. A newspaper report of the 1934 Christmas lunch mentioned that the Earl and Countess of Plymouth were present with a party from Hewell Grange, that the Countess distributed Christmas presents, and children from Tardebigge School sang items from their recent school concert.

When the Village Hall was no longer available after WW2, a meeting room for the officers of the newly created Borstal was built on Hewell Park and this was used for the meetings of local organisations, including the W.I., for many years. Latterly meetings were held in the Church Hall. After 75 years in existence the Tardebigge Branch closed down in December 1992 due to the fact that the membership had declined and there were no volunteers to take over as officers to run the branch. However the Bentley Branch of the W.I. has continued to flourish, its meetings being held in Bentley Village Hall.

The MOTHERS UNION was started in a small way by Mary Sumner, the wife of the Rector of the parish of Alresford, near Winchester, in 1876, as a group of mothers meeting together to support each other in their marriages and in the care of their children. The idea caught on and by 1892 there were over 60,000 members in 28 dioceses of the Church of England. In 1897 Queen Victoria in her diamond jubilee year became patron of the movement. Today there are over three and a half million members in 78 countries of the world.

It is likely that by 1900 the MU was established in the Parish of Tardebigge. In the 1920s and 1930s it met in the Village Hall. In August 1930 the branch organised a pageant in the grounds of Hewell Grange in which other local branches took part. The pageant depicted the history of the MU and its work in many countries throughout the world, and it attracted a very large audience, many having to stand. After WW2 the MU met in the weaving room behind the Village Hall and later in the Hewell Officers Recreation Hall. In the Revd Reginald Underhill's time it met monthly, usually in the Vicarage, at 2.30 pm on a Wednesday, and its Enrolling Members (presidents) included Mrs Hill of Holyoake's Farm, Mrs Rock-Evans from Finstall, and the vicar's wife, Mrs Underhill. By 1965 there were problems, for at both the September and October meetings the future of the branch was under discussion. In December there was a joint meeting with the Women's Fellowship of the Methodist Church in Redditch, and during 1966 the MU at Tardebigge ceased to be and was replaced by a Ladies Fellowship which met monthly and was well established by the time the Revd David Copley became Vicar in March 1967. The Tardebigge MU banner which was given in 1951 by Miss D Boultbee Brooks, has been preserved in the chancel of the church.

The TARDEBIGGE BRANCH OF THE BRITISH LEGION was formed soon after WW1. It met in the Village Hall between the wars and then, following WW2, it met at the Cross Inn, Finstall. In 1951 the Tardebigge Branch closed and its members moved to amalgamate with the Aston Fields Branch, which has continued to be active, its meetings being held in the local Working Men's Club. John Allcock served as secretary for over 40 years, first of the Tardebigge Branch and then of the Aston Fields Branch. His wife Lucy was secretary of the ladies' section.

CHAPTER 5

Tardebigge Village Hall

TARDEBIGGE VILLAGE HALL was conceived by the Earl and Countess of Plymouth as a community centre for the Parish of Tardebigge and as a memorial to their son, the late Viscount Windsor, who had died in India in 1908. It was designed by the architect Francis Bayliss of Redditch under the personal instructions of the Earl. The builders, Messrs J & A Brazier of Bromsgrove, started work in September 1910. The walls were constructed of special thin red bricks made on the Hewell Estate in the brickyard of Mrs Anne Frisby, which was situated on the offside of the Worcester and Birmingham Canal between the top lock and London Lane.

The main doorway of the building led into a through entrance hall with access to the courtyard at the back. On the left of this, through an archway, was the great hall with a high barrel ceiling and a removeable stage at the far end. To the right of the entrance hall was a billiard room and, beyond it, a men's reading room. In the wing behind the great hall was a women's room and toilet, and beyond it a spacious kitchen. In the wing behind the men's reading room there was a bathroom and men's toilets and, beyond this, accommodation on two floors for a resident caretaker with its own private entrance.

Above the men's reading room and reached by a separate staircase was a room, partly in the roof, intended to be used for carpentry and wood

Tardebigge Village Hall as it was until the 1960s (Linda Butler).

carving, and a store room. There was hot water central heating and electric light throughout.

Amongst the many persons present at the opening ceremony, held on Thursday 9 November 1911 in the evening, were the Earl and Countess of Plymouth, Lady Paget, Lord Windsor, Lady Phyllis Windsor-Clive, Mr and Mrs L F Lambert, members of the Dixon family, and the Revd Canon Dickins. In an opening speech the Earl of Plymouth said he hoped the hall would be used widely as a centre for both recreation and instruction and that it "might benefit many generations long after those who were now present had played their part in life and passed away." The Earl was thanked for his generosity in speeches by Canon Dickins, Mr Frank Rowles and Colonel Matthew Dixon. There were refreshments and the proceedings concluded with an orchestral and vocal concert.

At its opening the hall already had a membership of 327, consisting of 153 women and girls, 151 men, and 23 youths. From the outset it was administered by a committee under rules laid down by the Earl of Plymouth, whose property the site and buildings remained, and who, as president, had ultimate control, being ex-officio chairman of the committee. Membership was by election of the committee and was restricted to men and women resident in the ecclesiastical parish of Tardebigge together with residents and employees of the Hewell Estates. Membership subscription was 4d per month for men and 2d per month for women and for boys aged 14 to 18. The hall was open each weekday and on Christmas Day from 2 pm to 10 pm, and on Sundays and Good Friday from 2 pm to 5 pm and 8 pm to 10 pm. No intoxicating liquor was allowed on the premises, except on special occasions, and betting, gambling, bad language and disorderly conduct were forbidden. The caretaker was expected to provide refreshments at such times and prices as the committee might determine. The refreshment tariff included tea at 1d a cup or 3d per pot, coffee 1d per cup, Bovril 2d per cup, lemonade or ginger beer 1d per bottle, bread and butter 1d for two slices, bread and cheese 2d per portion, and cake 1d per slice.

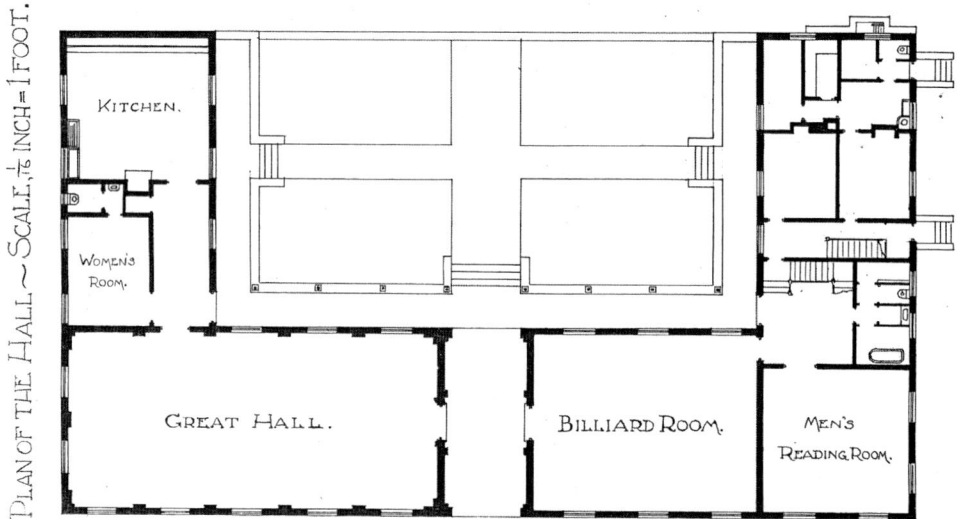

Ground floor plan of the Village Hall (Committee Minute Book, 1911-14).

The first committee, appointed by the Earl of Plymouth, consisted of himself as president, A A Pettigrew (secretary), Henry Bate (treasurer), the Countess of Plymouth, Canon Dickins, Miss Barbara Dickins, Mr and Mrs Hugh Dixon, Mr and Mrs L F Lambert, Messrs Fred Buckley, Frank Rowles, J Beattie, J Johnson and A Johnson. This committee, with the addition of the Countess of Plymouth as lady president, continued in office throughout 1912 and 1913, those due to retire, four each year, being re-elected at the A.G.M. held each January.

During the first three years of its existence, from November 1911 to October 1914, when it became a military hospital, membership remained at around 350 and the hall was generally well used. However, because attendance on Sundays in 1912 was minimal, it was closed on Sundays from January 1913. A variety of activities took place there, especially during the winter months. There were monthly lectures, the first three of which in 1912 were given by Lady Paget, Lord Windsor and Mr A C Dilks, Headmaster of Tardebigge School. There was a weekly social night with entertainment, a badminton club using the great hall, dances, concerts, plays, whist drives, and cookery and sewing classes. The billiards table was popular and a second table was soon purchased. The men's and women's reading rooms were well stocked with newspapers, magazines and library books, and on Friday evenings the men's bathroom was well patronised. Organisations which used the hall for their meetings included the Hewell Cricket Club, the Bowls Club, Tardebigge Choral Society, the Foxlydiate and Hewell Flower Show Society, and also the Hewell Boy Scout Troop, founded in November 1912 with the Revd M Davis as Scoutmaster, which used to meet upstairs in the carpentry room.

The Hewell Bowls Club was founded in 1914 after the Earl of Plymouth had the bowling Green made behind the back of the village hall. The green,

The opening of the Bowling Green and Bowls Club on 16 June 1914, with the names of some of those present, including Lord Plymouth standing on the green, and Margaret Dickins. (Hugh Dixon's Scrap Book)

40 yards square, was laid upon a foundation of ashes and sand by workmen from Hewell gardens under the direction of the head gardener, Andrew Pettigrew. It was opened by the Earl, with many local personalities present, on 16 June 1914. He had provided sets of bowls, mats and rubbers for two of the six rinks, and a bowls match which took place between a visiting team from St Fagan's and a novice Hewell team was, unsurprisingly, won by the visitors. The bowling green and the bowls club today remain the sole surviving sporting activity from the days of the Village Hall.

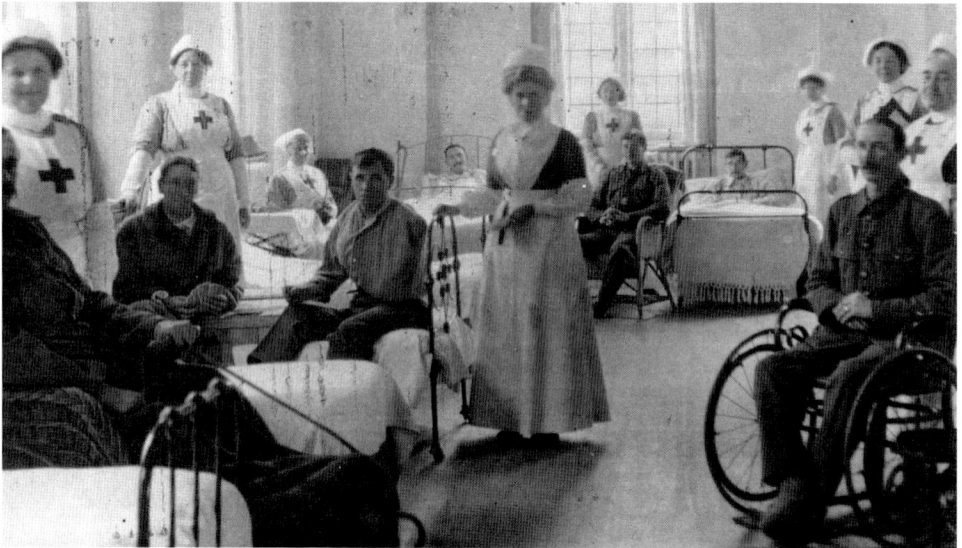

The Village Hall in use as a VAD Red Cross Hospital during WW1. (Linda Butler)

In October 1914, following the outbreak of WW1, the Village Hall was taken over as a VAD (Voluntary Aid Detachment) Red Cross Hospital for the treatment and care of wounded soldiers. It was cleaned and scrubbed out by local volunteers and stocked with the necessary equipment, beds, blankets and bed linen. The first patients arrived by Red Cross ambulance from Bromsgrove Railway Station early in 1915. Initially in charge of the hospital, with the title of Commandant, was Mrs Hugh Dixon. Amongst her VAD nurses were Mrs Ralph Dixon and Lady Phyllis, daughter of the Earl of Plymouth. Miss Walford was Commandant in 1916. Up to about forty wounded soldiers were there at a time, with influxes following the battles of the Somme in 1916 and lengthy Passchendaele in 1917. For all these men, after the hell of the trenches, Tardebigge was a peaceful haven in the midst of lovely countryside as they experienced the loving care of the nursing staff and the generosity and friendship of local people and organisations.

Nurses and patients at the VAD Hospital, the servicemen apparently well on the road to recovery. (Margaret Barnett's scrap book)

During their stay the soldiers wore a blue uniform to distinguish them when outdoors. Those able to do so, on foot or in wheelchairs, were able to visit the grounds of Hewell Grange or the canal and New Wharf area, and some came up to Tardebigge Church on Sundays, with some of the nurses, and to Holy Communion at Christmas and Easter. At Christmas there were gifts from firms such as Cadburys and from local organisations and people, and also at various times there were concerts and other entertainment. The last major event at the end of 1918, following the Armistice of 11 November, was the Christmas celebration, Christmas dinner and tea. Soon after this the hospital closed and reverted to its use as the Village Hall.

From 1919 until the beginning of WW2 in 1939 the hall continued in use under the same regime as before. The original caretaker, Mr F Wade was succeeded by Mr Alf Skudder and the hall continued to provide social and educational facilities for its members. Behind and beside the hall there were grass tennis courts and the bowling green. In addition to the regular social events, including Saturday evening dances and concerts, there were pantomimes in the 1930s organised by the Vicar, the Revd Scott Warren, involving local people and children from the church school. On Friday afternoons the older girls from the church school came over to the hall for cookery and laundry lessons given by Mrs Frisby (better known by her maiden name Netta Bate), and the girl guides met there in the evening, the guide captain being Mrs Noel Thompson. The late Mrs Madge Guise wrote thus of her memories of the Village Hall in the thirties:-

In 1935 I had the privilege of becoming a member of Tardebigge Village Hall for the amazing subscription of 2/6d (now 12.5 pence) per annum, privileged because, to become a member, you had to be either employed by the Plymouth Estates or your house was built on Plymouth Estate land. I fell into the second category as my father had our house built on land in Birchfield Road, Webheath, purchased from the Plymouth Estates in 1935. Membership included the use of the library, the opportunity to play badminton in the winter and tennis and bowls in the summer, and also to engage in various crafts carried on in the workshops. Tennis dances were organised to the music of Irving Frith and his band and the local band of the Beszant Brothers.

It was an excellent hall for badminton because the high dome in the ceiling enabled players to hit the shuttlecock upwards with force. There were few cars available to take us to away matches but we managed to pile in somehow. Jack and Gerald Hill, Peggy and Howard James, Nancy Dixon, Mrs Hugh Dixon, Tony Wilson-Jones, Bert Skinner, Kath Yapp and many more played in the team and we all had such a happy and enjoyable time. The Webheath members often missed the last bus and so we walked, often through the snow, singing and laughing all the way home. Mr and Mrs Skudder were the resident caretakers, and Mr Skudder appeared in the doorway on the stroke of ten to ensure we were all out of the badminton hall immediately. Any delays, apart from match nights, were not very popular. Excellent refreshments were provided by Mr and Mrs Skudder for summer and winter sports matches – fruit set in jelly, I remember, was always a favourite item on the menu.

In the thirties we had many money-raising efforts for the provision of a hard tennis court. This was created where the car park of the Tardebigge Hotel now is at a cost of about £98, including a high netting fence. We already had six grass tennis

---

"THE SLEEPING BEAUTY," 1938.

LIST OF CHARACTERS.

The Princess	LADY GILLIAN WINDSOR-CLIVE.
The Prince	MR. P. DIXON.
King of Hearts	MR. W. E. BASELEY.
Queen of Hearts	MRS. MOUNTFORD.
Knave of Hearts	MR. J. SIMPSON.
The Joker	MR. R. COZENS.
Lord Chancellor	REV. P. SCOTT WARREN.
Witch of the Woods	MRS. EADES.
The Fairy Queen	MRS. SMITH.
Nurse	MR. R. C. DIXON.
Cook	MRS. HAWKINS.
The Landlord of the "Slug and Lettuce"	MR. R. A. WILSON JONES.
Gaffer	MR. B. COOMBES.

Chorus—MRS. SHRIMPTON, MISS K. CHAMBERS, MISS D. WEBB, MISS I. SPIERS, MISS K. GRIFFIN, MISS D. EVANS, MESSRS. E. H. HUGHES, H. FRAZIER, W. LONG.

Fairies—WINIFRED PERKS, MARGARET PERKS, ALICE PHILLIPS.

Imps—ROBERT WILSON, FRANK STANLEY, DENNIS CLARK, VINCENT CLARK.

Understudy—MISS M. MANN.

Musical Director—MR. A. DAVIES.

Accompanists—Piano		MISS J. MORTIBOYS.
Violin		MR. J. GRAHAM COX.
		MR. BERNARD FRANKLIN.
Hon. Electrician		MR. J. V. WILSON.
Hon. Secretary		MR. C. G. BURMAN.
Assistant Hon. Secretary		MR. A. T. KNIGHT.
Prompter and Curtain		MR. G. L. FRAZIER.

CHOCOLATES on Sale in the Hall, arranged by MISS D. VAN BYLEVELT, MRS. C. G. BURMAN, MRS. A. GWYNNE, the MISSES J. COOK, D. COLLEDGE, R. DAY, W. HARRIS.

The centre pages of the programme of the fifth pantomime staged in the Village Hall. It was written and produced by the Revd P Scott Warren, and he played one of the parts in it. (Doreen Underhill)

Actors in one of the pantomimes in the Village Hall.

A pantomime in the Village Hall. Centre, Revd P Scott Warren, second from left, Nancy Dixon. (Jo Casey)

courts. I remember helping at a jumble sale, to raise money for the hard court, held in the weaving room at the back of the village hall and having great fun dressing up in Mr L F Lambert's cast-off plus four suit and cap. Mr Lambert was a local magistrate and Agent to the Earl of Plymouth, and he lived at Hewell House, where Mr and Mrs Joe Beckett now reside. Of course, Mr Lambert happened to walk into the weaving room when I was parading round in his suit. However, he laughed and thought it suited me. Mr Lambert's son inherited a family title and became Sir Greville Lambert.

In the 1970s the Bowling Club opened its doors to lady members. When we played tennis in the thirties we used to look over the hedge at the men bowling and I thought what a slow, dull game it was, but I soon realised when I joined what a fascinating and absorbing sport it is.

Between the wars the craft workshops at the village hall encouraged various handicrafts and produced some fine artefacts. Behind the hall a two-storeyed brick building with one room on each floor housed the glass studios. Here the beautiful east window in St Bartholomew's Church was made by Alfred Pike in 1922, the upper part depicting the Ascension of Jesus to Heaven having been designed by the Earl of Plymouth, the lower part showing the disciples having been left to Pike himself, who is said to have included the faces of local people. Pike also designed and created other windows in local churches. These included the three east windows of St Mary's, Bentley, in memory of Maude Mary Cheape, the "Squire of Bentley", and her two daughters Kate and Daisy who were both tragically drowned. Other examples of his artistry and skill are the window in St Monica's Chapel in Hewell Grange, a window in Holy Trinity Church, Belbroughton, and the War Memorial window in St George's Church, Redditch, installed in 1920. Pike is remembered as a tall man, single and fond of the ladies. He became engaged to Netta Bate, cookery mistress at the village hall, before disappearing to the USA around 1928, following which he then sent Netta a Christmas card each Christmas. Others who worked in the glass studios included Wallace Hughes who continued there after Alfred Pike left, and Sid Wall, both of whom were ex-scholars of Tardebigge School.

Between the glass studios and the village hall there was a wooden building known as the Weaving Shed where fabrics were produced. For some years a Mrs Warner was in charge, helped by local girls. The hut was used during WW2 as Headquarters of the local Home Guard.

The other main crafts, which took place in an upper room in the hall itself, were carpentry and wood carving. In charge of this workshop was Alf Westover. Alf had been summoned to Tardebigge at the age of eighteen in 1899 by Lord Windsor to add intricate carving to an oak table made by the then Hewell estate carpenter, Henry Tremlett, the table being intended as a gift from the Windsors to the Viceroy of India. Alf's father had a furniture manufacturing business in London and Alf had become a skilled wood-carver. He succeeded Mr Tremlett and married a local girl, Florence Styler, daughter of the Bentley village postman whose round included the Foxlydiate area. Some fine furniture was produced by Alf Westover including, in Tardebigge Church, the reredos, the altar rails and choir stalls in the chancel, donated by the Earl of Windsor around 1907. Later, in the village hall workshop, Alf took on an apprentice, Fred Gwynne, and they gave lessons in woodworking to local men and lads, besides producing many items themselves, including the wooden candlesticks which stand on the table below the War Memorial in Tardebigge Church.

During WW2, when Hewell Grange and its grounds were used by the Royal Army Ordinance Corps as an ammunition and armoured vehicle depot, the large body of troops stationed there used the Tardebigge Village Hall as an amenity. Also during the war a baby clinic was held there, to which mothers from Finstall and other nearby areas brought their young children.

Following WW2 when, because of death duties, the Hewell Estate was put up for sale in 1946, the Village Hall was included in the property acquired by Plymouth Estates Limited. The Hall was then offered to the parishioners of Tardebigge to purchase at the valuation price, but the cost of its upkeep following purchase would have been beyond forseeable resources. A meeting of parishioners was held in the church school early in December 1948 to consider renting the hall, but this possibility was prevented by a successful offer, that month, by Ralph Edwards Enterprises to buy the premises together with the weaving shed and tennis courts for use as a Country Club. This was a great disappointment to the local people who had hoped that it could have remained their village hall. The hall actually remained empty and unused for two or three years until bought by Ansell's Brewery and converted into a Public House as it now is. It underwent extensive internal alterations, including the removal of the central hallway. It was refurnished and reopened in March 1988 as "The Tardebigge" under the efficient management of Gerard and Valerie Ludden. With its restaurant it was run on traditional lines, with a waitress service, and during the 1990s used for some church social functions and the provision of Sunday lunch for visiting preachers at the morning services at St Bartholomew's Church.

When the A448 dual carriageway was constructed in the 1970s it covered the site of some of the old tennis courts and the glass studio and it cut across a footpath over what was known as the pleck between Church Lane and the Hewell dairy, used in earlier years by the children who collected milk for the school. Fortunately the bowling green escaped and it has continued to be well-used.

CHAPTER 6

Tardebigge School

EARLY YEARS; THE NINETEENTH CENTURY

The church school at Tardebigge has a long history. It came into being in 1815, following the appointment of the Revd Thomas Blackwell as vicar of the parish. He had been the tutor of Other, Earl of Plymouth, and he was keen to start the village school on the lines set out by a new society formed in 1811, "The National Society for Promoting the Education of the Poor in the Principles of the Established Church throughout England and Wales". For many years there had been a public house, "The Magpie Inn", situated where the School House now stands. To house the school, the "Magpie Inn" was closed and the premises became the residence of the school master and his family. A room in the building was retained for use as a courtroom, as it had been, for the trial of local miscreants, and an upstairs room became the boys' schoolroom. The girls were taught in a separate building on the vicarage side of what was now the school house.

The school continued in the old "Magpie Inn" and the adjacent building for 28 years. Then in 1843, Lady Harriet Windsor-Clive had these buildings demolished to make way for a new school house for the schoolmaster and his family, built on the foundations and over the cellar of the Magpie Inn, together with two adjoining school rooms, one each side of the school house. In the early nineteenth century it was usual for boys and girls to be segregated and many schools were built with separate entrances and rooms for boys and girls. At Tardebigge the left hand school room with its porch and cloakroom was for the girls. It still exists today as the front and kitchen area of the Church Hall. A similar room for the boys, with porch and cloakroom, on the other side of the school house has undergone alterations as extensions took place in later years. Between the entrances to the two school rooms there was a canopy extending in front of the school house, providing shelter in bad weather.

In 1866 it was decreed by the government that children below the age of seven, classed as infants, should be taught separately from the older children. As a result, the infants now occupied what had been the girls' schoolroom, and the older boys and girls were taught together in what was previously the boys' schoolroom. The two departments were known as the Infants School and the Mixed School. Because of increasing numbers, the Mixed School room had to be extended in 1870 and an extra classroom was added in 1884. Also in 1884 the large existing extension was built onto the Infants School room to create an extra classroom, separated from the other by a moveable wooden sliding screen which was only removed in recent years during improvements to the Church Hall.

From 1815 to 1900 there were only three successive resident school masters. The first, William Turner, was appointed at the age of 25 and he stayed for 43 years. He was assisted throughout by his wife Alice, who was in charge of the girls, and later by an assistant, George Hiscox. The second master in charge, John Wilson, remained for 32 years, from 1858 to 1890. He was likewise assisted by his wife, Ann. Also now helping with the teaching there were several pupil teachers. These, in accordance with a government scheme which started in 1846, were older pupils, boys and girls, who were selected by the head teacher to stay on from 13 to 18 years of age to teach. At first they taught full time and were trained outside of school hours by the Head Teacher. Later they spent half time at a pupil teacher training centre and taught only half time. At the end of their five years' service they could, if they wished, take an examination for a Queen's Scholarship which, if gained, entitled them to attend a three-year course at a teacher training college to become certificated teachers. The Head Teacher at Tardebigge from 1890 to 1900 was John Campbell. After his ten years service he left to become Principal of the Pupil Teacher Training College in Worcester. His wife Ann taught sewing part-time and his daughter Margaret taught for a time in the Mixed School.

During the nineteenth century the school continued on its steady course. Until 1891, parents had to pay 2d per week per child, with a reduction to 1d for a third child or more. From September 1891 fees were abolished and replaced by a government grant based on attendances registered at the beginning of each school day. Hence, from that time onwards, the importance of good attendance and of punctuality, and that children should not arrive late after the calling of the register. Previously, and especially before school attendance became compulsory for children from 5 to 10 years old under the Mundella Act of 1880, pupils would stay away from school when they were needed to help at home or on farms. In really bad weather, such as when there was deep snow, and at harvest time, or on local Fair Days, the school would close.

TWENTIETH CENTURY CHANGES; FROM ALL-AGE SCHOOL TO FIRST SCHOOL

The twentieth century brought many changes to this country's educational system, and to Tardebigge School in particular. The 1902 Education Act created Local Education Authorities (LEAs) in place of the School Boards which had been set up in 1870 to provide elementary schools where needed. The teaching in all elementary schools, including church schools, was now to be state-aided, paid for out of the rates. But the premises of church schools, their repair and extension where necessary, remained the financial responsibility of the church or other providing benefactor. In the case of Tardebigge, it was the Earl of Plymouth who owned the school, his predecessor Lady Harriet having had it built. From the beginning, the management of Tardebigge School had been in the sole hands of the vicar. Canon Dickins, vicar since 1855, had faithfully fulfilled this duty. Now under the 1902 Act there had to be a body of six managers, of whom two were nominated by, and represented, the LEA, the other four, known as foundation managers, being appointed by the church. The first four foundation managers were Canon Dickins (chairman), Mr Joseph Hodgetts of High House Farm, Mr Edward Tustin of Broad Green and Mrs Elizabeth

An aerial photograph of Tardebigge Church and School. (Heli-Photos of Elstree)

Thompson of Stoney Lane Cottage. Under the Act the managers of church schools were allowed to appoint or dismiss teaching staff, subject to the approval, on educational grounds, of the LEA.

One stipulation of the 1902 Act was that in a church (or "non-provided") school, religious instruction had to be "in accordance with the provisions (if any) of the trust deed relating thereto, and shall be under the control of the managers". At Tardebigge there had been no trust deed setting out the legal situation in regard to the ownership and tenancy of the school, together with the School House and surrounds, staff conditions of service, and the nature of the religious teaching. To remedy this, a trust deed was drawn up, agreed and signed by Robert Lord Windsor, and dated 14th March 1903. In accordance with the terms of this trust deed, the premises were restricted to the use of a public elementary school for the parish of Tardebigge. A yearly rent of one shilling was payable for the use of the building and one shilling for the use of the surrounding land (1420 square yards). The education provided was intended for the children, or children and adults, "only of the labouring, manufacturing and other poorer classes" in the parish. It was laid down that the school "shall always be in union with and conducted according to the principles and in furtherance of the ends and designs of the Incorporated National Society for promoting the Education of the Poor in the Principles of the Established Church throughout England and Wales".

A major consequence of the 1902 Act was the establishment of secondary schools by LEAs. These, to some extent modelled on the existing grammar schools, extended the educational opportunities of children hoping to enter colleges and universities and the professions, including teaching. In the early 1900s most of the children at Tardebigge School stayed on there until the leaving age of 13 or 14, boys mainly to go into apprenticeships or farm work, girls into service. But an increasing number of youngsters entered for scholarships to one or other of the new local secondary schools, Bromsgrove County High School or Redditch County High School.

The other important twentieth century Education Act, which transformed the educational system, was that passed in 1944 towards the end of WW2. Under the Act the description "elementary school" was superceded, as schools taking young children up to the age of eleven were now termed primary schools, and in future all children were to transfer at the age of eleven to one of three types of secondary school, grammar, secondary modern, or technical. So Tardebigge became a primary school and more of its pupils began to move at the age of eleven to secondary schools. It was not until 1958 that the new Ridgeway Secondary School, Astwood Bank, was completed. Until that year, Tardebigge School continued to retain many pupils up to the age of 14. As a result pupil numbers were reduced from some 130 in 1958 to around 80 the following year.

A further change in the status of the school occurred between 1972 and 1974, as the three-tier structure of schools came into operation in the Redditch area. Tardebigge now became a First School for children aged 5 to 9, and since then children have had to leave at the age of 9, most moving to Ridgeway which became a Middle School (for pupils aged 9 to 13). As a consequence of this, pupil numbers, having risen to around 100, now dropped to about 80 by 1975.

The major event in the life of the Parish which affected the ownership and administration of the school was the departure of the Plymouth family and the sale of the Hewell Estate properties in 1946. Since its foundation in 1815 the school, its premises and the land around it had been owned and maintained by the Windsors, and the school had been known over the years as "Lady Harriet's School" in her time, and then "Lord Windsor's School". On 14 July 1947 the school, the school house and land were given by, and conveyed from, the Plymouth Estates Ltd to ownership by the Worcester Diocesan Board of Finance, but with control vested in the Parochial Church Council. Following this change of situation it was soon necessary for the PCC to decide how the upkeep of the school property should be financed. The choice was between "Maintained" status, with upkeep entirely financed by the LEA and only a minority of the school managers appointed by the church, and "Aided" status with the church partially financially liable for maintenance but able to appoint a majority of the school managers. In 1950 the PCC opted for "Aided" status, and that has continued since.

THE INFANTS SCHOOL, 1867-1931

From 1867, when it came into being as a separate department, until 1931, when it was merged again with the Mixed School, the Infants School at Tardebigge remained a separate department in its own separate building and with its own Head Teacher. From 1867 to 1891, the teacher in charge was Mrs Ann Wilson, wife of John Wilson, the Headmaster of the Mixed School. When the Wilsons retired at the end of 1890, Miss Mary Ann Garnham, who had been an assistant mistress in the Mixed School since 1884, was appointed Head Mistress of the Infants School by Canon Dickins. At the same time Miss Eliza Worgen, who had been a pupil at the school and had served as monitress in the Infant School since the building was extended in 1884, was appointed as assistant infants teacher. When Miss Garnham and Miss Worgen eventually retired together in February 1931, they had each served a total of 46 years at Tardebigge, six in the Mixed School and 40 in the Infants School.

During her time at Tardebigge School, Miss Garnham lived conveniently close to the school at Plymouth Guest House, owned at that time by Alfred Whitmore. Miss Worgen lived in Middlefield Road, Aston Fields. She walked to and from the school, two miles each way, picking up children in the morning on her way through Finstall and seeing them safely back on her way home. Both ladies were tall and slim, wore long skirts and were a little forbidding. Discipline was strict, and a cane kept on teacher's desk was used on the hand and remained a visible deterrent to bad behaviour. Nevertheless both teachers were respected and remembered by their former pupils as being caring and kindly disposed.

Tardebigge Infants School in 1920, Miss Garnham on the left, Miss Worgen on the right.

The curriculum in the Infants School concentrated, as in the Mixed School, on the 3 Rs and the scriptures. Singing was encouraged; there were special songs for each school year, as well as poems and passages to be memorised and recited, and there were weekly topics to add interest and variety to the curriculum.

FOUR HEAD TEACHERS, 1900-2000

Over the years, Tardebigge School has been fortunate in having head teachers, as well as a number of assistant teachers, who have given long and devoted service to the school and have also been involved in the life of the church and the local community.

The Vicar and Headmaster with the School Cricket Team in 1928. From the left, back row: The Revd F G Ellerton, Frank Broom, Doug Wall, Mr Dilks. Centre: E Coote, J Laten, Jack Drew, Arthur Davis. Front: Bill Callow, Ron Tongue, Frank Colledge, Percy Wall, G Drain. (Bromsgrove Messenger)

ARTHUR CHARLES DILKS, who succeeded John Campbell as Head of the Mixed School in 1901, remained in office for 32 years until 1933. Soon after his appointment he studied for and obtained the degree of B.Sc. in physics of London University. Following the building of the Tardebigge Village Hall by the Earl of Plymouth in 1911 he was a leading light in its activities and in charge of the lantern slide projector. He was keen on cricket and was a member of the Hewell cricket team. He built a 3 inch gauge model railway in the School House garden with a steam locomotive he himself constructed, and this was a source of interest and wonder to the pupils who peered over the garden wall to see it working. As a teacher Mr Dilks was especially remembered by his ex-pupils for inspiring them with a love of literature, through the books he read to them and the poetry he made them learn.

The Mixed School, c.1930, with the children dressed as a pack of playing cards. On the left, the Vicar, the Revd F G Ellerton. (Vi Empson)

In the early 1900s the Mixed School was overcrowded with around 90 children and, after severe criticism by HM School Inspectors of this and the open fires, in 1912 the school summer holiday was extended until the end of November whilst the Mixed School building was demolished, all but the facade to the right of the School House, and replaced by three new classrooms and a new additional side entrance (now the main entrance). The new maximum number of pupils was set by the board of Education at 150, allowing as many as 50 pupils per room, but numbers in the school remained at about 90 in subsequent years.

The teaching staff in the early 1900s, with the exception of Mr Dilks, were all unqualified. In 1904 assistants were Morton Rowles and Gertrude Allbut, both pupil teachers, and Mrs Frances Dickins, wife of the vicar, who was sewing mistress. Mrs Dilks assisted when needed. In 1911 Harriet Platts, who had been a pupil and pupil teacher was appointed as an uncertified assistant. She was married in 1916 and as Mrs Badger she went on to teach until she retired in 1944, only to be called on to return in 1946. She finally retired in 1950. She was one of a number of long-serving teachers remembered affectionately by former pupils of the school.

World War 1, 1914-18, occurred during Mr Dilks' headship. Many former pupils and fathers of children at the school were away on active service and there was sadness when casualties amongst them were reported. As part of the war effort, the school collected and sent vegetables to naval ships, and in 1917 part of the school field was cultivated by the boys and the vegetables grown were supplied to the VAD military hospital in the Village Hall. This was the beginning of the inclusion of gardening in the timetable, which continued along with handicrafts for many years. During the war, cookery and laundry classes for the older girls, which had commenced in 1912 in the Village Hall, were held elsewhere. They were held again in the Village Hall after the war, during the 1920s and 1930s, under the tuition of Mrs Frisby.

The next Headmaster, ARTHUR THOMAS KNIGHT, arrived in September 1933. He had been Headmaster of Martley School, and he remained at Tardebigge for 26 years until his retirement in 1959. Arthur Knight was a musician. He sometimes played the church organ for services, and he organised many school concerts, some to raise money for school items, such as a new piano and a radiogram or for other good causes. He played an active part in the life of the church and the local community, being at various times parish magazine secretary, secretary of the parochial church council, and chairman of Tutnall and Cobley parish council. He was a member of Hewell Bowling Club.

Arthur Knight was Headmaster during the war years, 1939-45. During this period a number of evacuees from Birmingham, who came to live locally, swelled the school population. When air raids on the Midlands began to intensify towards the end of 1940, twenty evacuees were sent from Birmingham, together with a teacher, Miss Griggs, to join the school. Though Tardebigge had little serious damage from air raids, there were nights when the air-raid warning siren sounded and the children lost their sleep and arrived at school the following morning extremely tired. As the war continued and the dangers seemed to be less, some of the evacuees began to return to their own homes. During the war and after, Mr Knight was involved with the Redditch Air Training Corps as Flight Lieutenant in charge. It was to provide extra food for the children in the time of wartime food rationing that Mr Knight in March 1940 started the provision of school dinners. These cost 4d each, and 22 children began to take advantage of them. Kitchen equipment was installed in the old infants school room,

Mr A T Knight, Headmaster 1933-59. (Ron Knight)

including a sink and a large electric cooker, and the children ate their meals in part of one of the main school classrooms. From 1943 to 1962 the meals supervisor was Miss Van Bylevelt, and from 1962 until 1982, when the provision of school dinners ceased, Mrs Doris Warner was in charge. By 1982 the amount charged for school dinners had risen to 45p.

As already mentioned above, the 1948 Education Act made secondary education compulsory for all pupils, as soon as could be, but it was not until the Ridgeway School opened in Astwood Bank in 1958, the year before Mr Knight's retirement, that it finally came into complete operation at Tardebigge. Now all pupils, instead of being able to stay on to the age of 14, had to leave at 11 to attend a secondary school. As a result the school population dropped from a steady 130 or so to around 80, and this was a significant change both for the school, which lost its senior pupils, and also for the pupils themselves.

Meanwhile, in July 1958 Mrs Eades, a former pupil of the school, who had been appointed to the staff in 1931, retired, and in the following September she was replaced by Miss Phipps who came from Bentley School, following its closure, with twelve children from there. She soon married, and as Mrs Lamb she continued to teach and eventually retired after 40 years service at Bentley and Tardebigge in 1967.

JAMES HUTCHINGS, who became the Head of Tardebigge School in April 1959, began his teaching career after war service as a navigator in the RAF. He taught at St George's School in Redditch before being appointed to the staff of Tardebigge School in 1953. In the summer of 1958 he left to teach at the new Ridgeway Secondary School, but was soon selected from 62 applicants to return to Tardebigge as Head Teacher. Mr Hutchings had evidently made a good impression during his previous five years at Tardebigge. During his 23 years as Head, his enthusiastic involvement in the life of the school, and also the church and local community, continued to impress. He was a great nature lover and was especially knowledgeable about birds and their songs. He shared this interest with his pupils and often took small groups of them on Saturday mornings along the canal or into the grounds of Hewell Grange. Another of his interests was country dancing which he taught to the children. They danced round the old oak tree near the barn when the weather was fine, and in the former infants school at other times. One of the occasions when they performed in public was in 1977 at the Queen's Silver Jubilee celebrations in Hewell Park. Soon after taking over as Head Teacher Mr Hutchings organised the school football team which played other schools on Saturday mornings, and money was raised to purchase the necessary kit through coffee mornings and raffles.

Jim Hutchings and his wife Patricia lived, as did previous headmasters and their families, in the School House, which made it convenient for them both to participate in church activities. Mr Hutchings was a member of the PCC and he also served on the Tutnall and Cobley Parish Council. Patricia, who was not a qualified teacher, served as school secretary, also as unofficial "School Mum" to whom the children turned

Headmaster Jim Hutchings and his wife Pat, prizewinners at Tardebigge Show, August 1981. (Bromsgrove Messenger)

when accidents happened or other problems arose. She helped children with their reading and she looked after classes when Jim was called away.

During Mr Hutchings' time as Head Teacher, the school population fluctuated greatly. There were around 80 children, 5 to 11 year olds, until 1965, when an influx of children of the staff from the newly opened Brockhill Remand Centre swelled the number to as many as 110. To accommodate this increase the new infants classroom was built and came into use in 1966. Pupil numbers remained buoyant until the three-tier system was introduced in the area, between 1972 and 1974, and children now had to leave Tardebigge at the age of nine. Then pupil numbers dropped to around 80. They fell still further to around 50 by 1979 due to there being fewer children in the catchment area. For some time there was a fear that the school might have to close, but fortunately it survived this apparent threat.

The children of prison officers brought a mixed assortment of dialects to the school population, as the families came from various different parts of the UK. A few children were allowed to attend from Whitegates Children's Home at Tutnall. Four coloured children from there, two boys and two girls, already problem children, caused disciplinary problems at a time when coloured people were still a small minority in the local population. At first they were alienated by other children and called "wogs". But they were soon integrated and one of the boys, Herbie, kept in touch with the school until after his marriage in Redditch.

During the 1970s power cuts and strikes causing shortages of coal and coke were frequent occurrences and led to many schools having to close. But Tardebigge had the reputation of remaining open at such times and in snowy weather. During power cuts school dinners continued, potatoes were boiled on the coal fire in the dining room and other food was cooked on the vicarage Aga. During snowy weather farmers brought children to school on their tractors and a gang of Borstal boys would be sent to clear the snow from the school approaches.

In 1981, with a view to his early retirement the following year, Jim Hutchings received permission from the school managers for him and his wife to move out of the school house into their own home in Finstall. After only 5 years of retirement, Mr Hutchings died in 1987.

In September 1982 Mrs JANET CROOK began her 18 years' service as Head Teacher. Like her predecessor, Jim Hutchings, she had been an assistant teacher at the school, in her case from 1973. She had studied part-time and had obtained the degree of B.Ed. in 1979. Following her appointment as Head Teacher she and her husband Geoffrey continued to live in their own house in Fairfield, and so the School House was available to let, at first to Peter and Maureen Frowley, then to a succession of other tenants who have kept a watchful eye on the church and school premises and have also been helpful in other ways.

During Mrs Crook's headship the number of pupils in the school increased steadily from around 50 to around 135, and from just two members of staff in 1982 (Mrs Crook and Mrs Slater) the staffing level rose to six (including the Head) by the year 2000. By 1994, when a mobile classroom had to be installed in the playground because of repairs to the school buildings, there were four classes for children covering ages 5 to 9, with just over 100 pupils. The retention of the mobile classroom after the completion of the repairs provided the opportunity to start a reception class of 4 year olds, and this enabled the school population to rise to around 135. Also in 1995 a change was made in the time of entry of children to the school, which was changed from the previous intake of rising fives each term to a single yearly intake in September each year. The rise in the population of the school and increasing pressure upon places have been due, not only to the Brockhill development in the parish, but also to a large extent to the increasing popularity of the school with its Christian ethos, its family atmosphere and its good reputation following excellent OFSTED reports.

It was at the beginning of Mrs Crook's time as Head, in 1982, that the provision of school dinners came to an end and the old infants school, which had been used for cooking and serving the meals, became the Parish Room or Church Hall. With an increasing school population it was a good thing that the hall could now be used by the school for its early morning and other assemblies for all the children, as well as for church meetings and social events. But the use of the Church Hall for P.E. was very limited, and so for some years children were transported to Rigby Hall Special School in Aston Fields to use their gymnasium. This inconvenient arrangement was rendered obsolete by the opening of the Tardebigge Community Hall which is now used extensively by the school.

A number of significant events occurred during Mrs Crook's term of office. In 1983 the school obtained its first computer (BBC model) used at first in the office for administrative purposes. A video recorder also acquired that year enabled TV educational programmes to be saved for use in the classroom. In 1985 children with special educational needs (SEN) were first admitted to the school, with provision for their needs. In 1993 the school premises were extended to include a Head Teacher's office, a staffroom and a staff toilet. (One wonders how the teaching staff had managed previously without these amenities!). In 1994 the church and school car park near the entrance to the churchyard was constructed and made available. In 1997, following the Dunblane tragedy, when a gunman entered a school and shot dead a teacher and some pupils, security at Tardebigge was strengthened by the construction of the inner lobby and office window to monitor visitors to the school.

One outstanding event which took place in church on 17 and 18 July 1996 was the excellent performance by the school children of the musical "Joseph and the Amazing Technicolour Dreamcoat". It was produced by Mrs Carter and Mrs Downes, and the accompaniment on the piano was by Mrs Downes and Mrs Atkinson. Many children were involved and the main parts were played by Charlotte Hollis (Joseph), Alenka Lamare (Jacob), Tom Pope (Pharaoh), Henry Myatt and Harriet Wood (Mr and Mrs Potiphar), Miles Tibbins (Butler) and Lucy Crisp (Baker). Mrs Denise Carter has been the longest serving full-time member of staff in recent years, having been appointed in 1991. Mrs Sue Atkinson has also given long service as the school secretary since 1995. Another long-serving member of staff is Julie Clarkson, who has been a part-time teaching assistant since 1991.

In 1998 "A Review of Educational Provision in Redditch" was published by the LEA. It included the shattering proposal that Tardebigge School should be merged with Holyoakes Field School in Redditch and should move from its premises at Tardebigge. Needless to say, there was a great outcry and determined opposition on the part of the Governors (led by the Chairman, Mrs Vivien MacKenzie), parents, church members and many other interested people. As a result, the good news was received in January 1999 that the school had been saved from closure at Tardebigge and would carry on into the 21st century.

Mrs Jan Crook retired from her headship at Tardebigge at the end of the year 2000, to take on less arduous teaching duties elsewhere. Under her successor, Mrs Susan Helps, who served until 2009, the school has maintained its success and popularity, and has benefitted greatly from being able to use the new Community Hall.

SCHOOL LIFE

Insights into various aspects of life at the school are to be found in the memoirs of Ken Clarke, Kate Eades, Roy Hims and Ivy Broomfield in chapter 11 of this book. They include having to walk to and from school quite long distances along country lanes in all sorts of weather, impressions of the head teachers and others who taught them, the organisation of school dinners, and details of what was known as "Lady Plymouth's Treat", the Christmas party held each year early in January at Hewell Grange until the start of WW2.

Holidays from school to mark special events were quite a feature of the school calendar in the earlier years of the century. In 1904 there was a whole week's holiday to celebrate the coronation of King Edward VII, and in 1911 another likewise to celebrate the coronation of King George V. Whole or half-day holidays were given on the occasion of special local events, such as the baptism in church of Other Robert George Windsor-Clive, son and heir of the Earl of Plymouth on 21 November 1923.

Coming from a scattered rural community, many children were in demand at fruit gathering times and some holiday times were chosen accordingly. Before WW1 instead of the usual Whit-week holiday, children at Tardebigge School had a fortnight's holiday at the beginning of July each year for strawberry picking. In September some children were allowed days off school to help with the harvest.

In the 1920s, starting in 1922, there was an annual "Children's Day" in June organised by the Tardebigge Women's Institute and hosted by Lady Plymouth, when the school was closed in the afternoon for the children to attend and enjoy the fun and games.

The School Production of "The Wizard of Oz", July 1999, in Tardebigge Church. Jan Crook, headmistress, congratulating the children involved, together with the staff, parents and musicians, on their splendid performance. Some of the principal parts were played by Katie Radburn (Dorothy), Esme O'Loughlin (The Wicked Witch), Jonathan Marsh (The Scarecrow), Joe Underhill (The Tin Man), and Sarah Townsend (The Cowardly Lion). (Jan Crook)

Empire Day, 24 May, if on a school day, was observed with due ceremony, if fine at a gathering around the flagpole. In 1916 the occasion was attended by five wounded soldiers from the VAD Hospital in the Village Hall.

Soon after the Village Hall opened in 1911, girls from the school were given cookery and house-keeping lessons in the kitchen there and this continued between the wars, taught by a succession of ladies. Boys were taught woodwork and other handicrafts at the school from around that time, and both girls and boys took part in gardening in the school grounds at various times. Unfortunately, as the school log book records, the occasional invasion of sheep or cows brought damage and destruction to the school garden.

Because of the relatively small number of pupils, always below the 150 mark, and through its Christian ethos as a church school with daily prayers, often led by the vicar, its generally strict but benevolent discipline and caring family atmosphere with insistence on good manners, many generations of scholars have enjoyed a sound education at Tardebigge School and have retained happy memories of their time there.

CHAPTER 7

Webheath and Foxlydiate

WEBHEATH

The district of Webheath, as its name suggests, was formerly an area of heathland which lay mostly west of Birchfield Road and north of Heathfield Road towards Foxlydiate. In 1894 the Local Government Act gave the name Webheath to a large civil parish extending eastwards as far as Headless Cross, and westwards as far as Tardebigge Church and Tardebigge Farm, and it included Sheltwood Farm, Holyoakes Farm, Tack Farm and Banks Green. This civil parish, besides covering part of Tardebigge Ecclesiastical Parish west of Heathfield Road (formerly known as Webheath Lane), also included part of St Luke's, Headless Cross, Parish east of Heathfield Road. Webheath civil parish lasted until 1930 when it ceased to exist and most of the area we now know as Webheath became part of the Urban District of Redditch.

In the early part of the nineteenth century, as the tithe map shows, the area was entirely rural. But this began to change when, around the 1840s, due to the growth of the needle and other industries in and around Redditch, dwellings began to be built along Birchfield Road as far as, and

The Rose and Crown Public House, Webheath, in the early 1900s. ("Rose and Crown")

St Philip's Church, Webheath. (AW)

along, Heathfield Road. About 1850 a public house, the Rose and Crown, was opened and it probably then also served as a shop. By 1870 the local population had risen to around 500, sufficient to warrant the building of the district church of St Philip's, Webheath.

In 1849 a little Baptist Chapel was built in Birchfield Road a little way towards Redditch from the Heathfield Road junction. It was a small unpretentious building, sponsored independently by Esau Harris, a blacksmith, and it was the first Baptist place of worship in the Redditch area, since the Baptist Church in Redditch town did not open until 1862. In 1864 the Webheath chapel was purchased by the Worcestershire Baptist Association, and it continued in use until WW2. In 1947, having not been used for some years, the chapel was put up for sale. It was bought by the

Redditch Meeting of Christadelphians. Formed before the war, the Christadelphian group had been meeting in the Masonic Hall, Ipsley Street, Redditch, since 1940. In 1947 this venue was no longer available to them, so they were glad at that time to be able to buy the redundant chapel at Webheath, each member contributing to the purchase price. It took a great deal of hard work on the part of the members to renovate, repair and decorate the building. Electricity was installed and, over the years since, the building has been extended at the back, the original wooden pews replaced by chairs, and it continues to be used for worship, Sunday school and other meetings.

In 1868 a needle factory was started in Webheath towards the Redditch end of Birchfield Road by Thomas Harper, and it later became Thomas Harper and Sons Ltd. Thomas Harper lived at The Birches adjacent to his factory. The factory made sewing machine needles and various other needles, and it continued in production until 1931 when it was absorbed into the Milward Group whose main works were in Studley.

In the early 1900s there was a plant nursery in Webheath, George Ecclestone and Son, and a coal dealer, Thomas Simons, at the Hill Top end of Heathfield Road. Several local shops included that of grocer Thomas Cashmore, bootmaker George Johnson, and a laundry run by Mrs Emma Ecclestone.

A bakery was soon built and opened by the Langston family in Birchfield Road facing Heathfield Road. The Langstons lived over the shop and, besides selling and delivering bakery products, they sold groceries and also petrol from two petrol pumps in front of the shop. Following the closure of the bakery around 1979, the shop was occupied by Harris Tool Hire business until, in 1984, Robert Biddle established the present Biddles grocery and general store there. Robert's father, John Biddle, had worked a milk delivery round from Crumpfields Lane from the 1930s to the 1970s, collecting milk from local farms.

During the twentieth century a number of shops and businesses existed at various times in houses built along Heathfield Road. They included the post office and shop, half-way along, run by Mrs Patricia While, first in the 1920s in her white cottage and then in the nearby present premises for many years. In the white house opposite the post office, a bakery business was first established by the Pritchard family, followed by a Mr McClenn, and then from 1931 until 1959 by Charles Shepherd. Next door neighbours were John James, butcher, who eventually moved to Astwood Bank, and a greengrocer. At the Hill Top end of the road there was until around 1970 a general store. Also at Hill Top, inside Church Road, there was the coal and firewood business of Thomas Simons. This was taken over by D E (Joe) Pollard who also owned the timberyard and sawmill along Pumphouse Lane. The timberyard and sawmill business was in turn taken over and has been run in recent years by David Partridge who lives in the adjacent picturesque old cottage.

By 1900 a Webheath Village Club and Institute had been established in Bromsgrove Road (not the present Bromsgrove Road which used to be called Red Lane, but that part of what is now Birchfield Road from Biddles Shop to the Foxlydiate Public House). Secretary of the Club and Institute around 1900 was Ernest Jones. There was also a Working Men's Club which by 1900 had been in existence over twenty years, and its premises were in all probability the corrugated iron building which was the residence of the Hands family featured in the book "The Tin House" by Elizabeth Owen. This very unusual house which belonged to a Mr Adams who owned other local property, including Sycamore Farm at the top end of Heathfield Road, was rented by the Hands family from around 1935 until 1974, after which it was soon demolished to make way for new houses. In the Tin House there was a cloakroom, 5 ft by 12 ft, with clothing pegs. It was a roomy building and would have been suitable for meetings and the residence of a secretary/caretaker.

In 1926, after much local fundraising, a new timber-built village hall opened, the land on which it stands having been bought and donated by local manufacturer Victor Woodfield. It was, and remains, the meeting place of a number of organisations. These have included Brownies, Guides and Ranger Guides; the White Heather Derby and Joan Club which started in 1960; the Webheath Women's Institute which closed in 2003 through lack of volunteer officers; and church groups, including the Sunday School. Because of pressure on the hall's usage, an additional room was built as an extension at the rear in 1974 at a cost of £4750, following much local fundraising.

SALTWAYS CHESHIRE HOME

In 1967 a group of local people, Mr Martin Davies, Mr Halsey and Mr Quigley, were in touch with the Leonard Cheshire Foundation with a view to setting up a Cheshire Home in Redditch. With the encouragement of the Foundation an open meeting was held in September 1968 to generate support. By 1970 the purchase of a site at Hewell was being negotiated. However, in 1971 Redditch Urban District Council offered the site at Webheath on more favourable terms, and this offer was accepted. In 1972 planning permission was obtained and a fundraising appeal was launched. Building work started in 1974 and "Saltways" Cheshire Home was officially opened on 22 November 1975 by a trustee and former chairman of the Leonard Cheshire Foundation, Lord Edmund-Davies. Initially the Home provided a self-contained unit for five residents, with staff accommodation. Extensions followed, first in 1978 with increased communal space and bed sitting rooms for twelve residents, then in 1983 a new wing which brought occupancy up to 21. In the 1990s respite and day care services were introduced and a new block was built to include a staff room and an activities room. Currently Saltways offers support services for young physically disabled adults and for people with learning disabilities. Its situation in Church Road close to Webheath Church makes it convenient for resident disabled people to attend church services.

WEBHEATH SCHOOLS

Until 1946 there was no day school in Webheath for the local children to attend. They had to travel, usually on foot, to schools at Tardebigge, Bentley, Headless Cross or Redditch. In 1946 a school was started in the village hall by the Redditch Council. Mrs Marion Jarvis, from St Luke's School, Headless Cross, was appointed Headmistress. It was not until 1959 that the school moved into new school buildings in Downsell Road. Mrs Jarvis retired in 1966 and she died in 1974.

On 11 November 1968 Our Lady of Mount Carmel Primary School moved from the centre of Redditch to new buildings on the opposite side of Downsell Road. The Head Teacher at the time was Mr Francis Donelly who served as Head from 1948 to 1975. Arrangements were made with the Midland Red Bus Company to transport children to the school from places around Redditch, with the exception of Batchley. From around 150 pupils at first, the number of children attending what is now a First School (for ages 4 to 9) has risen to approaching 300.

WEBHEATH CHURCH

The foundation stone of St Philip's Church was laid on 11 May 1869 by Canon Dickins, Vicar of Tardebigge. The church was consecrated by Dr Henry Philpot, Bishop of Worcester, just over nine months later, on 22 February 1870. The land for the church was given by the local landowner, Richard Hemming of Bentley Manor, and the £3,000 cost of the building was the gift of Lady Harriet, Baroness Windsor of Hewell, before her death in 1869. It was constructed of local sandstone from Hewell and Finstall quarries. As it was being built, Baroness Windsor gave a dinner on 19 August 1869 at the Fox and Goose Inn at Foxlydiate for the fifty work-people engaged in its construction. Various features of the church, its furnishings and monuments, have been provided by generous donors over the years including, initially, the reredos by the Hon Robert Windsor Clive and stained glass windows by the Revd A S Porter. The two-manual hand-pumped pipe organ built by Nicholsons of Worcester was installed in 1890. It remains with some modifications, including the electric blower in 1951.

For over a hundred years St Philip's remained a daughter church within the parish of Tardebigge. It had a succession of curates-in-charge and, until a parsonage was built in Church Road across from the church in 1920, these clergymen were provided with board and lodgings in Pumphouse Farmhouse. This large rambling two-storied farmhouse had, for some time in the nineteenth century, been a workhouse for local vagrants who, in return for their labours on the farm, were given shelter and were fed. The bell, which was used to summon them for meals, still exists in the possession of farmer Lionel Tongue. Also up in the farmhouse there exist clothing pegs and a rack for inkwells and it may well have been that the curate held a Sunday School there.

Eventually a schoolroom was built onto the end of the farmhouse nearest to Pumphouse Lane, and this served for many years as a meeting place for the Sunday School and other church groups. The schoolroom which, together with the rest of the farm, was Hewell Estate property, was given by the Plymouth family to the church in 1947. In 1970 it was sold for £450 to help raise money for the new church car park. The Jazz Group which bought it as a practice room made so much noise that it was soon bought back by farmer Lionel Tongue's sister Sylvia for £500. In a dilapidated state it now serves as a store room.

In 1954 the new vestry, built at a cost of £1,250, was dedicated by the Bishop of Worcester, Dr W W Cash. It was needed because the organ had largely occupied the original vestry, and there was little space for the choir, at that time, of 15 boys and 4 men. A fund for the building had been started before WW2, but due to the war the project had been shelved. It was not until 1952 that the Priest-in-Charge of St Philip's, the Revd T Edwards, revived the idea and the necessary fundraising was then enthusiastically undertaken. The new vestry has served, besides clergy and choir, also children during church services.

When the centenary of the church was celebrated in 1970 with special services and events, the curate-in-charge was the Revd Fred Coley. He and his wife and son arrived at the parsonage together with a steam roller in 1968, after the previous curate, the Revd Roy Lodge, had left, after just over a year in office, to become the warden/chaplain of the new probation hostel for young male delinquents at Upper Norgrove. In February 1970 another steam vehicle, "Goliath", a massive traction engine, which had been used from 1921 to 1954 to tow the fairground equipment of Pat Collins, arrived to grace the parsonage. Other features of Fred Coley's popular ministry included the introduction of family services and the endless collection of jokes he included in the Webheath section of the monthly Tardebigge parish magazine.

By the time Fred Coley left in October 1972 to become the vicar of three parishes in the Teme Valley, the Church Council of Webheath was proposing that Webheath should become a separate parish, independent of Tardebigge. It was to be another nine years, during the ministry of priest-in-charge the Revd Eric Thomas, that, in May 1981, the Queen in Council authorised the creation of the Parish of Webheath, to be included in the new Ridge Team Ministry from 1 June. This Team Ministry covered the parishes of Headless Cross, Crabbs Cross and St Georges, Redditch, as well as Webheath, and it remained in being until in 2006 the Holy Trinity Team Ministry was established, which included Tardebigge and Webheath.

FOXLYDIATE

Now the name of the hotel on Birchfield Road near to its junction with the A448 Warwick Highway, Foxlydiate is historically the name of a small hamlet which was in existence long before the expansion of Webheath into the area in the latter part of the twentieth century. It consisted of the Foxlydiate Farm together with a small cluster of cottages, a public house "The Fox and Goose", and a post office and stores. Before the building of the dual carriageway, the location was busy with traffic on what was the main road from Bromsgrove to Alcester. This road, originally a country lane, had been widened to take motor traffic.

Around 1990 the late Madge Guise recorded these memories of the area:-

Early 1900s view of Birchfield Road looking towards Bromsgrove and showing, on the left, old cottages and Foxlydiate Farmhouse, on the right the village shop and post office and, projecting into the road, "The Fox and Goose" public house. "The Fox and Goose" was demolished in 1947 when the road was widened. (Alan Foxall)

"The Fox and Goose", a peaceful scene in the early 1900s. (Alan Foxall)

Foxlydiate was an attractive little Worcestershire village situated between the villages of Webheath and Tardebigge. Many changes have, however, been made since my young days.

The "Fox and Goose Inn", demolished in the thirties, was situated on the main Bromsgrove Road, opposite Foxlydiate Farm. It was a long low building with its front entrance facing Foxlydiate Hill. It was in this inn that the locals enjoyed playing the board game of quoits. The licensee was then my great uncle, Herbert Chambers, having married my grandmother's sister Mrs Chesshire. There was a private hedge-maze behind the inn and the post office, which always scared me to go round as a child.

After the demolition of the inn the Foxlydiate Hotel was built on the site of "Foxlydiate House" by Dare Brothers. The opening ceremony was performed by the actress Evelyn Laye in 1939.

"Foxlydiate House" was the home of Mr and Mrs W L McCandlish. The house was covered with creeper, thus making it an attractive and colourful building in the heart of the village. Mr McCandlish bred Chow dogs, and I remember he gave my cousin, Peggy Humphries, one of these beautiful dogs.

The Post Office, where my grandmother Lee was postmistress, is now closed, but it still stands. Originally it had cobbled stones in front, with two rustic seats. In front of the wall between the post office and the inn were the mounting steps and water trough for the horses. It is only recently that the mounting steps finally crumbled away. My grandmother had an unfortunate trap accident in front of the post office and when she regained consciousness the first thing she said was "Where's my transformation?" A wig or hair piece was called a transformation in those days.

Foxlydiate Farm, when I visited my grandparents, was farmed by the Hughes family. Happy days for my Grandfather Lee and Mr Hughes senior were trips by horse and trap to Crowle or Chaddesley Corbett races. Off they went, each resplendent in yellow waistcoat and watch and chain, complemented by a well-trimmed moustache. They returned, needless to say, looking very rosy. The Hughes family retired to "Hill Cottage", Foxlydiate Hill, and in 1951 Mr and Mrs Fred Shrimpton went to live at the farm. Fred, who was also a builder, kept a dairy herd and specialised in calf rearing.

Another great change in the village was the construction of the Bromsgrove Highway by R M Douglas Construction Ltd. I was asked by the Redditch Development Corporation to open the road. The cutting of the tape and the official ceremony took place under the bridge opposite the Foxlydiate Hotel on 25 October 1979. I was presented with the scissors and an inscribed silver tray. My husband Harry and I were then taken by bus to see the whole of the completed Bromsgrove Highway.

Many attractive houses have been built down the Lane, now Heathfield Road, creating a different look from the quiet rural scene with the stream babbling away at the foot of the hill. One of the features of the village was the Meet of the Worcestershire Hunt, a sight I shall always remember.

Foxlydiate House, mentioned by Madge in her memoirs, was a large house which was originally built for William Hemming, needle manufacturer and purchaser of the Manor of Bentley, in the 1830s. In the early 1900s it was the home of Sir Montague Margesson, private secretary to the Earl of Plymouth. From around 1910 until 1935 it was the main residence of William McCandlish and his family. McCandlish was a wealthy businessman who moved from Bristol to involve himself in the financial affairs of the Bromsgrove Guild of Applied Arts. He was for many years managing director and chairman of the Company. Dogs were his hobby and he was an official of the Kennel Club. He often visited the workshops of the Guild in Station Street, Bromsgrove, and was remembered for his use of a monocle. In 1935 he moved with his wife Millicent to Hampshire and he died in 1947.

LOCAL FARMS

Foxlydiate Farm, with 40 acres of land, used to be part of the Bentley Estate. In 1947 it was sold by auction and purchased by Aner Shrimpton, a member of the Shrimpton Family building firm established in Mount Pleasant, Redditch, in 1860. Aner farmed it for four years, but the house, meanwhile tenanted by farm workers, was in bad shape and in 1951 Aner's nephew, Fred Shrimpton, also a builder, and his wife Beryl took over the house and farm. Fred built up a dairy herd and a milk business, but later changed to rearing calves for the meat trade. Meanwhile Webheath was expanding and around 1985 the barns were sold and converted into three dwellings. In 1987 the farm house was sold and half of the farm land was sold off for housing and road developments. The remaining 20 acres, situated in the Bromsgrove Council area, were retained and let out, in part, for the grazing of Shetland ponies. The farmhouse still stands, the Foxlydiate Lane having been deviated around it.

Two other farms in the Foxlydiate area which came to an end through housing development as Webheath expanded were Springhill Farm along Foxlydiate Lane and Boxnot Farm facing the end of Foxlydiate Lane near Webheath Church. Springhill Farm was rented from the Bentley Estate. In the early 1900s and until around the end of WW1, it was farmed by Howard Hill, who moved from there to Holyoakes Farm, Tardebigge, around the end of WW1. His two sons Jack and Gerald were born there. The last to farm at Springhill was Ralph Farmer. He retired in 1969 and moved after over 30 years there. Ralph and his wife were very active members of Webheath Church and he was a churchwarden for over 26 years. After their departure the farmhouse and part of the land were sold by the Bentley Estate and since then the farmhouse has been altered and modernised by subsequent owners and the surrounding land used for the keeping of horses.

Boxnot farm has completely disappeared, the partly timber-framed farmhouse having been demolished in the late 1990s to make way for housing. The last farmer there was Arthur Partridge. He bought the farm from the Bentley Estate about 1940, after the previous tenant had been evicted for bad farming. During the early part of the war he was an agricultural contractor, engaged in ploughing up land for food production. One relic from the farm is a 5 ft high mantrap now in the County Museum at Hartlebury. It held its intruder victim in its dangerous jaws, and it used to be situated on a wall by the granary at one side of the farmhouse.

Tack Farm today is separated from the rest of Foxlydiate by the A448 dual carriageway overbridge, but before that came into being, the farm was just a little way down the main road and a closer part of the Foxlydiate community. It was Amy, one of the daughters of farmer Walford of Tack Farm in the 1840s and 1850s, who created the unique lectern in Tardebigge Church and the memorial window to the two wives of Thomas Dixon. In the 1890s and until 1925, when he died, Charles Owen was the farmer and he played a prominent part in local affairs. He was followed by Alfred Goulbourne until the beginning of WW2 when he died, and his wife was only able to keep the farm going for a time with the help of three land army girls, including Mary Morris, whose story is told in chapter 11. Around 1943 the farm was rented from the Hewell Estate by Dr H E Houfton of Redditch. When the Estate was sold in 1946, Dr Houfton was one of the consortium of four which purchased all but Hewell Park and the Grange. He chose to keep the farm and took up residence there. In 1966 the farm was sold to Mr Jones and his wife who came from Telford. Following her husband's death, Mrs Jones, who had served in the land army during the war, carried on with the help of her overworked handicapped son. This unhappy situation ended when, around 1992, the son murdered his mother, and then, for a number of years, the farm buildings remained in a dilapidated state. In due course the farmhouse was restored and modernised and the outbuildings attractively converted to residential use.

Lanehouse Farm along Curr Lane was farmed from before WW1 until his death in 1926, aged 83, by Thomas Tongue whose wife was a member of the Cookes family of Bentley. His son Harvey Tongue then took over the farm and continued to run it until in his eighties. In his younger days Harvey had worked as a gardener at Hewell Grange, helping with the layout of the garden there, and he remained throughout his life a keen gardener. His son Ron, who was born in 1916 and attended Tardebigge School, also began his working life away from the farm as a carpenter on the Hewell Estate before eventually joining his father, in the 1940s, as a partner on the farm. Following Harvey's death in December 1969, Ron moved away from the farm to manage a riding school in Beoley and, as happened so often elsewhere, the farmhouse became a private residence and the land has since been used by other local farmers.

CHAPTER 8

Other Local Communities

BANKS GREEN

The area around the junction of Copyholt Lane with the road southwards to Upper Bentley has long been known as Banks Green. It was, way back, a clearing in the Forest of Feckenham and took its name from Thomas Banckes who lived in the area in the seventeenth century. Banks Green Farm in Copyholt Lane near the road junction was a smallholding of some 10 to 15 acres. From the 1930s onwards it was the home of Austin and Kate Eades, rented at first from the Hewell Estates, then bought in 1946. Kate Eades' mother, Mrs Wilson, the widow of John Wilson who had been the Hewell Grange electrician, lived in the adjacent Banks Green Cottage. More recently Banks Green Farmhouse has been the home of John King who married Janice, the daughter of Austin and Kate Eades.

Amongst the longest established residents of Banks Green are Roger and Peggy Boss who have lived at Bradley Cottage since its purchase in 1963. The cottage takes its name from the Bradley family who at one time were the tenants of what was a smallholding belonging to the Hewell Estates. When the land became part of New House Farm the cottage was used, until 1963, to house farm workers.

Apart from farming, two businesses were established on opposite sides of Banks Green Road in the latter part of the twentieth century. In the 1960s

Aerial view of Bentley Garage and, over the road and opposite, Banks Green Garden Centre, c.1970. (Richard Kendall)

and 1970s there was Bentley Garage. Its proprietor was T W Pritchard who undertook to carry out repairs to all types of vehicle. There were two petrol pumps in the forecourt and, behind, a large repair shop. Mrs Pritchard sold sweets and cigarettes. The business was eventually taken over by John Wood and used for the servicing of heavy goods vehicles, before being sold and the site cleared and used for the building of two houses. Banks Green Garden Centre was started at "The Haven" by Richard Kendall and his mother Eileen in 1982. Since Eileen died in 1998, it has been developed by Richard and his wife and they have continued to supply bedding plants wholesale and retail over a wide area.

BLACKWELL COURT

Blackwell Court lies just outside the boundary of Tardebigge Parish, but within the civil parish of Tutnall and Cobley on the east side of the Lickey Incline, between Vigo and Blackwell Golf Course. It owes its existence to George Unite, a wealthy Birmingham business man who, in the 1860s, following the completion of the Birmingham to Gloucester Railway in 1841 and the building of the station at Blackwell, decided to make his home in

Blackwell Court. (AW)

the Worcestershire countryside near to the station. He purchased the large area of farmland bounded by lanes and the railway, built his large house "Blackwell Court" together with its coach house and stables, created the drive and developed the parkland. From the house there was a footpath to the station, from which he was able to commute to Birmingham.

Some 40 years later, in 1906, the house was let by the Unite family to Boultbee Brooks. He was the eldest son of John Boultbee Brooks, founder of the leather firm in Birmingham which had produced the famous Brooks bicycle saddle, adopted by cycle manufacturers Rudge Whitworth, Raleigh, and others world-wide. In 1896, John, now well-to-do, and his family, had come to live at Finstall Park, near Bromsgrove. The following year his son Boultbee, having joined his father's firm at the age of 17, was made a director at the age of 21. Nine years later, following his marriage and the birth of his baby daughter, he was able to make his home, not far away, as the tenant of Blackwell Court.

As George Unite had done, Boultbee Brooks travelled by train between Blackwell and Birmingham. Trains, it is said, used to whistle at the bottom of the Lickey Incline to give Mr Brooks time to get to the station to catch his train from Blackwell to the city. The train on which he returned would also whistle on the approach to Blackwell to alert a servant to take the donkey cart to pick him up at the station. To shield his home from the railway and maintain his privacy, trees were planted on his land alongside the railway.

In 1911 Boultbee Brooks had two tennis courts made alongside the entrance drive to his abode, and he had part of the old kitchen garden converted into a croquet lawn. In 1919 after WW1 he bought the property from the Unite family, and in 1921 he had electricity from his own generator installed. Also at that time he added the east wing to the house, carried out major improvements to the gardens and converted the stables into garages. During WW2 the family moved out and the house was let to the Josiah Mason Orphanage. Mrs Brooks died in January 1945 and in June of that year Boultbee and his daughter moved back into Blackwell Court and began a long uphill struggle to bring the house and the gardens back to their pre-war condition. Boultbee died in 1952, just after mains electricity had been installed. His daughter, Miss Dorothy Boultbee Brooks, carried on alone until around 1970 when she moved away. She was a keen horse rider and an active member of St Bartholomew's Church, Tardebigge, until she died.

In 1971 the County of Birmingham Scout Association acquired the property with its 52 acres of land as a conference and activity centre and camp site. It was initially known as "The Douglas and Mary Turner Scouting Centre" after the couple who donated generously to its purchase.

The first manager of Blackwell Court Scout Centre was Bill Shorto, until 1975. He was succeeded by Brian Kimberley who served from 1975 to 2000. Together with Pikes Pool, used for canoeing, Blackwell Court has been extensively used by scouts and guides for camping and other activities, and for the training of scout and guide leaders. Over the years facilities have been added, including an outdoor swimming pool and the conversion of the old stable block into a bunkhouse. International events have been held there, including an International Guide Camp with a royal visit from Princess Margaret.

BROAD GREEN

For many years there has been a small community at Broad Green, where the road from Tutnall to Cobley, along the Holloway and up Stoney Lane, crosses Hewell Lane. Hewell Lane, on the way between Alcester and The Lickey, was part of one of four coach routes from London to Holyhead and was classed as a mail road. Also, before the road from Tardebigge New Wharf to the gates of Hewell Grange was constructed around 1811, road traffic from Bromsgrove to Redditch usually travelled through Finstall and Tutnall, along the Holloway to Broad Green, then right via the slip road onto Hewell Lane and left along Brockhill Lane. So Broad Green used to be quite busy with horse-drawn traffic, as it has been with motor traffic in recent times. Welcome amenities there, both for travellers and local people, were the old timber-framed inn, the "Black Boy", at one corner of the cross-

Formerly "The Black Boy" public house at the crossroads, Broad Green. A notice outside the "Black Boy" in Cartway, Bridgnorth, states that it was named in honour of the Restoration of King Charles II, so-called because he had a dusky complexion. This suggests that the "Black Boy" at Broad Green was in existence in the seventeenth century. (AW)

roads, the building still standing with its entrance from Stoney Lane, and the old Forge close by in Hewell Lane where the blacksmith's job included that of farrier and wheelwright. Also at Broad Green there used to be the Pound, a useful wooden-fenced area where stray farm animals could be impounded and kept until claimed by local farmers.

By 1900 the "Black Boy" had closed as a public house, probably at the same time as Lord Plymouth closed the "Plymouth Arms" and other public houses on his estates around 1879. It had previously served partly as a shop for travellers and local people, and subsequent occupants continued this service. Mrs Eliza Tustin, widow of Edward Tustin of the Old Wharf, kept shop there for some years until her death in 1917, and she was followed by Mrs E G Large whose husband Jack was a tractor driver for T & M Dixon and then for Tardebigge Orchards. The shop, as remembered, was in a small building at the side of the old Black Boy and sold sweets and items of grocery.

Back in the 1860s and 1870s the blacksmith at Broad Green was John Turley. When he died in 1883, Edward Thomas Tustin, his apprentice, then aged 21 and known as Ted, took over the business. Ted's parents were the above-mentioned Edward and Eliza Tustin, who lived on the Old Wharf where Ted was born in 1863. They were shopkeepers; Edward worked as a groom for T & M Dixon, and they continued to live on the Old Wharf until Edward died in 1904. Their son Ted, living at the Forge, was married twice. His son Edward William, by his first wife, died of war wounds in 1917 and his name is on the War Memorial in Tardebigge Church. Ted's son Harry by his second wife, Sarah, went to Tardebigge School and then began work as a blacksmith with his father in 1911. When Harry married, he and his wife Gladys lived at Tutnall, and then, when Ted died, a widower, in 1945, they moved into the Forge house. Eventually Harry retired at the beginning of 1971 after 60 years in the business. He died in 1973, and Gladys in 1985. The Old Forge has since been modernised and adapted as a private residence.

Between the old "Black Boy" and the Forge, "Laundry Cottage" was where, for many years, the residents, Mr and Mrs Coote, ran a laundry service for the families of T & M Dixon. Their two sons, Eric and Ted, went to Tardebigge School.

In 1922 two semi-detached bungalows were built by Dixons on the slip road at Broad Green for their employees. Of these "The Heathers", nearer Hewell Lane, was first occupied by Thomas Evans, stockman for Dixons, his wife Florence, and their children, Tom, Florence and Doris. The first tenants of the other bungalow were Joel Williams, fruit foreman, with his elderly mother, his wife Alice and their family, and they were there until the 1960s. Nearby, now the site of new houses, there were Dixons' offices with a forecourt with three petrol pumps and, nearby, fruit and egg-packing sheds, erected soon after WW1. The first resident caretaker at the offices was Mrs Houghton, mother of T & M Dixon's long-serving secretary Jack Houghton. She was followed by Thomas and Florence Evans who moved from their bungalow and were there until 1951. Their daughter Doris worked in Dixons' nearby egg-packing premises for many years. At the offices, the directors of T & M Dixon used to meet regularly, employees went there to receive their wages, and fruit-pickers, in season, called there to receive payment in return for the tokens they had been given by the fruit foremen.

During the period of the existence of these timber-built offices at Broad Green, two men who worked there from the beginning until their retirements in the 1970s were Howard Bird and Jack Houghton. Both had worked as clerks or secretaries for T & M Dixon at the Lower House. Howard Bird rose to become a partner in Dixons' farming business and a director of their Redditch coal business, and he subsequently became chairman and managing director of Tardebigge Orchards, and he played a prominent part in local affairs. Jack Houghton retired in 1972. Others who worked with Jack Houghton over the years included Fred Bird and Charles Wall.

The offices were used by Dixons' successors, Tardebigge Orchards, until around 1970, when, following the closure of the cattle market in Bromsgrove, Fred Duggins took over the site and constructed an abattoir. After about 25 years, Duggins sold out to Bakers of Northampton, and the abattoir continued until 2000/2001, when the company, hit by the outbreak of foot and mouth disease in cattle, closed down. This is when the site was soon developed and the present houses were built.

Memories of Broad Green during and between the wars include gatherings of the local hunt. The horses and hounds regularly assembled on the Green at around 10 am before moving off. During WW2 there was an Anderson type air-raid shelter installed on the Green for the local inhabitants. Ray King remembers acting as a casualty during a training exercise by the Red Cross at Broad Green during the war, and being taken by ambulance, driven by the singer Mavis Bennett, to Smallwood Hospital, Redditch.

Just along Stoney Lane from Broad Green, The Cottage (so-called, but actually a large family house) was the home of three generations of the Dixon family. First to live there, from 1857 until his death in 1896, was Thomas Dixon, the elder of the two brothers of the T & M Dixon partnership, who was twice married but had no children. The Cottage was then occupied by Colonel Dixon, bachelor son of the younger partner Matthew Dixon, until he died in 1932. With him, in his later years, also lived his widowed sister Elizabeth Thompson and her family. They were,

The Coronation of Queen Elizabeth II on 2 June 1953 was marked by local representatives at Broad Green. From the left: Jack Large, Jim Mitchell, Tom Evans, Howard Bird, Alf Westover, Mrs Gwendoline Tustin, William Perry, James Williams, Len Banner. The wooden plaque was evidently the work of Alf Westover. Mrs Tustin, wife of blacksmith Harry Tustin, was a Bromsgrove Rural District Councillor. Howard Bird was Chairman of Tardebigge Orchards. The other persons were employees of Tardebigge Orchards, formerly T & M Dixon.

A meeting of the Worcestershire Hunt at Broad Green. In the background are the offices of Tardebigge Orchards, formerly T & M Dixon. The only surely identified person is, beside the telephone box, Mrs Gertrude Large of the nearby shop and post office. ((Birmingham Post and Mail)

Harry Tustin, blacksmith, at The Forge, Broad Green, just before his retirement. He started working for his father at the smithy on 1 January 1911 and retired 60 years later on 31 December 1970. (Birmingham Post)

in turn, succeeded by Honor Dixon, and her husband Allan Macdonell, until the latter's death in 1954. The property then passed into the ownership of Alfred Preedy of the well-known firm of tobacconists, and he also acquired part of the property at the Broad Green crossroads, the tenants of which, Mr and Mrs Fox, worked for him at The Cottage. Around 1970 The Cottage was bought by John Terry and he had it enlarged and converted into a private hospital for cosmetic surgery. As such it had a chequered history, involving John Terry's private circumstances, and it was eventually taken over and further impressively developed to become "Dolan Park" private hospital.

An interesting large house along Hewell Lane between Broad Green and Hewell is "The Elbows". In 1812 the property was held by John Hunt, the licensee of the Navigation Inn opposite Tardebigge Old Wharf. It may have become licensed premises when the Navigation Inn closed. From around 1850 until 1872, when she died aged 81, Elizabeth Billings was the occupier. She was quite a character. She was a licensed beer retailer. She farmed some 15 acres of surrounding land belonging to the property. She had a reputation as a "wise woman" with a knowledge of herbs and medicines. Her grave in Tardebigge churchyard is situated opposite the chancel door.

In 1873 The Elbows farmhouse and outbuildings, garden, meadow and pastureland, totalling 16 acres, were sold for £1,500 to James Harris of Redditch. He and his wife Emma and their son Augustus, who farmed the land, were there until soon after 1900, when Hugh Dixon, one of the sons of Matthew Dixon of T & M Dixon, took up residence with his wife Mabel, and the land was farmed as part of the family business. Fruit grown at The Elbows included blackcurrants which were contracted to Carters of Coleford for the making of Ribena. Hugh died in 1931, but Mabel Dixon continued to live there until her death in 1953. She was a graduate of Girton College Cambridge, a sportswoman and a JP, and she was active in local affairs.

From 1953 to 1973 The Elbows was the home of Howard Bird. Born in 1888, Howard began working for T & M Dixon in their office at the Lower House as clerk around 1908. He was joined by Jack Houghton as his assistant in 1911 and, as mentioned already, the two continued to serve the business after the new offices were built at Broad Green. Howard's business ability was rewarded in the 1930s by his promotion to be a director of Dixons' coal business and a partner in their farming business. His part in local affairs included serving on Redditch Urban District Council and Worcestershire County Council. When the Hewell Estate was sold in 1946 Howard was one of the syndicate of four which purchased most of the land and property, some to retain and some for resale, and he acquired the Lordship of the Manor of Bromsgrove.

COBLEY

The area known as Cobley, which includes Cobley Hill, extends eastwards from the hill top down Grange Lane over the canal and railway bridges as far as the River Arrow. It is a rural area with just a few scattered properties including two farms, Cobley Hill Farm and Grange Farm (see Chapter 10), and most of the land used to be part of the Hewell Estates before their sale in 1946.

On the left-hand side of Grange Lane as one descends from the hill top to the canal bridge, lies "Keeper's Cottage". This was the residence of those appointed to manage the pheasantry which was located in Andrew's Coppice, the woodland which is on the opposite side of the lane and now stretches down to the canal. Although pheasants have long ceased to be reared there, they are often still to be seen in the fields on Cobley Hill. Whereas Keepers Cottage was double-fronted, having rooms either side of the front door, the under-keepers cottage, now "Top Cottage" on the brow of the hill, was only single-fronted, thus marking the distinction between those of greater and lesser rank in the Hewell Estate employment hierarchy. The last tenant, before the property was bought by John and Rosalind Chambers, was Thomas Jackson who worked for T & M Dixon.

On Cobley Hill, Top Cottage and, over the road, the former windmill pump. (Rosalind Chambers)

From the early years of the century until around the year 2000, a prominent feature on the top of Cobley Hill was a tall windmill pump. It was used by Cobley Hill Farm for raising water from a well. The well is still there, but wind-power has been replaced by a submersible pump.

HEWELL VILLAGE

For many years at Hewell there has been a small community of people, mainly estate workers and their families, living in tied cottages. On the north-east side of Hewell Lane are the estate lodges, the buildings of the Home Farm and further towards Redditch, beyond the drive to the Kennels and Paper Mills, the row of four attached cottages known as Park Cottages. Before the Hewell Estates were sold, the Home Farm was managed by estate staff. The farmhouse was occupied by Lionel F Lambert, agent to Lord Plymouth, and then by his successor John F Mellor. In 1946 Joe Beckett, one of the consortium of four who purchased all but the Grange and surrounding parkland of the Hewell Estate, moved from Shortwood Farm to the Home Farm at Hewell with his wife Janie and

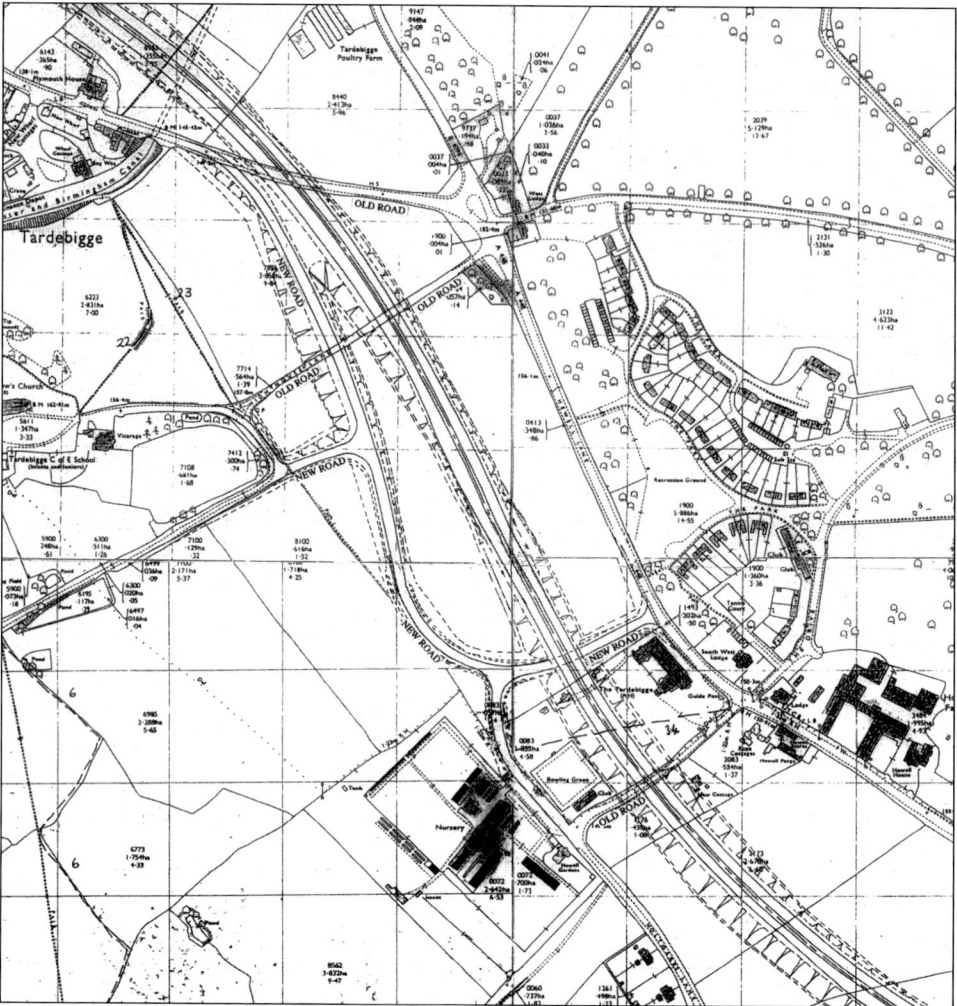

Map of Hewell Village showing the dual carriageway, constructed in the 1970s, and the changes it caused to the road system. Also marked are the walled vegetable garden (which supplied Hewell Grange), Hewell Home Farm, and the many houses on The Park which were built for officers of the Hewell Grange Borstal and Brockhill Prison and their families.

young daughter Elizabeth. For some twenty-five years, Joe, with the help of George Scoltock who lived at the nearby lodge (formerly the Dairy), worked the Home Farm at Hewell and also Brockhill Farm which he now owned. Then around 1971 he decided to retire from farming, as the A448 dual carriageway began to be constructed across his land. Both farms, covering altogether some 700 acres, of which 200 acres were woodland, had been run as dairy farms. In recent years the farmland has been let,

The farmhouse and outbuildings of the Hewell Home Farm before the out-buildings were converted for commercial use. (Michael Price)

partly to local farmers including Jim Wormington of Patchett's Farm, and partly to the Home Office.

Once the cowsheds and most other buildings surrounding the Hewell farmyard became redundant, they began to be converted and let to small businesses. The first to be established there was the partnership of Geoff Bayliss and Geoff Whitehouse whose business was supplying exhibition stands. The farmyard area, together with the adjacent large barn, is now known as Tardebigge Court, and after 30 years it has become a successful out-of-town group of small, mostly specialist, craft shops, including metal-work and upholstery.

Between the farmyard and the dairy lodge, the open area was the estate timberyard. At the far end of it there was an electrical sub-station building. Also in the timberyard were the sawing shed and the carpenters' shop where furniture, farm gates, fences and other wooden items were made and mended, and from there carpenters went round the estate property, to farms and cottages, to replace or repair wooden items such as floor-boards, window frames, doors and gable ends. In the 1930s the foreman at the timberyard was Ray Squires. The head carpenter was Bill Palmer, and he eventually stayed on to work for Joe Beckett. Bill and his assistants, Charlie Platt and, for three years, Ron Tongue, started work, as did other estate employees, at 7.30 am. Bill Palmer lived with his sister at Palmer's Cottage, and, whilst working for Joe Beckett, he sometimes made wooden toys for Joe's daughter, Elizabeth, when he should have been otherwise busy. Charlie Platt, who was deaf-as-a-post, lived with his schoolteacher sister, Mrs Badger, at the Papermills. Ron Tongue was appointed by Mr Lambert straight from Tardebigge School in 1930. He earned only half-a-crown a week at first, and just 17/6d later, which was why in 1933 he decided to leave to work at the Austin Factory where some of his former school friends were earning around £5 per week. The carpenters' shop is now used as a rented garage doing car repairs, and the sawing shed is in use as a depot for the maintenance of rented property.

The two black and white lodges each side of what, for many years, used to be the main entrance to Hewell Grange, were built in the mid 1880s following the completion of the new mansion. The Dairy Lodge, next to the timberyard, was for many years the Home Farm dairy, where butter and cheese were made and milk was supplied, a small amount free to estate workers and their families, the rest sold locally or sent to Redditch. On school days, two of the older children from Tardebigge School used to be sent to the dairy to return an empty milk churn and collect another with the day's supply for the school children's free third of a pint as decreed by the Government. In the early 1900s the dairy was run by John Laugher and his wife Esther, together with their dairy-maid daughter Mary. In the 1920s, 1930s and 1940s, it was run by Miss Dorothy van Bylevelt, with the help of two dairy maids. Following the takeover of the Home Farm by Joe Beckett, George Scoltock and his wife lived in the lodge and their daughter ran the dairy until it closed. George Scoltock had earlier worked for Joe Beckett's father on the family farm near Shrewsbury for many years, almost as one of the family, and when Joe moved to Shortwood Farm in 1939, he invited George to come with his wife and family to help to run the farm. At Hewell George served as Farm Bailiff, setting the work for the farm workers to do each day. Later, when the farming had finished, he was in charge of the maintenance of the Tardebigge Court buildings and he took on the care of the Beckett's extensive garden. Altogether he served the Becketts, father and son, for 66 years.

Until the sale of the Hewell Estate in 1946, the north-west lodge on the other side of the drive was occupied in turn by Estate Bailiffs. In the 1900s the position was held by Peter Gowan. By 1916 the Estate Bailiff was Henry Spiers, and in the late 1920s he was succeeded by his son Raymond Spiers who served until the 1946 sale of the Hewell properties but continued to live in the former north-west lodge with his wife and daughter Eileen for several more years.

Further along Hewell Lane, where there used to be a T-junction with the old lane to the church (which disappeared with the building of the A448 Highway), there are two single-storey former lodges which served the old Hewell Grange. Together they were occupied by one family, their living quarters being in one lodge and their bedrooms in the other. For many years the Wall family lived there and endured this inconvenience. Frank Wall was a groom to the Plymouth family and to their agent L F Lambert. His son Sid Wall, born 1913, attended Tardebigge School.

On the south-west side of Hewell Lane facing the later two lodges is the lane which, before the dual carriageway turned it into a cul-de-sac, used to be the direct route from Hewell Grange to the walled kitchen garden in Holyoakes Lane which supplied the Grange with flowers, fruit and vegetables. Estate workers lived in the cottages along this lane and also in the three sets of semi-detached cottages in Holyoakes Lane. Since the end of WW2 and the takeover of Hewell Grange by the Home Office, the gardens have been tended by the inmates of the Grange under supervision and the produce has been used not only by the Borstal, and then by the prisons, but it has also been available for sale to the general public.

In Hewell Lane opposite Hewell House and alongside the road is the building which housed the old forge which served the Estate. The blacksmith/wheelwright around 1900, following John Gittus, was Henry Symonds. In the 1920s and 1930s the blacksmith was James Morris, who lived in the last of the six estate cottages in Holyoakes Lane. He had been a Regimental Sergeant Major in WW1. There was stabling behind the forge for six horses and also, nearby, a tan-pit which was used at one time for the tanning of animal hides to make leather. The circular tan-pit, about four feet in diameter was brick-lined and several feet deep, and underneath it was a furnace accessed by steps down. Before chemicals came to be used for industrial tanning in the twentieth century, tan-pits containing a solution of crushed oak bark in water, which contains tannis acid, were widely used. Animal skins from which hair and flesh were as far as possible removed, were soaked for several weeks in the pit to process the skins and turn them into leather. At Tardebigge this local leather was sent to Barratts, then located in Redditch, to be made into gaiters and other articles for use on the estate. In the first half of the twentieth century the tan-pit, no longer used for tanning, was used for the immersing of wooden farm gates and fencing in creosote. Eventually the pit, a safety hazard, was filled in with rubble from the construction of the dual carriageway. Since the forge closed around 1940 the buildings have been used as workshops for making metal boats and for repairing cars, and latterly by a computer software firm. The two forge fireplaces still remain and the building has been little altered. By the entrance from the road there remains a very old oak tree with a massive trunk.

The building attached to the forge, which extends to the roadside, was for some years a shop. From 1964 to 1971 it was a general store rented from the Estate and run by Michael Farrin and his wife Rhona, then living in Upper Bentley. It was open from 8.30 am to 6.00 pm on weekdays, and until 5.00 pm on Saturdays. Much of its trade came from prison officers and their families living on the Park, and in the later years from labourers constructing the dual carriageway. Whilst there, Rhona used to provide teas for the nearby Hewell Bowling Club. Before the Farrins took over, the shop had been started and run by Mrs Jackson who lived in Holyoakes Lane and whose husband worked for Joe Beckett. When the Farrins left due to Michael's ill health, it was taken over by Hodson and Breeze, two wives of prison officers, who advertised in the Tardebigge Parish Magazine from July 1971 until 1974 when, it seems, the shop closed.

In 1964/5 the Hewell community was suddenly increased by the building of the present cluster of 65 houses known collectively as "The Park". These, together with a hostel for about 6 single men, were built under supervision by many of the Borstal boys, who received training in building and other vocational skills. The houses were let by the Home

Office mostly to staff of the newly opened Brockhill Remand Prison who had families, but some were available to officers of the Borstal and others moving out of the twenty-five prefabs (prefabricated bungalows) which had been constructed during the war in two rows beside the Hewell Lake. These prefabs, which were accessed via a spur lane off the main drive to the Grange and had been used to house some of the Borstal staff, had served their purpose, they had been warm and cosy, but they were not designed to be long-life structures. They were demolished, one by one as the tenants moved out, and by the 1980s they had all gone.

In 1984/5 the Home Office began to sell off houses on "The Park" to sitting tenants, as well as to other purchasers, and by the year 2000 very few of the original residents remained.

PAPER MILLS

Paper Mills is the address of a small out-of-the-way cluster of cottages which, together with a former lodge to Hewell Grange, includes the remains of what was a paper mill. The paper mill is known to have been in existence in the seventeenth and eighteenth centuries. It was advertised to let in Berrows Worcester Journal in 1752, and it was John Holyoake, described as a papermaker in 1771, who produced paper there until his death in 1812. Evidence for this is a scrap of paper dated 1808 with the watermark J Holyoake. The mill closed in 1817 and its buildings were subsequently converted into several cottages. After the mill closed, the water-wheel which had driven the machinery, together with the rollers which were used to squeeze and press the paper, lay in the Hewell timberyard for over 80 years. The remains of a basin used for making pulp from disused clothing fabric can still be seen in one of the cottage gardens.

The Papermills Lodge was built in 1876, this date being visible on the gable facing the drive to the house. Like the other two lodges on Hewell Lane it is partly timber-framed. At one side of the front entrance to the lodge there is a peephole or squint, which enabled the lodge-keeper to keep an eye on people and vehicles entering or leaving the Park. This entrance to the Park would have been used by Papermills residents and other people using the track from Tack Farm at the Foxlydiate end of Hewell Lane.

SHOOTING GROUND

The site of the Hereford and Worcester Shooting Ground, with its entrance in Hewell Lane, was within part of the Hewell Estate acquired by Joe Beckett in 1946. From that date it was rented for use by three firms of gunmakers and by the Redditch Gun Club. In 1981 Ian Butler, who had worked there for one of the gunmakers, took over as owner of the Shooting Ground Company. Since then the grounds have been redeveloped to include a shooting school, gun shop, restaurant and gunsmith's workshop. The Club there now has some 500 members, and the many users of the facilities include several public schools.

TUTNALL

Tutnall has remained a small hamlet around what was a busy junction of highways from Bromsgrove to Redditch and to Alcester. Situated at a

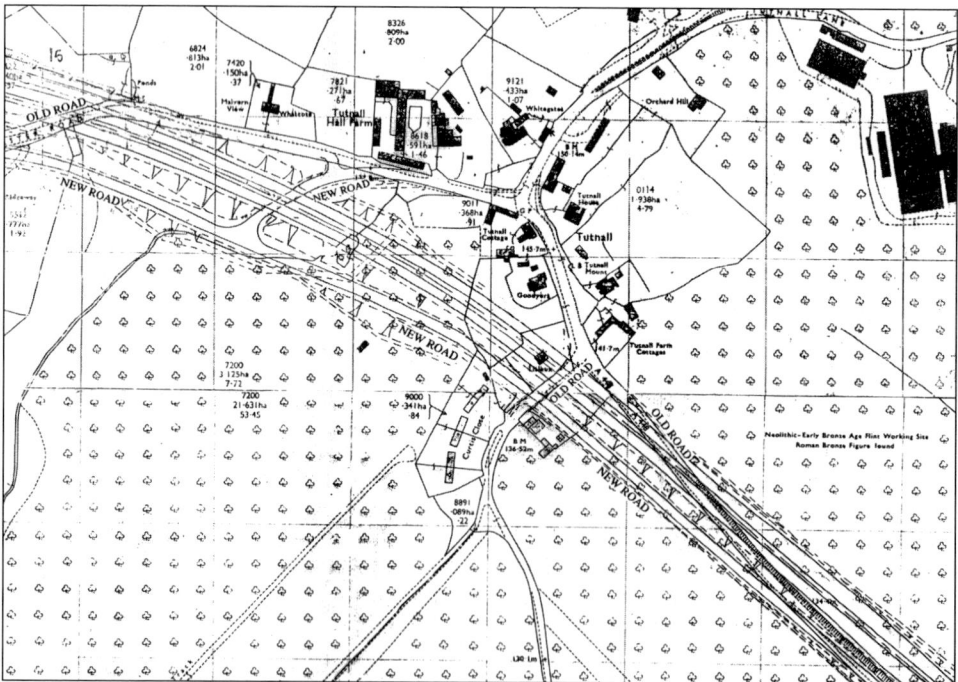

Map of Tutnall showing the dual carriageway, constructed in the 1970s, and the changes it caused to the local road system. Part of the old main road, south of the junction, became a cul-de-sac. The map shows the surrounding area covered with the orchards of Tardebigge Orchards.

The hunt outside the Toll House at Tutnall. In the background are the buildings of Tutnall Hall Farm. (Stewart Fletcher)

corner of the T-junction where the narrow Holloway to Broad Green turns off the Alcester road, there was for many years a turnpike toll house, with turnpike gates across the road from Bromsgrove. After the ending of turnpikes, the house and garden were sold in 1872 by the Trustees of the United Trust of the Alcester Roads in the Counties of Warwick and Worcester to Mr Thomas Parkes of Surrey. The house was tenanted until 1936 when, because of its situation, right on the corner, limiting the visibility of vehicles turning at the junction, it was demolished. Last to go, long after the house, was the outside toilet at the end of the back garden. The last occupants of the toll house were George and Mary Clarke, whose daughter Gladys married Edgar King, the father of Ray King of Broad Green. The iron tollgate from Tutnall, with its "sunburst" design which was introduced by Telford on his turnpike roads, may now be seen outside Tardebigge Old Vicarage.

Besides the projecting toll house, another hazard was that the T-junction was on a sharp bend and this was a cause of frequent accidents. Especially at night, cars travelling too fast towards Bromsgrove from Redditch often landed up in the vegetable garden of Tutnall Hall Farm. It is said that a white line which Ralph Dixon caused to be painted in the centre of the road to separate the two-way traffic passing on the bend was the first of its kind in the country.

The local history of Tutnall in the earlier part of the twentieth century has taken some sorting out because of changes in the names of several of the larger houses. The house now known as Tutnall Farm House used to be known as The Cottage and it housed senior farm workers of Tutnall Farm. The actual farmhouse was Tutnall House on the bank facing the junction on the opposite side of the road. The house which, in 1968, became a children's home called Whitegates, was previously known as Tutnall Mount but, strangely and confusingly, there is another old house also called Tutnall Mount with its entrance just up a little side road to the left beyond Tutnall House. Tutnall Hall Farm has retained its traditional name, but in some documents, including the 1901 census, it is wrongly referred to as Tutnall Farm.

In 1900 Tutnall Farm was in the ownership of John Moore whose ancestors had owned and farmed a large area from Alvechurch to Tutnall for over 300 years. He was living in Tutnall House with his wife Harriet and two teenage sons John and William. The house had been built by his predecessor John Moore, together with Tutnall Mount nearby, in the 1790s. The barn alongside the road opposite is more recently built, having been designed by the Bromsgrove architect John Cotton, and on its east end can still be seen the initials JM of John Moore.

When John Moore finished farming around the beginning of WW1, neither of his sons wanted to take over the farm. The elder son John had poor health and he and his first wife eventually moved into Goodyeres, a bungalow built around 1930, with a lot of land including an orchard before the building of the A448 road across it. He spent much of his time creatively in his garden and in his work shed where he made toys, garden furniture and other things including the big cross at St Peter's RC Church in Bromsgrove. In front of the bungalows was the bus stop which helped to provide customers to whom John and his second wife Marie sold sweets, cigarettes and tobacco. Their small Austin "Ruby" car which was cared for by Len Banner, went eventually, after Marie's death, to the Patrick Collection at Kings Norton. John's younger brother William made his career in the army and moved away.

Following John Moore, T & M Dixon added Tutnall Farm to their farming empire and it became a poultry farm with incubators in the roadside barn. During and just after WW2 Ralph Dixon's widow Florence, her son Crispian Dixon and their housekeeper, were living in Tutnall House. Crispian was in charge of the poultry farm and it was in the incubator barn that, soon after the war, he committed suicide in August 1948. Meanwhile The Cottage was the home of Harry Tustin from the date of his marriage in 1924 until 1945, when he moved to Broad Green to live and to work at the forge there. During his time at Tutnall, besides assisting his father at Broad Green he also had a smithy of his own in one of the Tutnall Farm outbuildings. Following the war Alan Voller and his wife moved into The Cottage and, with other members of his family, helped to manage the poultry farm.

In recent years there have been two barn conversions at Tutnall. In 1987 Derek Bullivant and his wife Jaqueline, who had lived at Tutnall House since 1964, moved into their converted "Tutnall Barn" just along the Holloway nearby. In 1992 Robert Swann and his wife Connie, who had purchased Tutnall Farm House (formerly The Cottage) in 1980 and had lived there since, now moved into the adjacent barn after its conversion, and it was named "Tutnall Corner".

Whitegates Children's Home, located in the large house previously known as Tutnall Mount adjacent to Tutnall Hall, was established in 1968 by a charity, the Endeavour Service Council Limited, to care for about ten children who were deemed unsuitable for fostering and were recommended by various local authorities. It was run on family lines under the supervision of houseparents and their deputies, and there were domestic staff and a gardener. Successive houseparents were Mr and Mrs Ayres, Mr and Mrs Barry Jones and Mrs Christine O'Leary. The children were able to play in the spacious grounds and they were encouraged to help with the growing of fruit and vegetables on their own allotted patch of ground.

There was no upper age limit and some of the children, totalling some three dozen over the years, formed lasting friendships and acquired an affection for this their old family home which they came back to visit. The home closed in 2004. Before the house became Whitegates, its previous occupants, when it was known as Tutnall Mount, included in the 1920s and 1930s Harvey Dixon, the youngest son of Ralph Dixon, who was a dental surgeon and who moved from there to a newly built house, "Orchard Hill" located up a drive off the Holloway, around 1932.

Inhabitants of the other Tutnall Mount have included, from 1830 to 1872, Captain Emmott of the Worcester Yeomanry, followed by his widow Mary Ann. Captain Emmott had served in the Peninsular War and at Waterloo and was adjutant to the regiment of Yeomanry formed in 1831 by Lord Plymouth. When he died in 1865 he had a large military funeral. His impressive grave and monument facing the west door of Tardebigge Church has been well looked after in recent years by Stephen Orr-Cooper who has lived at Tutnall Mount since 1993 and is the producer of Tardebigge Cider. A barn and stables belonging to Tutnall Mount were demolished in the 1960s.

Tutnall Hall Farm House was built in 1720 in the Georgian style of red brick with giant pilasters at each end of the frontage and the front door. Its occupants in the early 1900s before WW1 were George James, his wife Sarah and son George. They were followed by Leonard Jeffery until 1933 when Edward Godfrey Ashwin, his wife Nancy and their young son Godfrey moved in from their farm at Whatcote near Stratford-upon-Avon. One visitor to the Hall in their time, around 1960, was John Betjeman, invited to tea by Mrs Ashwin, and he was especially impressed by the staircase. Soon after the Ashwins came the two semi-detached houses, named Whatcote and Malvern View, situated along the old road beyond the farm buildings, were built for their farm workers, one of whom, Charlie Pearce, served for many years.

Tutnall Hall Farm has, over the years, specialised in milk production with its dairy herds. Edward Ashwin had an extensive milk round in the early years up to and including WW2. Thereafter most of the milk was collected, at first by lorries, which picked up the churns from a roadside platform, then later by tankers. By the 1960s the business included, besides

Tutnall Hall Farmhouse and the outbuildings, well before the house became a nursing home.
(Rosemary Ashwin)

milk, turkeys plucked and dressed for Christmas, and eggs packed in large wooden boxes and collected weekly by the egg marketing board. There were also private sales to shops and local people.

Edward Ashwin never kept a bull. The previous farmer had apparently been gored by one, and this may have led Edward to become one of the first to use the insemination services of Avoncroft Cattle Breeders. Until the construction of the A448 dual carriageway cattle had to cross the busy road at milking times between the farm and fields opposite, and road traffic, frustratingly, had to be held up.

153

Godfrey, who was married in 1959, took over the running of the farm from his parents the following year. His parents continued to live at the farm, and Edward continued to help. Edward died in 1969, and a tribute in the Tardebigge Parish magazine mentioned that he was a regular churchgoer and read his Bible daily, and that he had been vice-president of Bromsgrove British Legion.

The construction of the A448 dual carriageway around 1971 took a large chunk of land from the farm's 90 acres. It was this that helped to persuade Godfrey to move away from farming and support his wife Rosemary, a nurse, in the running of a new nursing home at Battlefield House along Kidderminster Road near Bromsgrove.

From 1971 to 1983 Tutnall Hall was privately owned as a residence, but the farm buildings and the land were taken over by Derek Moss of Astwood Bank who, with his son Keith, has farmed it since and whose dairy herd has supplied milk to the Ford Group and to Dairy Crest. In 1983 the Hall was reportedly sold with four acres of land and a shrubbery for £125,000. The new owners, Bradburys and Murphys, turned it into a nursing home. Mr and Mrs Murphy soon bought out the Bradburys and later added the extension to create the present successful care home from which they eventually retired.

CHAPTER 9

The Worcester and Birmingham Canal and its Tardebigge Wharves

HOW THE CANAL CAME TO TARDEBIGGE

On 10 June 1791 an Act of Parliament was passed, authorising the making of a canal from Birmingham to Worcester to pass through the parish of Tardebigge. As the news reached the scattered inhabitants of this rural parish and the surrounding area, it must have aroused a good deal of interest, concern maybe on the part of the landowners along its route, welcome perhaps on the part of householders and farmers looking forward to the use of canal transport for the delivery of coal and other goods and the carriage of local produce to urban markets. The news, however, would have come as no surprise, knowing that previous attempts to obtain an Act for such a canal had been made in 1786 and 1790. These, however, had been unsuccessful due to the opposition of local landowners, rival canal companies, and the owners of watermills anxious about the impact of the canal upon the streams supplying their water power. This time it was the Earl of Plymouth, Other Hickman, who was actually in favour of the canal passing through his Hewell Estate, who was instrumental in achieving the narrow majority in the House of Lords for the passing of the Act. He held twenty of the original £100 shares in the canal company and he was chairman of the proprietors (shareholders) at their first meeting in July 1791 and at their fourth meeting in January 1793. The concession he and his successors received of the toll-free carriage of coal and goods was later of great benefit to T & M Dixon, whose Tardebigge wharves were on Hewell Estate land and who carried goods on behalf of their noble landlord.

Because the canal is level for fifteen miles from Birmingham to Tardebigge New Wharf, work on its construction began at the Birmingham end so that, as sections were completed, the canal could be increasingly used. It was opened as far as Selly Oak in 1795, to Kings Norton in 1796, and through the long West Hill Tunnel to Hopwood in 1797. By this time the amount of money permitted by Parliament to be raised for its construction had been spent. It was a time of monetary inflation, partly due to the war with France, but mostly because of the high demand for bricks and other materials, for labour, and for specialist engineers and craftsmen, as many canals were being built at the time. So in 1797 construction work on the canal came to a halt, and for the next ten years Hopwood remained the southern terminus of the canal. Before the canal could be extended from there to Tardebigge, extra money had to be raised as allowed by an Act of Parliament in 1804. Work restarted early in 1805 and the canal was completed through Bittell cutting, across the Bittell Valley and through Shortwood Tunnel and opened as far as Tardebigge Old Wharf in March 1807. By this time, partly due to the cost of constructing five reservoirs to appease water-mill owners on the Rivers Rea and Arrow which were crossed by the canal, the company had again run out of money. So construction work ceased, leaving the Old Wharf at Tardebigge, for the next four years, the busy terminus of the canal. More money had to be raised by another Act of Parliament in 1808 to enable Tardebigge Tunnel to be completed and the New Wharf prepared for its opening in January 1811.

It had taken fifteen years from the start of work on the canal in 1792 to reach Tardebigge Old Wharf. In the early years there had been some work done on the section between Hopwood and Tardebigge. In 1794 the approach cuttings at both ends of Shortwood Tunnel had been excavated.

In 1796, three tunnel shafts had been sunk and, before work ceased in 1797, a headway along the line of the tunnel had been made through the clay soil. A start on Tardebigge Tunnel was also made in 1796 when the southern end was exposed and a shaft was sunk to the level of the tunnel through sandstone rock. After these early signs of progress it must have been disappointing and frustrating for the people of Tardebigge to have to wait ten years for the opening of the canal to the Old Wharf, and then another four years to the New Wharf.

It was to take nearly five more years for the canal, with its 58 locks from Tardebigge down to the River Severn at Diglis, Worcester, to be completed and officially opened on 4 December 1815. The original Act of Parliament was for a broad canal to take barges up to 14 feet wide, so all five of its tunnels were made to a width of 16 feet. But in 1809, to save money, it was decided to construct the canal from Tardebigge down to Worcester with narrow locks 7 ft 3 in wide, thus limiting the passage to narrow boats.

From 1809 to1814 an experimental canal lift, designed by engineer John Woodhouse, was in use where the deep top lock at Tardebigge now is. The idea of using such lifts was to save water since, by the Canal Act, reservoirs were forbidden to be made north of Tardebigge Parish. Water was at that time not available from the Birmingham Canal system, and it looked as if water would have to be obtained by pumping it up from the River Severn in three stages to the summit level. However, when it later became clear that the canal would be able to receive surplus water from the Birmingham system, it was decided to complete the canal with locks.

GRANGE WHARF

For many years the house adjacent to the humpback bridge over the canal in Grange Lane had its own towpath wharf. Here from 1850 until 1889 Noah Knight and his wife Charlotte lived and kept shop and maintained a coal business. Noah possessed his own working boat and he employed George Withers as boatman to fetch coal from Midland collieries. Noah died in 1889 and his wife in 1891, and both are buried in Tardebigge churchyard opposite the chancel door. Their son Thomas continued to run the shop and coal business, probably with the help of his sister Alice Knight, until WW1.

THE OLD WHARF

When the Old Wharf opened in 1807, boats brought mainly coal for the surrounding area, it being carried from the wharf on horse-drawn wagons to Redditch and Bromsgrove, and as far as Alcester and Droitwich. Most of the boats returning to Birmingham carried farm produce which was allowed to pass free of toll by the canal company. Of six businesses which were initially allotted boat lengths on the wharf for mooring and stacking their merchandise, mainly coal, only one survived until the mid 19th century, namely that of Thomas Dixon, which grew into the business partnership of T & M Dixon and continued to use the wharf and its canal boats until around 1950.

Amenities on the wharf as it opened included a warehouse and a weighbridge with its machine-house. The weighbridge has long been removed, but the weighbridge house is still there, extended as a residence. For the convenience of traders some small private warehouses were allowed to be built on the wharf, but these have long gone. The canal company soon applied for a licence for a public house, and one was built on land on the other side of Brockhill Lane opposite to the entrance to the wharf. Called "The Navigation Inn", it was well used at first, but as the New Wharf and its inn, "The Plymouth Arms", became established and creamed off trade from the Old Wharf, "The Navigation", after about thirty years, eventually closed. Its licensee, John Hunt, and his wife Catherine continued to live and run a farming and coal business at the Old Wharf, followed by their son Richard and his wife Emma, for many years until the early 1900s. There is now nothing to be seen of the Navigation Inn in the field where it once stood.

Soon after the Sharpness New Docks Company took over the Worcester and Birmingham Canal in 1874, it set about legalising the terms under which Dixons occupied properties on the Old and New Wharves. Maps of the wharves were produced by the new canal engineer, Francis Hobrough, showing the occupiers of the various wharves and properties. In 1879, an indenture was drawn up between Thomas and Matthew Dixon and the canal company for the lease by T & M Dixon of most of the cottages, gardens, stables and warehouses, together with the lime kilns and an old turnpike house. This lease, as usual for 99 years, would have expired in

In 1993 Malcolm Johnson, who had lived with his parents at the post office and shop beside the canal at the Old Wharf during and after World War 2, sent these three photographs, together with a covering letter, to Ron Barnett of The Park, and they were kept in Ron's family scrap-book.

The post office and shop taken in 1942. Mrs Emma Netta Johnson was the post-mistress from 1935 to 1953. The white bench was made by Malcolm's grandfather, Ernest Chambers, of Crabbs Cross. By this time the adjacent donkey stables were used as coal house and garden sheds. The Edward VII post-box remains on the back wall of the donkey stables.

Taken from the Johnson's garden in 1942, is of the tug Worcester *crewed by Percy Hawkins and John Colledge, towing a Severn and Canal Carrying Company boat. The tug is now preserved and maintained at the Ellesmere Port Boat*

Museum. The buildings at the top left of the photograph are Dixons old pig slaughterhouses which were blown down in a gale a year or so later. The building to the right of them was Bill Chapman's humble abode of which little now remains.

Taken in the summer of 1940, is of young Malcolm and his next door neighbour's daughter, Barbara Maskell, trying on their gas masks for the first time. Malcolm wrote "I well remember this photo being taken - within seconds we were all steamed up and couldn't see a thing, the smell of rubber was horrible and quite stifling, and we were both jolly pleased to remove them after the photo had been taken. They were issued at Tardebigge School by the Headmaster, Mr A T Knight. We had to take them each day to school neatly packed in a little square box fitted with a shoulder strap."

1978, and during its tenure the cottages, weighbridges and other property on both the Old and New Wharves were occupied by tenants who were employed by Dixons.

Behind and beyond the Old Wharf, Dixons rented land from the Hewell Estate on which free-range poultry were kept in large numbers. By the 1900s there was a mechanised piggery where the pigs were fed by means of an overhead tramway which conveyed pig-food, brought from a brewery and other sources in Birmingham by canal boat, to a row of pens. Pigs were killed and processed in a slaughterhouse, later replaced by the use of the disused lime kilns nearby. Coal, stacked on the wharf, milk and dairy products, vegetables and meat were sold from the wharf. Tommy Carter from the New Wharf, and after him Len Banner from Broad Green, were in charge of the piggery and also the wharf weighing machine, which was in use until WW2.

Living in the weighbridge cottage from 1923 to 1940, were Harry Sumner and his wife. He was ostler and waggonner for Dixons and looked after some dozen horses kept at the Lower House. Whilst serving in the army in WW1 he had been wounded and underwent 23 operations in hospitals back in the UK. His wife Elizabeth used to make tea for the many fishermen who came from Birmingham on the train to Blackwell at the weekends and walked to the Old Wharf to fish between there and Shortwood Tunnel. She charged 6d for a pot of tea for four people. Following the Sumners, Alf Warman and his wife Henrietta lived in the weighbridge cottage for many years until he died in 1985. He worked for Dixons and Tardebigge Orchards with Ray King on the fruit production and packing. Following an accident he was disabled in one leg and his friends adapted a bicycle for him with one fixed pedal.

Between the weighbridge cottage and the wharf entrance there was a tiny cottage (long demolished), with only one room on each floor. Miss Green who lived there did sewing for Dixons. Further beyond the weighbridge cottage and at the back of the wharf there was a small one-storey dwelling where Bill Chapman lived in the 1900s. This derelict building has gradually disintegrated over the years.

On the west side of the canal, the present boat-hire business incorporates in its premises two former semi-detached cottages, which were in existence well before 1900. The one further from the road bridge was tenanted in the early 1920s by fruit foreman Hubert Knight, his wife Gertrude and family, then until 1937 by another fruit foreman, Edgar King, his wife Gladys and family (parents of Ray King), then by Mr and Mrs Ainge (he worked for farmer John Whittaker). The other adjoining cottage was for many years a shop, one of a number at wharves along the canal which supplied working boat crews and local inhabitants. The shopkeepers in the early 1900s were Edward and Eliza Tustin whose son Ted became the blacksmith at Broad Green. From around 1919 until 1935 Fred and Annie Davies lived there; Annie ran the shop, which from 1922 was also a post office; Fred, an ex-naval man, was gardener to Colonel Dixon at "The Cottage". From 1935 to 1953 the shop and post office were in the hands of Sydney and Emma Johnson. Emma was the postmistress and ran the shop, Sydney worked at High Duty Alloys in Redditch. Their son Malcolm went to Tardebigge School and eventually in 1993, from his home in Holland, he sent the three photographs taken at the Old Wharf and the accompanying information (page 159).

In the 1920s and 1930s, between the wars, there were still usually some half dozen working boats tied up at the wharf. One, built in 1906 for T & M Dixon, was the "Enterprise", driven by a Wolseley car engine, which used to take farm produce and milk picked up at Harris's Bridge near Stoney Lane Farm to Birmingham daily, in only half the time taken by horse-drawn boats. It was crewed in earlier years by George Colledge, later by Ernie Jones and Ray King's uncle, Jim Williams.

The first hire-boat business established on the west side of the wharf was the Tardebigge Boat Company in the 1970s. This was followed by Dartline in the 1980s and then in 1997 by the present establishment, a branch of Anglo-Welsh Holidays.

THE NEW WHARF

When the New Wharf opened in 1811 its moorings and 90 feet square basin were soon busy with boats bringing in coal for dealers, including Jenkins and Wright, Bolding, Chair & Co., and Dixon & Co. The weighbridge house at the wharf entrance and several other cottages were provided for the machine clerk, wharfinger and other canal workers. Five lime-burning kilns were constructed behind the basin, soon after the opening of the canal to Worcester making it possible for boats to bring up limestone from quarries at Dunhampstead. As the use of the wharf by canal carriers, coal merchants and other traders grew, it became necessary to excavate, in 1831, the canal arm from a corner of the basin, two boat lengths long and two boat widths wide, thus providing additional moorings for four vessels.

In 1874 the Worcester and Birmingham Canal Company was taken over by the Gloucester and Sharpness Canal Company and it became part of what was now known as the Sharpness New Docks Company (SND). The new company soon decided to introduce tugs, one for towing boats through the Tardebigge and Shortwood Tunnels and another for towing through the West Hill Tunnel. The tugs came into use in January 1877. By this time T & M Dixon had occupied the warehouse, had monopolised the coal and lime business, and had leased from the canal company all the wharf cottages, with the exception of the weighbridge house, for their employees on the wharf. So it was necessary for the SND Company to

At Tardebigge New Wharf Maintenance Depot, the former crane, used for lifting timber, alongside the timber store, and also, behind Malcolm Ward's boat, the fitting shop. (Malcolm Ward)

build the terrace of four split-level houses (soon known as "Tug Row") on the road outside the wharf, for the tug crews and their families.

The first four tugmen at Tardebigge were recruited from the Gloucester area, Frank Rowles, Isaac Boulton, William Veale and William Hawkins. These young men settled down, married, and by 1900 they and their families were established members of the canal community at the New Wharf. Their children attended Tardebigge School, and some of their sons sang in the church choir. Frank Rowles eventually became the Section Inspector of the canal at Tardebigge, and his son Morton Rowles became a teacher at Tardebigge School and later Head of the village school at Upper Bentley. Two sons of William Hawkins, Charlie and Percy, found employment with the Canal Company as tug crew and engineers, and likewise Percy's son George between the wars. William Veale's son Philip became a bricklayer and he worked on the canal until he died, aged 79, in 1942.

On the wharf itself, by 1900 the weighbridge house, no 1, just inside the entrance, was occupied by Walter Leighton, who was quite a character. He was reputed to be the best fisherman on the canal; he always knew where to fish and where not to fish. He was also notorious for being able to walk to "The Shoulder of Mutton" in Bromsgrove and back within the hour. He was succeeded at the weighbridge house by Fred Warner, who eventually moved, around 1915, to Astwood lower lock cottage. The weighbridge with its mechanism in the front cellar of the house, was moved, when no longer needed at Tardebigge, to Stoke Wharf in 1920 to replace the one there which had been condemned. The iron rim of the weighbridge can still be seen in front of the house. In cottage no.2 on the wharf lived Harry Such who was in charge of Dixons' animal and poultry feed mill in the old warehouse. He was assisted by his son Walter who carried on working there until WW2 and the closure of the mill. No.3 cottage was the shop and post office, as it had been for many years. The postmaster from 1881 until he died in 1918 was officially Thomas Colledge. He could neither read nor write. His wife Mary ran the post office which was open from 7.00 am to 8 pm on weekdays. He was in charge of Dixons' fleet of canal boats and the ordering and transport of coal from various collieries. Following the death of his wife, his married daughter, Fanny Smith, ran the post office until she emigrated to New Zealand with her husband in 1922. Then the post office moved to Davies's on the Old Wharf. Cottage no.4, around 1900, was the home of Bill Archer, who had been the miller before Harry Such. In no.5 lived John Colledge, one of the sons of Thomas Colledge, with his wife Emma (nee Lewin) after their marriage. John Colledge also worked as a boatman on Dixons' boats before eventually owning his own boat.

In the early 1900s, a house just inside the wharf entrance opposite to the weighbridge house was occupied by Edwin Hunt, wharfman, and his wife Harriet. Following his wife's death in 1909, he moved and the canal company let the tenancy to John Colledge who, with an increasing family, lived there for about three years. In 1912/13 the house was demolished and replaced by the present one which was built as a more appropriate residence for Frank Rowles, the newly appointed Section Inspector in charge of the canal. He had evidently shown himself to be a capable engineer and organiser. He was a member of Tardebigge Church choir and over many years he continued to play an active part in local affairs. The section inspectors following Frank Rowles were Edgar Spiers (1931-49), Leslie Thompson (1949-59), George Colledge (1959-74), and Stuart Perry (1974-89). From 1989 until 1993 the canal was managed by Glyn Phillips and with Stuart Perry serving under him and retiring to Cheshire in 1993. In 1993 British Waterways combined the management of the Worcester and Birmingham Canal with that of the Stratford-upon-Avon Canal and the northern section of the Grand Union Canal. Andrew Stumpf became manager and the office and administration was centred at Lapworth, leaving the New Wharf as just a subsidiary works depot.

At the back of the warehouse and attached to it, a small two-storey dwelling, in recent years ivy-covered and in ruins, was the home of one of Dixons' workmen employed as a lime burner and in other ways. Limestone continued to be brought by canal from quarries at Dunhampstead to be burnt in the lime kilns behind the basin, and the lime produced was sold to local farmers for use on their land and to local builders. In the 1860s and early 1870s the lime-burner was Thomas Worgen, whose daughter, Miss Elizabeth Worgen, became a teacher at Tardebigge School. He was succeeded in the late 1870s by Thomas Carter, who lived in the hovel behind the warehouse for many years. His wife Martha died in 1918, he remarried at the age of 76, and he died in 1938. Use of the lime kilns came to an end around 1900. They were soon filled with rubbish and a topping of earth, and the draw holes from the lane below were covered over and concealed with a bank of earth. The bank has recently been dug away and the draw holes exposed. It is hoped that at least one of the kilns can be restored and preserved.

The years 1909 to 1911 saw changes on the wharf as the maintenance depot was transferred in stages from Stoke Wharf to Tardebigge. This was long overdue, as it made sense to locate the canal workshops where the tugs were based, but the move had been delayed until the retirement, in 1908, of the canal's engineer and manager, Francis Hobrough, who lived in the large white house by the bridge at Stoke Wharf. First to be erected in 1909 was the large building alongside the basin. In it were situated the carpenters' shop nearest the canal, in the middle the company's own stables and, at the end beside the canal arm, the fitting shop. In 1910 the office building at the entrance to the yard was built; and in 1911, within the yard and beside the canal arm, the smithy. Other buildings were soon erected on the other side of the canal arm, the wooden open-sided timber store and the brick buildings housing the sawmill and general stores. Two cranes were installed, one by the entrance to the canal arm for loading and unloading timber, its base still visible, the other where the present crane is situated in the yard, it being used for lifting heavy items such as lock gates made in the carpenters' shop. The canal arm was converted into a dry dock in 1924, being no longer needed as a coal wharf since Dixons' coal business had, for quite some time, been based at the Old Wharf.

The building of the new maintenance depot meant that the canal company's craftsmen and labourers, many still living in the vicinity of the old Stoke depot, now had to commute to Tardebigge. This was because Dixons still held the lease on most of the wharf cottages which housed their employees. One of the canal craftsmen was Herbert Bate, foreman carpenter, who lived with his wife Jane and his family in the middle cottage of the row of three beside the canal below Whitford Bridge at Stoke Pound. When his assistant, Charlie Wright, enlisted in the army early in WW1, Herbert's son George, who had recently left school at the age of thirteen, joined his father in 1915 and soon became a skilled craftsman. When his father retired, George succeeded him as foreman carpenter. Another arrival from the old depot was Thomas Insull, foreman blacksmith. He was able to move with his wife into the former weighbridge house, no.1, on the wharf, and following her death and his retirement he continued to live there until he died in 1961. The following tenant in no.1 for over 20 years was Phil Barnard who worked on the administrative side of British Waterways. He also ran his own hire fleet of small boats, at first from Tardebigge, then from Gas Street Basin.

Other employees of Dixons have occupied New Wharf cottages over the years. In no.2 lived Albert Bluck, his wife Gertrude and step-children, Fred and Nancy Skillern, in the 1930s and 1940s. Ernest Jones and his wife lived at no.4 in the 1920s and 1930s, followed by Tom and Ethel Bennett, the latter long surviving the death of her husband. Living in no.5 were Bill Skillern and his wife Kate. Bill Skillern was a lorry driver for Dixons as were his brother Matthew and Matthew's son Fred. Eventually, following the demise of Dixons after the war, some of the cottages were occupied by canal employees, including no.2 by Bill Harbach and his wife Mary until his death in 1981, and since then by Mike Hansford, canal bricklayer, and his wife Paula. The little cottage behind the warehouse was finally occupied by George Bate and his wife in the 1970s.

The use of tugs, one to pull trains of working boats through Tardebigge and Shortwood Tunnels, another to do the same through the long West Hill Tunnel, continued until soon after WW2, by which time most of the dwindling numbers of working boats were motor-powered.

Whilst the tugs were in use, it used to happen on Saturdays that two or three of the local school children were taken, as a treat if they had been well-behaved, on the tug which worked from Tardebigge. As the use of the tugs came to an end and the Tug Row houses were no longer needed for tugmen and their families, they were tenanted by other canal employees. In the 1980s and 1990s, in no.1 nearest the wharf lived Arthur Goode, and his wife Annie; in no.2 Edgar Shrieves, retired canal maintenance man, his wife Annie and their son Philip; in no.3 Mrs Anderton, widow of canal carpenter Len Anderton; and in no.4 David James, for over 40 years canal foreman, and his wife Norma.

One notable happening on the wharf was the arrival of "Cressy", a converted narrowboat, in 1941. Its occupants were Tom and Angela Rolt, and it remained at its Tardebigge mooring during the war and until 1946. Tom Rolt was a civil-servant/engineer working for the government locally in Bromsgrove. He was interested in the future conservation and preservation of the canals, and had written a book entitled "Narrow Boat" which was published in 1944. This book sparked off a widespread concern for the future of the canals, and in 1945 another canal enthusiast, Robert Aikman, met Tom and Angela Rolt at Tardebigge and they decided to found an organisation "The Inland Waterways Association", which has done so much over the years since to save, conserve and restore many of the waterways in the UK. A plaque on a brick plinth beside the canal between the basin and the top lock commemorates the meeting and the formation of the IWA.

Another small plinth and plaque near the basin is a memorial to Norman Cox. He was a founder member and first chairman of the Worcester and Birmingham Canal Society, which came into being in 1979.

Causing a sensation locally at the beginning of February 1958 was a report in the Bromsgrove Messenger under the headlines "STRANGLING AND SUICIDE IN HOUSEBOAT", "COUPLE'S VIOLENT END AT TARDEBIGGE". The bodies of the man, Ernest Spencer, and his wife Edith were found by police on Saturday 31 January in the curtained front compartment of the vessel "Lady Luck" moored at the New Wharf, after a note stating the man's intention had been received by his brother in Birmingham. The woman had been strangled by her husband and he had died from an overdose of aspirin. At the inquest in Bromsgrove it was learnt that Spencer had had a relationship with a married woman, Mrs Morris. He had killed his wife on Wednesday 29 January and hidden her body under coats behind a wardrobe. Later that day he had fetched Mrs Morris from Birmingham and forced her to spend the night with him. On the Thursday he told Mrs Morris he had done something he had been waiting to do for 32 years. She was able to persuade him to take her home that evening by car. On the Friday he left a suicide note before taking his own life.

The funeral of the victims took place a week later at the graveside in Tardebigge churchyard, being conducted by the vicar, the Revd. R W Underhill.

In recent years there have been a number of people living on narrow boats moored permanently at Tardebigge, mainly on the off-side of the canal above and below the accommodation bridge no.56. The longest established canal-boat resident is Malcolm Ward, who has lived on board his boat in the basin alongside the workshops since 1968. An electrician by trade, he came from Tipton. In 1974 he changed his boat to the one he has lived on since. He has been a helpful source of information about people and happenings on the New Wharf in recent years.

The year Malcolm arrived, 1968, was the year canal carpenter George Bate retired to work part-time as lock-keeper and lengthsman. From around 1965 lock gates were no longer made at Tardebigge. They and other items have since been made at Bradeley workshops in the Black Country and elsewhere. During and following the 1970s the workshops were further run down, and the depot was reduced to being, as it is today, basically a canal office and a place for the storage of canal gear and materials. Some of the redundant buildings have been used by businesses. For some time the ground floor of the warehouse was used by Cliff Chester of Precision Tools and Dyes. The upper floor was used by Arthur Gibson, pattern maker until he moved first to the old wooden timber store and then to Burcot. Following Arthur Gibson, the timberstore and brick-built joinery shop have been occupied by fibre-glass businesses, first Perks and Dolman, then N & M Fibre-glass. It is hoped to turn the New Wharf into a Canal Centre and Museum, making use of the warehouse which has been reroofed but needs a new upper floor and much renovation, some of the workshops, and no.3 New Wharf, as it has remained, a typical early 1900s dwelling.

In December 1989 a trip boat owned by Nick Fazey was used for the first of the Santa Trips, since held annually over weekends before Christmas. These, run from the old carpenters' shop on the New Wharf, have been very popular with families. Father Christmas, usually in the person of jovial Mike Hansford, is stationed on a beautifully decorated and illuminated narrow boat in the centre of Tardebigge Tunnel.

In 1999 the restored hull of "Birmingham", one of the motor tugs which had worked on the canal, was placed on show on the wharf, and forms a visitor attraction.

There are now good facilities for boats visiting the wharf. A notice board carries details each week of services and events at Tardebigge Church, and at these it is always pleasing to welcome people from the boats.

PLYMOUTH HOUSE

Soon after the canal opened to Tardebigge New Wharf in 1811, the "Plymouth Arms" inn, almost opposite to the wharf entrance, was built to serve the needs of travellers and tradesmen as well as local people. It was provided by the Earl of Plymouth at the time, together with the coach house and stables on the other side of the road. Over the years it was the venue for many festivities and it was well patronised until, in 1878/9, it was closed by another member of the Windsor family, the young Lord Robert Windsor-Clive, who was concerned about the dangers of alcohol and drunkenness and decided to close all licensed premises on his estates.

Following the departure of the last publican, Andrew Moythan, the tenancy passed to John Cund, parish clerk to the Parish of Tardebigge, and the premises became known as Plymouth House. John Cund and his wife had been living on the New Wharf. He continued as clerk to the parish of Tardebigge which, until the creation of the civil parishes of Tutnall and Cobley and of Bentley Pauncefoot in 1894, was responsible for local services. During his tenancy, which lasted until 1892, he farmed 20 acres of surrounding land, as had the licensees of the hostelry before him.

The next occupants of Plymouth House, from 1893, were Alfred Whitmore, his wife Elizabeth, and their four sons. He continued to farm the land, but also worked for the Bromsgrove Rural District Council, as Sanitary Inspector from 1895, and as Surveyor from 1898. By 1906 his eldest son Frank had started up in business, using the coach house and stables, as a funeral undertaker and carriage proprietor. He later also undertook furniture removals. This situation continued until Alfred died in 1928.

During Alfred Whitmore's time at Plymouth House, some of its many rooms were occupied by paying guests, one of whom was Miss Garnham who, for many years, was the head teacher of Tardebigge Infants School. She continued to live there after her retirement until she died in 1932. In the meanwhile Plymouth House was taken over by Mrs E Palmer, sister of Mrs Coney of High House Farm, and she ran it as a guest house until the 1950s.

An advertisement of Frank Whitmore's funeral business, showing his four horse-drawn vehicles displayed in front of Plymouth House. (Bromsgrove Almanac 1914)

It was Mrs Palmer who had part of the stable building opposite converted as a residence and she moved to live there. In the mid 1950s Plymouth House was sold to Mr and Mrs Lucas who had it converted into 6 flats and lived in one of them with their two sons. Then, in 1981 Plymouth House was bought by Mrs Margaret Ursall and her husband Frank and turned into a nursing home which opened in November 1982 and has since continued to serve successfully as a nursing and care home for about twenty, mainly elderly, people.

THE TOP LOCK AND LOCK HOUSE

From Tardebigge New Wharf down to Stoke Wharf there are thirty narrow locks on the canal within two miles. They comprise what is known as the Tardebigge Flight, although only the top three locks are actually in the Parish of Tardebigge. Most of the locks on the canal give a change of level of 7 feet, but the top lock is exceptionally deep and provides a change of level of 12 feet. This is because, as the canal was nearing completion, the lock replaced an experimental vertical canal lift which raised or lowered boats through 12 feet. In the garden of the lock house can be seen the remains of a side pond into which, to save water, half a lockful could first be diverted as boats descended, and this same water emptied first into the lock as boats ascended. The side pond was in operation until around 1950. The side pond paddle was removed by George Bate in 1957, but the paddle-gear frame remains in place.

Lock-keepers at the top lock from around 1900 were Henry Harrison until his death in 1906, then William (Joe) Warner until the 1950s. The lock-keeper's duties included the gauging of commercial boats to assess the weight of their cargoes, the collection of tolls and keeping of records, as well as the upkeep of their lock and section of towpath. Subsequent tenants of the lockhouse were not canal employees. Amongst them was a lady who claimed to be a witch, dressed accordingly, kept a red light burning, and was a cause of concern to some locals and passers by.

FRISBY'S BRICK WORKS

Just below the top lock there is an accommodation bridge originally built for the use of Cherry Trees Farm. At each side of the bridge, under the arch,

Two views of Frisby's Brickworks, c. 1905. (Andrew Tandy)

Lines of bricks drying. (Andrew Tandy)

can be seen insulators which used to carry the telephone wires of the system used by the canal company until the 1930s. Between this bridge and the London Lane road bridge, on the off (non-towpath) side of the canal, there was a busy brickworks in operation from 1896 until 1912. The brickworks was established there by Samuel Frisby at the invitation of Lord Windsor, the site being on his Lordship's land. Lord and Lady Windsor had often visited Italy and had been impressed with Italian decorated terra-cotta pots, vases and garden ornaments. Samuel Frisby had produced such items at his Perryfields brickworks in Bromsgrove, which was about to close because the claypit there was exhausted. He agreed to set up the new brickworks and pottery and he built for himself and his family a four-bedroomed house, known as "The Brickworks Cottage", at the north end of the site.

The brickworks included an office, a potter's wheel, a large drying shed, two round kilns, each about 20 feet in diameter and with its adjacent chimney. There were two boilers; one supplied steam for the machinery used to winch small wagons by wire hauser up from the claypit, the other was for machinery which included a machine for granulating hard clay, a conveyor belt to take it to where it was mixed with water to the required consistency, and a brick press. There was also a machine with wire cutters (like a giant egg slicer) for cutting the unbaked bricks to size. An agreement with the canal company allowed water to be taken from the canal for the boilers and brick-making. Coal for the engines and kilns came by canal using the brickworks' own horse-drawn boat, which was also used for delivering some of the bricks made. There was a stable for two horses. Many of the bricks bore the name "S Frisby, Tardebigge".

When Samuel Frisby died in 1904, aged 54, his wife Anne, who was a strong and capable person, took over the management. Their son John who was employed at the brickworks, was by this time married and living in Wellington Road, Aston Fields. Before the Frisbys moved to Tardebigge, John had been attracted to Minnie Jones who used to pass the Perryfields brickworks on her way to work in Bromsgrove. He was too shy to approach her himself, but one of the brickworks employees, Moses Brooks, acted as Cupid and brought them together. Anne continued to run the brickworks and she treated John like the other employees, paying him a weekly wage.

In its heyday, the brickworks employed about ten men, of whom two or three, including Moses Brooks, were full time, the others being casual labour. John's sister Lena, not married, worked in the office. Road haulage of bricks was mostly done by Tommy Jones of Finstall using his horse and cart.

Frisbys specialised in unglazed terra-cotta garden pots, vases and ornaments, many of which were attractively decorated and tinted with sand and yellow ochre, some being supplied to Lord Windsor. Local houses built at the time, many in Aston Fields, used Frisby's bricks in their construction. For the building of Tardebigge Village hall in 1911, special bricks, thinner than common bricks, were supplied by Frisbys.

By 1912 there was a building slump, Frisbys were owed a considerable sum by several local builders, the claypit was exhausted, and the brickworks closed. John found other employment. Anne and Lena continued to live in the brickworks cottage until about 1930, when they moved to Hewell Lane. They lived on the proceeds of the sale of the plant and machinery and by letting part of the house to holiday-makers and students.

The derelict brickworks gradually fell into decay, remaining items such as tools and wooden moulds were destroyed, the waterlogged claypit was used in part by the canal company for disposing of dredgings and eventually the whole area was cleared and tipped over to make an extensive garden. From about 1930 until 1946 the brickworks cottage was occupied by Ellis Penrice, cowman at nearby Cherry Trees Farm, his wife and large family. When the Windsor Estate properties were sold off in 1946, the farm and brickworks site were bought by the farmer, John Green. In 1951 he sold the brickworks cottage to the first of several subsequent owners, including Mr and Mrs John Hedley and Mr and Mrs Markovic, who developed the house, now called "The Bridges House", into a pleasant property with its extensive canalside garden.

THE ENGINE HOUSE

Tardebigge Reservoir with its large dam was created during the years 1822 to 1826, in two stages, to store water to supply the canal when needed, at a time when commercial traffic on the canal was rapidly increasing. At the same time, in 1823, the Engine House was built and a 50 horse-power engine was installed to pump water back from the reservoir through an underground culvert to the summit level of the canal above the top lock. However, following the completion of the Upper Bittell Reservoir in 1832 and the decline in commercial traffic on the canal in the latter half of the nineteenth century, the use of the Tardebigge pumping engine was needed less and less and by 1900 it was no longer needed. It was last in steam in January 1914 on a maintenance test, and in the winter of 1915/16, during WW1, it was dismantled, the engine and boiler were broken up and the metal parts were sent for the making of munitions. The chimney was eventually demolished in the winter of 1937/8.

The Engine House cottage beside the canal was for many years the home of John Allbutt, foreman bricklayer on the canal, his wife Mary and their two sons. When he died in October 1943, aged 84, he had lived at the Engine House cottage for 58 years, he had been in the employment of the canal company for 68 years, and he had carried out his normal duties until the day before he died. He had been a member of the Tutnall and Cobley Parish Council for forty years, and there was always a welcome at his home for friends and neighbours.

For many years the Engine House remained unused and derelict until, in 1961, it was taken over from British Waterways, together with the adjacent canalside cottage, by a Birmingham businessman, Martin Hone. He and his wife Patsy, then in their early twenties and just married, lived in the cottage and eventually, with difficulty, obtained planning permission in 1974 to turn the Engine House into a night club which opened in 1975. Following complaints from local people about the noise and rowdiness of its patrons late at night, the night club closed in 1980. The next tenant of the Engine House, Alan Tyler, renamed it "Tylers Lock" and turned it into a waterside restaurant, a convenient place for passers-by, boaters and walkers, to find refreshment. In the 1990s and early 2000s, under new tenants Andrew and Karen Tait, Tylers Lock continued as a licensed restaurant and an attractive venue for special occasions. For a number of years the Worcester and Birmingham Canal Society held a popular May weekend "Gathering of Boats" on the canal adjacent to "Tylers Lock", and the Taits generously allowed the Society to use the facilities of their premises.

THE RESERVOIR LOCK HOUSE AND ADJACENT COTTAGE

The reservoir lock house, opposite lock 53, was where Pat Warner, the author of the book "Lock-keeper's Daughter" was born in 1924 and lived until she left home in 1941 to train as a nurse. Her father John Warner came, with his wife Agnes and several small children, to be the lock-keeper there in 1910. He had a sad life for he lost by death four young daughters and a son, and then, three years after Pat was born, his beloved wife. Pat was brought up by her 20 year older sister Isobel who came to look after her and her father. One of John Warner's duties was to issue fishing permits for the reservoir and also for the canal as far as Alvechurch. His brother William was lock-keeper at the Tardebigge top lock. John Warner died, still at the lock house, in 1952. Since then the house has been purchased, altered and occupied by non-canal people.

Adjacent to the reservoir lock house, at a lower level and end on to the canal is the cottage where for some years George Bate and his wife lived. It was, it is believed, the brickyard cottage at the time the canal was being created.

CHAPTER 10

Farms and Farming

I N THE twentieth century tremendous changes took place in the management and methods of farming. In general the farming scene in 1900 was little different from what it had been for centuries, with many scattered mixed farms across the countryside, using mainly horse-power for haulage and field work, with outbuildings, barns, cowsheds, dairies and piggeries clustered around a farmyard adjacent to the farm house, and the use of intensive labour, especially at harvest time. The century saw the introduction and widespread use of mechanisation, with tractors, motor transport, combine harvesters and other machines, also the use of intensive production methods, especially on poultry farms, and pest control using chemical insecticides. By the end of the century the land of many smaller farms had been bought or rented by larger more enterprising and efficient farming businesses, able to survive in the era of supermarkets, with competition from cheap imports and, not least, the burden of government regulations and time-consuming forms for the supply of statistics.

Many farmhouses now no longer house farming families, having become desirable country residences, and many of the barns and other out-buildings have been converted into living accommodation, this latter trend having gained momentum from the 1980s onwards.

All these changes affected the farming scene in the Parish of Tardebigge. In 1900 there were over fifty working farms in the area, mostly rented from the Hewell or Bentley estates. By the year 2000 these had been reduced to some half dozen large independent farming businesses in the Tardebigge area and seven smaller farms, still rented from the Bentley Estate, in the Bentley area. The trend of combining smaller farms into larger businesses had already started in the Tardebigge area in the latter part of the nineteenth century in the case of the T & M Dixon farming partnership.

PEST CONTROL – A CULL OF SPARROWS

One of the problems farmers have always faced is depredation due to wild-life, especially rats, rabbits and birds. Rats and rabbits have always been controlled to some extent by trapping and shooting. Birds are another matter. In the early 1900s sparrows, especially, were a nuisance to tenant farmers on the Hewell Estate. At a meeting in the estate office on 11 May 1905 eleven farmers met under the chairmanship of Mr L F Lambert and decided to form Tardebigge Sparrows Club. Each farmer would pay an annual subscription of 3d per acre on all arable land on his farm. The Club would pay 3d per dozen for full-grown sparrow heads; 4 eggs would count as 1 sparrow-head and 2 unfledged heads would count as 1 full-grown head. Each member would be a receiver of heads and would send in his account at the end of each quarter. All neighbouring farmers were to be invited to join, the area of the club being limited to the civil parishes of Tutnall and Cobley, Webheath, North Redditch and Bentley Pauncefoot.

At the end of the first year, in April 1906, it was reported that 8,793 sparrows had been killed at a cost of £9.3.1d and there was a remaining balance of £4. The price to be paid per bird was increased henceforth from a farthing to a halfpenny, the subscription at the end of the year to be adjusted to cover the cost of the scheme. The following year it was reported that 15,476 birds had been killed at a cost of £32.4.10d, and to cover this the subscription was raised to 7d per acre of arable land. In 1908 it was decided to carry on for another year and that the half of the number of members who killed the least number of birds per acre should pay the cost of a club dinner for all the members, at 3 shillings per person, at the

Unicorn Hotel. In April 1909 it was decided to disband the club and donate the £3 left in the accounts to Tardebigge Nursing Society.

T & M DIXON

The extensive Dixon farming and commercial empire began, in a small way, when Thomas Dixon, a Birmingham canal carrier and coal merchant, became a tenant of the Lower House Farm in 1809. The Worcester and Birmingham Canal had been constructed and opened from Birmingham as far as Tardebigge Old Wharf two years earlier in March 1807. Thomas Dixon had applied for, and been successful in obtaining, one of the six boat lengths which were available, together with its adjacent stacking ground, on the wharf. In 1808 the Lower House in Stoney Lane, with 77 acres of farm land, had been purchased by the Hewell Estates and the tenancy advertised, and Thomas Dixon had applied and been accepted. So he came the following year, with his wife Rebecca and one of his three sons, Thomas, to begin a new life at Tardebigge. At first it was a struggle financially to stock the farm and maintain his canal-carrying business, but he overcame the difficulties successfully.

In March 1813 his son Thomas was involved in a runaway marriage in Birmingham with Mary, daughter of a well-to-do coal customer, Mrs Harvey of Weethley, near Alcester. They had seven children, two of which were sons, Thomas born in 1818, and Matthew born in 1830. These two sons eventually took over the business on the death of their father in 1856 and formed the partnership T & M Dixon. They worked together for 40 years, until Thomas, who lived at The Cottage, Stoney Lane, died, childless after two marriages, in 1896. During this time Matthew and his wife Anne lived at the Lower House and had a large family, five daughters and five sons. Three of the sons, Thomas, Hugh and Ralph, became increasingly involved in various aspects of the business.

During the years of their partnership, Thomas and Matthew Dixon increased the area of land they farmed to around 800 acres (over one square mile) by the renting of The Cottage, Horns Hall (now Robin Hill Farm) on the hill opposite, and other farm land on the Hewell Estates. When the branch railway from Barnt Green to Redditch was opened in 1859, Dixons seized the opportunity to rent a coal wharf just inside the gate of the

Redditch goods yard off Hewell Road. They had, from the outset, retained the family coal and canal-carrying business in Birmingham, and they now proceeded to establish coal depots and offices. Besides those at Tardebigge and Redditch, others were at Bromsgrove, Kings Norton, Alcester, Studley, Harborne, Barnt Green Station, and Camp Hill, Birmingham. Dixons took over the five lime-burning kilns behind the basin at Tardebigge New Wharf and the three beside the winding hole at the Old Wharf and sold the lime produced for use on farms and by builders. They also rented the old warehouse on the New Wharf as a grist mill for the production of animal and poultry feeds. By 1900 they had monopolised the Old Wharf for so long that it was known as Dixon's Wharf, and from there they sold coal, milk, eggs and other farm produce.

In January 1901 the whole business became a company, T & M Dixon Limited, its shares being owned by the family. Matthew of the partnership continued to be the chairman until his death at the age of 93 in 1924, and he was known as "The Governor". During the 1914-18 War, for financial reasons and as food production was so important, a new company, T & M Dixon (Farmers) Ltd was created as a subsidiary of the parent company, thus leaving the coal and other sides of the business within T & M Dixon Ltd. Three of the Governor's sons were actively involved, Colonel Matthew Dixon on the coal side, Hugh Dixon with the livestock, cattle, horses and milk production, and Ralph, who was innovative and enterprising, in managing the large piggery adjacent to the Old Wharf and in developing the fruit-growing business on such a large scale that Dixons were supplying, by road and rail, markets as far away as London.

The T & M Dixon farming business was at its zenith in the 1920s and 1930s between the wars. By this time they were farming some 3,000 acres, which included, in addition to the Lower House, The Cottage and Horns Hall Farms, also Stoney Lane Farm, Hollow Tree Farm, Dusthouse Farm, Tutnall Farm, Burcot House Farm and Ashborough's (Burcot) Farm.

Following the successive deaths of Hugh Dixon in 1931, Colonel Matthew Dixon in 1932, and Ralph Dixon in 1936, management of the various parts of the business passed to Howard Bird who had long served as company secretary at Dixons' office at Broad Green, Allan Macdonell, husband of Ralph's daughter Honor, and Bill Thompson, a grandson of "The Governor". They were joined by Ernold Dixon, another grandson of "The Governor", and by Crispian and Peter Dixon, two of Ralph Dixon's sons.

During WW2 T & M Dixon (farmers) Ltd was kept busy with vital food production, and Blackwell Golf Course (apart from the greens) was ploughed up for this purpose and in use until its restoration in 1947. To offset the shortage of manpower, due to the younger men being away on military service, four members of the Women's Land Army were employed, namely Mary Godrich, Margaret Hall, Christine Galletly and Nellie Myatt. As the war progressed, Italian and German prisoners of war were also employed under strict supervision, as on other farms.

Following the war, the T & M Dixon business empire began to disintegrate for various reasons. One was the sale of the Hewell Estates in 1946 which resulted in farms which had been rented by Dixons coming under the ownership of Howard Bird. Another was the death, in March 1945 towards the end of the war, of Peter Dixon, youngest son of Ralph Dixon. He had been awarded the Military Cross, and if he had lived would undoubtedly have had the drive to help maintain the business. His brother Crispian, who was involved with the poultry side at Tutnall and who had personal problems, committed suicide in 1948. The business continued under the partnership of Howard Bird, Allan Macdonell and Bill Thompson until 1952, when T & M Dixon under that name came to an end, and a new company was created under the title Tardebigge Orchards Limited.

In the meantime, Howard Bird's son John took an active part in the management of the business. From around 1948 he began to phase out the cultivation of soft fruit and the livestock side of the business to concentrate on the production of apples and pears. And so from then onwards, until late in the 1960s, vast areas of the farmland were given over to orchards. When in blossom in the spring, these orchards, covering some 600 acres of land and with around 50,000 fruit trees, were a beautiful sight, especially those viewed from the churchyard of Tardebigge Church. Unfortunately, due to subsidised competition from French fruit growers, the demand for English apples and pears slumped and Tardebigge Orchards Limited came to an end, its assets being divided equally between Howard Bird, John Bird and the family of Allan Macdonnell who had died in 1954.

FARMS IN THE BROCKHILL AND BUTLER'S HILL AREA

BROCKHILL FARM in 1900 was the centre of a thriving dairy business which had been built up by brothers Joseph and Thomas Cash, then in their sixties. Joseph died in 1903, leaving Thomas and his wife Matilda to carry on with the help of their son Thomas Edward, who eventually took over the business. He and his wife Emily were in turn succeeded by their son Edward (Ted) and his wife Rhona, who still traded as J & T Cash. Some time between the wars they introduced a bottling plant and developed an extensive milk round using a van and two electrically driven milk floats which were recharged at night and were used to deliver milk around the new Batchley Estate.

Following the sale of the Hewell Estates land and properties in 1946, Brockhill was one of the farms acquired by Joe Beckett, in addition to the Home Farm at Hewell where he and his wife and daughter went to live. Mr Beckett managed both farms for some 20 years and although George Williams, who lived in the farm cottage at Brockhill, was in charge there, Mr Beckett used to visit the farm each day. Ted and Rhona Cash continued to live in the farmhouse and carried on their dairy business at Brockhill until they retired in 1955 and went to live in Angel Street, Lower Bentley. Both were involved in local affairs and in the life of the church at Tardebigge. Rhona was chosen to be a member of the Redditch Development Corporation. Ted was a churchwarden at Tardebigge Church for many years.

In the early 1950s Mrs Irene Mason from Little Shortwood worked for Ted Cash on the accounting side. He had an old Armstrong Siddeley car in which he often gave the Mason family lifts to Tardebigge Church on Sundays. Their son Andrew Mason remembers that Ted was in the habit of gently crashing the front bumper of the car into the lower brickwork of the church school as he parked it.

Joe Beckett kept Brockhill Farm until 1966, when he sold it to William Tolley who, with his wife Gladys, and their two sons Edwin and Keith, took over the farm. They came, bringing 26 cows, Friesians, from Nene Savage near Cleobury Mortimer. They inherited five farm workers, and carried on the dairy and beef business. In 1978 it became a partnership, W E Tolley and Sons. By 1989 they had about 260 cows. In 1989 William died and Edwin decided to move away and farm in North Devon. The herd was split, leaving Keith at Brockhill with 150 cows. Keith and his wife Eileen have run the farm since in partnership as T K and E M Tolley.

When the Tolleys came to Brockhill the farm covered 290 acres. Of this, 38 acres of woodland were sold to Harris Brush Works for timber for brush handles, then eventually bought back by a consortium of ten, including Keith Tolley, in order to safeguard the woodland and to be able to use it for pheasant shoots, which take place about six times during the winter season.

In the late 1980s and in the 1990s, with large milking and beef herds, extra pasturage was needed. Fields were rented from Dial House Farm, Dusthouse Farm and Caspidge Farm; these in addition to 98 acres of Oxleasowes Farm, still used, bringing the total area then in use to over 500 acres. Dairy farming in the 1990s was beset by widespread epidemics of BSE, Foot and Mouth and Bovine TB which, though not occurring on Brockhill Farm, nevertheless devastated the farming industry. In addition, the price of milk wholesale dropped from 30p/litre to 18p/litre, making dairy farming uneconomic. In the year 2000 the decision was made to end many years of dairy farming at Brockhill. The milking herd was sold off and the farming limited to 200 acres arable (wheat, barley and oil-seed rape), about 220 sheep, and 25 suckler cows for rearing calves for beef. Farm buildings, including the dairy which needed restoration, came to be occupied by seven businesses.

In 1990 two small artificial lakes were created, near the farmhouse off Brockhill Lane, by widening and damming the natural valley, the source of water being a natural spring. This enabled the start of a fishery which is very successful and paid for its creation within two years.

Of BIRCHENSALE FARM, which covered some 200 acres between Brockhill Woods and Salter's Lane, Redditch, only the farmhouse and barn (grade 2 listed buildings) now survive, the surrounding land having been recently developed as the Brockhill Estate. Following the dissolution of the

Norman Neasom's drawing of Birchensale farm.

monasteries in 1539, what had been Bordesley Abbey land became part of the Hewell Estate, and it is believed that the first Birchensale farmhouse, later replaced, was built soon afterwards, around the time of Elizabeth I, since Elizabethan two-inch bricks were discovered in the pigsty some years ago.

In the early part of the nineteenth century Birchensale was tenanted by Thomas Sarsons, who was a churchwarden of Tardebigge Parish from 1794 to 1831. By 1858 the tenancy of the farm, together with that of LOWAN'S HILL FARM, to the north of Brockhill Lane, was held by William Neasom. It was William's son Thomas who, with a partner, Percy White, in 1856 founded the firm of Neasom and White, for many years Estate Agents and Auctioneers in Redditch. The farming business was continued by William's grandson Arthur. Following the death of William in 1913 and his widow in 1922, Arthur, together with his wife Ethel and their two young sons Thomas Arthur (known as Paddy) and Norman, moved from their cottage in Brockhill Lane into the farmhouse. Lowan's Hill Farmhouse had, in the meantime, been occupied by other members of the Neasom family. In the 1930s, during the depression, Arthur Neasom decided to give up the tenancy of Lowan's Hill Farm. The land there was hilly and sandy, suitable for sheep, but poor for arable farming

In 1946 Birchensale Farm was bought for £7,000, by Arthur, from the syndicate which had purchased most of the Hewell Estate land, and he continued living there with the help of his son Paddy until his death in 1966. Paddy and his son Timothy then ran the farm until Paddy's untimely death in 1988 due, it is believed, to his failure to protect himself from inhaling paraquet weed-killer spray used on the farm. In the 1980s grazing rights on the farmland were rented to Sagar Wood of Weight's Farm and his son Stephen for sheep grazing. Paddy's son Richard lived on in the farmhouse until 1996 when the farm was sold to the developers.

Norman Neasom, who grew up on the farm with his brother Paddy, and who became an art lecturer and illustrator, living in Redditch, has happy memories of life there in the 1920s, the 1930s and on through World War 2. *See chapter 11.*

WEIGHTS FARM takes its name from Edward Weight who farmed there in the seventeenth century when the farm was known as Sheepcroft. From the 1890s until 1936 Herbert French, his wife Mary and their two sons kept the mixed dairy and arable farm. During and just after WW2 the farm was in the hands of Fred Wright, whose brother had a butcher's shop in Redditch. Then on 29 September 1947, James Wood came down from Yorkshire and stayed with the Wrights until they moved out and he and his wife Sarah Ann and their three sons, Sagar aged 19, John aged 17 and Tom aged 16, moved in on 15/16 November 1947. With them came their farming livestock including a herd of pedigree Friesian cattle. At the outset James and Sarah Ann formed the partnership of J & S A Wood, by which the business is still known.

In the early years there was a concentration on dairy farming and pig rearing. Unfortunately in the mid 50s there was an outbreak of swine fever and no government compensation for the loss, so it was decided to sell the dairy herd and change to sheep farming and the growing of crops (barley, oats and beans), and this remained the main farming activity for many years until after the year 2000. James and Sarah Ann's three sons all worked on the farm at first, but John eventually left to go into transport and moved to Canada. Sagar and Tom succeeded their parents and as the business prospered they bought, in 1971, the land of Shortwood Farm from the Pridhams. The next major purchase was that of Astwood Farm, Wychbold, in 1976, and Tom and his family moved there in 1981, leaving Sagar and his son Stephen to run Weights Farm. Further purchases of farm land followed in 1985 with 250 acres of Grange Farm from the Shaws and in 1997 300 acres of Lower Park Farm, Bordesley. Other smaller acquisitions were Lowans Hill Farm (rented) and Ireland's Farm on Brockhill Lane (a small farm now occupied by new houses).

When Sagar Wood died in 1990 at the age of 62, there was a considerable gathering of local farmers and others in the congregation at Tardebigge Church for his funeral. Since then Stephen has carried out the development of the Weights Farm Business Park, which now occupies some of the land and old farm buildings. This began in 1990 with the provision of an "inert" landfill site on the nearby hillside and continued with the opening of various vehicle and construction businesses.

The extensive sheep farming continued in the 1990s with some 3,500 breeding ewes. In the mid 1990s hostile action by "do-gooders" against the export of live animals led to Weights Farm being targeted. The farming of sheep eventually came to an end in 2001 when all the sheep and cattle on the farm had to be slaughtered during the country-wide foot and mouth epidemic. Stephen and his son Adam then decided it would be more profitable to change to the rearing of beef cattle, and a range of new buildings has been constructed for this purpose.

SHORTWOOD FARM, adjacent to Weights Farm and Brockhill Farm, was tenanted by Joe Beckett from January 1939 until 1946 when, following his part in the purchase of the Hewell Estate, he moved with his wife Janie and their daughter Elizabeth into the Home Farm at Hewell. During the war years Italian prisoners of war were employed on the farm.

Joe Beckett was one of four brothers who became farmers. On leaving school at the age of fourteen he helped his father Alfred on their farm near Shrewsbury. Eventually, in 1932, he took on the tenancy of Ley Hill Farm, Northfield, Birmingham.

The owner of the farm was Mr Kunzle who lived at Ley Hill House nearby. Previous tenants had failed in the running of the farm, but Joe Beckett, through his hard work and enterprise, made a success out of his farming. He built up a dairy herd and started a milk round in the neighbourhood, and he marketed poultry, eggs and potatoes. He also built a piggery using offcut timber obtained free-of-charge from Vincents timberyard in Selly Oak. Kunzles had a high-class confectionary and restaurant business in the Arcade near Snow Hill Station in Birmingham. Joe Beckett supplied them with cream and milk in churns which were delivered by pick-up truck each day. Stale cakes from Kunzles were brought back to feed the pigs.

From 1946 to 1953 Shortwood, now owned by Joe Beckett, was farmed by Noel Arculus, who lived at the farm until 1949 when he moved to live and also farm at Butlers Hill Farm.

FARMS AROUND COBLEY HILL

LITTLE SHORTWOOD was a small farm of some 9 acres only, and its mid seventeenth century farmhouse may have been originally a gamekeeper's cottage. By 1900 it was probably a subsidiary of nearby Oxleasowes Farm, for it was tenanted at that time by George Powell, who was a poultryman, and his wife Elizabeth and young son George. There are none of the usual farm buildings there except pigsties. In December 1949 Edward Mason, his wife Irene and young family, came out from Birmingham to be the new tenants, following two families who had lived in the farmhouse. By this time the property was owned by Dennis Webb of Oxleasowes Farm. The 8 acres of surrounding farmland acquired by the Masons, including some ridge and furrow, had not been farmed for some years; it was rough and overgrown and was left so by Edward Mason who continued to travel to work in Birmingham by train from Alvechurch Station. However, he did take up bee-keeping.

The family and the farm cottage were in the news in the Spring of 1950, a few months after the Masons arrived. When they moved in, the house was without mains electricity or gas. After several accidents using oil lamps, Edward, who at that time worked for the Birmingham firm Joseph Lucas Ltd (which manufactured car components including dynamos and electrical equipment), decided to install a wind-powered electric lighting system. The source of power was a dynamo coupled to a twin bladed wooden propeller which, using a tailpiece, rotated to face the wind. It was mounted on top of a 40 feet high wooden pole with side brackets which, like those on traditional telegraph poles, could be used to climb up to access the apparatus. Two aerial wires connected the dynamo to 12 volt batteries in one of the bedrooms, and these charged the batteries which were wired to 23 light bulbs throughout the house and also supplied electric current to a wireless set. This humble innovation was a forerunner of today's wind turbines. It remained in use until mains electricity arrived in 1965.

OXLEASOWES FARM, with its drive off Brockhill Lane, was in the hands of George Taylor and his wife Elizabeth until his death in 1925. Then, for many years it was farmed by the Webb family, at first by Ernest Webb (died 1948), then by his wife and their son Dennis until his early death in

1959. In 1960 the farm was bought by Leslie Boffey of Cherrytrees Farm, and his son John Boffey moved in to manage the farm after his marriage to Valerie in 1961. Sadly John died of MS in 1974. Valerie's second marriage was to David Harrison, a Birmingham jeweller. They have continued to reside at the farmhouse, and their two children, Tim and Sally, following their marriages, have lived nearby in barn conversions.

Farming at Oxleasowes ceased after John's death, following which 120 acres of the land was sold, some to the Waterworks near the Old Wharf, some to John Whittaker of Stoney Lane Farm. Another 78 acres, including two fields on the east side of the drive, have been let to Keith Tolley of Brockhill Farm. Two redundant farm buildings are occupied by a car repair business. A film, "The Canal Children", was made on the farm by the BBC around 1980 for children's television. The line of vision between the farmhouse and nearby Blakenhurst Prison was deliberately blocked by the creation of a copse of various interesting trees near the house soon after the prison opened.

CATTESPOOL FARM, though adjacent to some of the T & M Dixon farms, escaped the Dixon net since it remained firmly in the ownership of the Peyton family until just after WW2. Way back in 1622 local landowner Robert Peyton of WHEELEY FARM had purchased the Cattespool estate. The timber-framed farmhouse was built by his son Robert around 1640. It soon had stonework additions, a porch and a western wing to the house, and stone walling round the garden. Over the years both Cattespool and Wheeley Farms have been farmed together by the Peytons or by their tenant farmers. The last tenant farmer at Cattespool in the 1930s was a Mr West and the last member of the Peyton family to own it was Mrs Gilpin Brown. By 1946 the house, which had been let during WW2 and occupied by evacuees, needed renovation and modernisation. This, including the installation of electricity, sanitation and running water, was carried out by Mrs Hilaire Hollick and her husband who bought the house and 100 acre farm in 1946 and then sold it in 1948 to surgeon Guy Baines and his wife Janet, who were just married.

Janet Baines came of a farming family. Guy Baines took up farming at Cattespool as a hobby whilst still practising as a surgeon in Birmingham. They managed the livestock farm with the help of various farm workers, some of whom resided in Cattespool Cottage or the newly-built Kitten-spool. They included Fred Besley of Burcot, and cowman Jack Grinter. Of the Baines' four children, the eldest, Robert, who became an accountant and a successful London businessman, had the barn behind Cattespool converted for himself and his wife to stay in at weekends. Guy Baines gave up farming in 1971 and died in 1984. Janet continued to enjoy life at Cattespool until moving to Chipping Campden in 2002.

Cattespool Farmhouse. (Dave Besley)

Following his father's death, Robert Baines inherited Cattespool and a year or so later bought Wheeley Farm. To manage both farms, he appointed a farm manager, Alan McKinnon, who has lived in the large tied cottage, known as Roy Green's Cottage, adjacent to Wheeley Farmhouse. Robert has continued to work during the week in London, but has spent time, mostly at weekends, at Cattespool. In recent years he has purchased more land, increasing the estate to some 500 acres, much of which is let to local farmers. In particular, he purchased Little Shortwood from Harris Brush, who used it to grow timber there for the wooden handles of their paint brushes before they were replaced by plastic handles. In recent times a game-keeper, Giles Jackson, living at Kittenspool with his wife Sue, has obtained six-week old pheasants and reared them and has organised shoots at Little Shortwood. He has also helped as a gardener at Cattespool.

One interesting feature of Cattespool is the quarry which existed on its land. When, in 1974, the A448 dual carriageway was being constructed between Bromsgrove and Redditch, the contractors quarried stone and gravel from the quarry and then landscaped the area with a dam to create a trout-fishing lake which is used by a syndicate. Cattespool farmhouse remains, much as it has been for over three centuries, a picturesque 17th century building.

WHEELEY FARM was tenanted and farmed in the 1890s and until around 1905 by James Brickley, then by Charles Taylor until his death in 1929, followed by his widow Elizabeth Taylor in the 1930s. Hubert Green then took over the farm and, after his death in 1954, his two sons carried on. The elder son, Beresford Green, lived at the farmhouse and he became long-serving chairman of the Tutnall and Cobley Parish Council in succession to Mrs Tustin of Broad Green Forge, who had also served for many years. The younger son, Roy Green, lived in the nearby cottage, newly built for him. It was in 1985 that the Green brothers retired and the farm was bought by Robert Baines. Beresford Green retained one field so that he could still continue to serve on the parish council. Roy Green's widow lived on for some years in a bungalow on Cobley Hill, now "The Shielling".

THE SIDNALLS was one of the granges (farms) of Bordesley Abbey, and at the dissolution of the monasteries it was included in the Hewell properties acquired by the Windsors. The old farmhouse was rebuilt around 1750. By the 1850s the farm land and farm buildings were used by nearby Wheeley's Farm, and Lady Harriet Windsor had the Sidnalls farmhouse converted into three farm workers' cottages. The cottages were still being used by the farm workers of H G Green and Sons of Wheeley Farm in the 1950s, having been bought by the Greens in 1948 soon after the 1946 sale of the Hewell Estate.

In 1954 the Sidnalls farmhouse, but not the farm buildings, was purchased by Mr and Mrs Amatt, and they spent the next few years converting the three cottages back into a single house. At the same time H G Green and Sons built the two semi-detached cottages next to the Sidnalls for their two stockmen who kept a herd of pigs using the farm buildings. In 1975 the Sidnalls was bought at auction by Tom Knowles and his wife Judith. They bought the farm buildings in 1978 and several acres of the farmland in 1985 when the Greens sold Wheeley Farm. Mr and Mrs Knowles added to the extensions and improvements to the property started by the Amatts, and they kept hens, ducks, bees, a couple of Jacob sheep and a Jersey house-cow. In 1989 their daughter Roberta (Bobbie), married to Philip Matulja, moved into the house and carried out renovations which took seven years of their early married life to complete. They are proud to be custodians of the lovely old house.

GORSEY LANE FARM had several tenants in the early part of the twentieth century, including Isaac Howard, who died in 1919 aged 80, and Leonard Lacey into the 1930s. In recent times its farm land has been part of nearby Fox Hill Farm, owned by Matthew Docker, a Birmingham industrialist, manufacturer at his Fisher Foundry of patent drinking bowls for cattle and of other metal products. Gorsey Lane farmhouse has, for many years, been a private dwelling.

GRANGE FARM was another of the granges of Bordesley Abbey and therefore it was included in the Hewell estate acquired by the Windsor family when they came to Tardebigge. In the 1890s and up to WW1 the tenant farmers were members of the Burman family, Charles Burman until around 1905, followed by William Burman. It is likely that they supplied meat to Bazely & Burman, butchers in Alvechurch. From 1926 and through the 1930s and 1940s Alfred Shaw was farming there and his two sons John and Colin followed in their father's footsteps in the 1950s, 1960s and 1970s. John continued to live in the farmhouse. Colin lived in a newly-built cottage "Cocot" adjacent to the farm. For their widowed mother, Evelyn, they built a bungalow nearby. In the 1960s John's wife Margaret ran a playgroup for young children in the farmhouse.

Around 1980 the Shaws decided to retire. The farm land was bought by Robert Baines and the farmhouse was bought by Arthur Cunninghame and his wife Rachel, Robert's sister. The Cunninghames eventually sold the farmhouse and moved to the Cotswolds around the year 2000.

COBLEY HILL FARM covers a large area of land from Cobley Hill down to the canal, together with fields around and behind the farmhouse. Two names are listed as tenants of this Hewell Estate property in the early 1900s, Isaac Howard and Thomas Green. Then for many years, up to and including WW2, the tenant was Vernon Taylor, and after his death his widow lived on there. When the farm was sold by Dr Houfton, who was one of the four who purchased the Hewell Estate farms and property in 1946, the purchaser was Roger Bence, an accountant, who has since farmed and managed the property for over 60 years. He was not married and in the early years his widowed mother helped to run the farm and took charge when he was busy in Birmingham during the week. She was a retired teacher, a slight lady but very strong. On one occasion she pulled a trailer using a rope tied round her waist! Latterly Roger has continued some of his accountancy work and has farmed in a small way. But in recent years most of the land has been let out to other farmers, including Richard Brittain of Bentley. Over the years Ron Perry, living in one of the two cottages opposite the farm, has helped Roger at weekends, whilst a series of contract milkers have occupied the other cottage. The large barn has been let to Robert Baines for lambing, and loose boxes for horses have been rented out to riders.

BLACKWELL FARM was situated on the east side of the Lickey Incline just beyond Blackwell Station. It was included in the Hewell Estates, and the tenant around 1900 was John Allsebrook who kept a dairy herd and other livestock on an area of undulating pasture land between Agmore Road and Blackwell Road. The farm buildings included stables and cowsheds around three sides of a spacious farmyard, together with the farmhouse, barns and a nearby cottage for a cowman.

Back in 1893, John Allsebrook agreed to allow a newly-formed golf club to use three of his fields, some 49 acres, for a nine-hole golf course, at a yearly rental of £15. The initiative for this, the beginning of Blackwell Golf Club, was that of the Revd Arthur Swift, Curate of Blackwell, together with four Birmingham businessmen who lived locally. Swift was a well-to-do bachelor and a sportsman, with more time on his hands than the others, and he undertook to be both secretary and treasurer of the initial committee. Members of the newly formed club had to endure the uneven ground, stray animals and cattle dung. There was no agreed length of tenure and for the first few years no club house in which to wash, shelter or change clothes, and no toilets. In 1899, a portable building, nick-named "The tin tabernacle", was erected in the farm's orchard, and in 1905 primitive lavatories were provided. It was soon clear that the long-term future of the club and its expansion to a full 18-hole course was dependent on the purchase of the farm. This move, however, was resisted by Lord Windsor, by John Allsebrook, and then by George Allsebrook, who took over the farm following his father's death in 1901.

Membership of the golf club continued to increase before and after the disruption of the 1914-18 War, and several limited-term leases were arranged, but it was not until 1921 that an influential and determined member of the club, Guy Bigwood, a Birmingham estate agent, was able to conclude an agreement with George Allsebrook, his widowed mother and the Earl of Plymouth, for the takeover of the tenancy of the farm. Bigwood found a house for Allsebrook and his wife, and they agreed to move by 1923. By this time the enlarged course of 18 holes was ready for use and it was opened with due ceremony on 4th August 1923 by the club's president, Ivor Miles, Earl of Plymouth. Fortunately the farm buildings were retained and adapted for use as the clubhouse with all the necessary amenities, including bar and restaurant. Over the years many well-known local people have been members and officials of the club which owes much to its pioneering and enthusiastic early members.

HIGH BARN FARM at Vigo, on the south side of the road between Broad Green and Burcot, was part of the Allbright's Finstall Estates until purchased by the tenant farmer, Norman Hall, in 1947. Norman and his wife Annie (nee Quinney) had succeeded the previous tenants, the Waldrons, in 1922. Their son Edward was born in 1924, and following his education at Tardebigge School and Lawrence's College in Birmingham, to which he travelled by train from Blackwell Station, he worked on the farm and eventually took it over after his father's death in 1959. Soon after his mother's death in 1966, Edward married Noreen, a teacher who had come to lodge at the farm and had become his dancing partner. In this he was encouraged by the Vicar of Tardebigge, the Revd Reg Underhill, who conducted their wedding.

Some of the High Barn Farm land is situated beside the Lickey Incline, and in the days of steam trains, the farm then being partly arable, the corn occasionally caught fire due to sparks from the steam locomotives. Drivers and firemen on banking engines descending the Incline were in the habit of throwing coal at the rabbits, which could be killed by a blow on the back of the neck, and some of them later retrieved. As much as two or three hundredweight of this coal could be collected from the land with a tractor in six months and used on the farm.

In his time, Edward concentrated on dairy farming and he had a local milk round until about 1960, when he changed to rearing beef cattle. He ceased farming in 1988, but continued to live at the farm until his death in 2006.

FARMS IN THE NEIGHBOURHOOD OF TARDEBIGGE CHURCH

CHERRY TREES FARM, situated below Tardebigge Church, had its land divided by the canal, which is why the accommodation bridge below the top lock was built to provide access. The farm was tenanted by Edmund Kemp in the 1890s and until 1904. From 1905 until the late 1950s it was farmed by the Green Family, by John George Green until his death in 1921, by Lionel Green in the 1920s and 1930s, then by John George Green until he died in 1953. The latter's wife, Edith, continued to live there until she died in 1958. In the meantime, in 1956, Cherry Trees was bought by Leslie Boffey of New House Farm, and he and his wife Gwyneth moved to live there in 1958. When they retired to Malta in 1971/2, the farmhouse with 9 acres of land was sold to gynaecologist Dr Elias Jones, and he lived there.

HOLYOAKE'S FARM, known as such since the seventeenth century, has a long history, having been one of the granges of Bordesley Abbey in the thirteenth century. When in 1827 the walled kitchen garden of Hewell Grange was made on some of the land of what had been Cutford Farm, the remaining few acres of this small farm, on which half a million bricks for the garden wall and buildings had been made from the clay soil, were absorbed into Holyoake's Farm.

In the early 1900s Holyoake's Farm had several short-term tenancies. Then, at the end of WW1, Howard Hill, together with his wife and two young sons, Jack and Gerald, moved there from Spring Hill Farm in

Foxlydiate Lane, Webheath. Holyoake's was a dairy farm and Howard is remembered as having ridden around it on a grey mare. He was a keen sportsman, a member of the Hewell Bowling Club to which he donated its original flag. When he died in 1952, son Jack took over the tenancy of Holyoake's Farm from the Bentley Estate which had purchased it when the Plymouth Estate properties were sold after WW2. His brother Gerald left to farm at Church Hill, Redditch, then later at Norgrove Court, and finally at The Sillins after it was sold by Leslie Gray-Cheape.

In their twenties, Jack and Gerald were reputedly great dancers and were much in demand as dance partners by the ladies. Jack continued his father's love of sport and hunting. He was in the county tennis and badminton teams and he bred and raced point-to-point horses. He died in 1970 after being ill for three years, during which time his wife Mollie ran the farm. His son Tim was only eleven when Jack died, hence the decision to relinquish the tenancy. The farmhouse and surrounding buildings were bought by Dennis Overton whose son has lived there since. Most of the farm land west of Holyoake's Lane was bought by Tony May, and that east of the Lane by Harry Gibbs. Tim Hill and his family have since lived at Cutford House, an extended version of Cutford Cottage, situated on what had been Cutford Farm land.

HIGH HOUSE FARM, in High House Lane, was, in the mid nineteenth century, in the hands of William Bradley. He was a Tardebigge church-warden in the 1840s. By 1900 it was being farmed by Joseph Hodgetts (died 1907), then by Frederick Buckley (died 1938) and then by his son Thomas Buckley. Following the 1946 sale of the Hewell Estates the property was owned by John Coney and he sold it in 1951 to Boxfoldia Ltd, one of whose joint managers, John Foyle, came and lived at the farm with his wife Eileen. Unfortunately in 1964 there was a fire there in which Eileen, who was alone in the house at the time, died. For many years the farm, owned by Boxfoldia, was managed by Heinrich Siodlioteck (known as Heinz) who had been a prisoner of war, together with his English wife Doreen and son Peter. Latterly the farmhouse has been a private dwelling, with adjacent barn conversions.

SHELTWOOD FARM was, in medieval times, a grange of Bordesley Abbey and it is believed to have been the location of a slaughterhouse for the deer of Feckenham Forest. At the dissolution of the monasteries it was granted to Edward Lord Clinton and included in the Manor of Tardebigge. In the 16th and 17th centuries it was the residence of various members of the Cookes family. In 1864 Lady Harriet Windsor-Clive had two cottages built on the site of the old tithe barn which had been demolished. These cottages, which are situated in the lane near the farm, are still known as Tithe Barn Cottages. By 1900 the farm was in the possession of the Manor of Bentley and it is still rented from the Bentley Estates.

In the early 1900s and until around 1935 the tenant farmers were Mrs Ann Brickley and her son Howard. They were succeeded in 1936 by George Frazier and his wife Lilian, who came from nearby Patchetts Farm together with their five children, Elsie, Leslie, Phyllis, Cyril and Herbert. At Sheltwood, sons Leslie and Herbert worked on the farm and by the end of WW2 they were both married; Leslie and his wife were living in Banks Green; and Herbert and his wife in Bentley. But they were now running the farm for their father. Herbert was in charge of the dairy herd, and Leslie managed the arable side, using shire horses as well as tractors.

George and Lilian Frazier, during their time at Patchetts and Sheltwood, were involved in the life of the local community. George was a playing member of Hewell Bowling Club. Lilian, described as "a tall formidable lady", was a founder member of Tardebigge W.I. which was formed in 1917; she was a committee member from 1921, secretary 1930-38, and president 1944-51.

Following George's death in 1955, the tenancy of Sheltwood was given up. Leslie, his wife Alice and family moved to a small farm with a milk round in the Forest of Dean; Herbert with his wife Allison moved to Wellingborough where he worked as gardener on a small estate.

Since 1956 Sheltwood has been farmed by Tony May who came from Gloucestershire, and latterly by his two sons, William and Martin. Some time after Tony May purchased, and moved into, Tardebigge Vicarage, his sons, who had been living in the Tithe Barn Cottages, moved, William and his family into Sheltwood Farmhouse, Martin and his family into Peplars Hill Farm which was created around 1980 by Tony May out of surrounding farmland. Although the Mays still rent Sheltwood from the Bentley Estates, extra adjacent farmland has been purchased and the farming business, which now extends to some 1000 acres, is now managed by William and Martin with the assistance of one man and modern machinery.

PATCHETT'S FARM. Although the farmhouse lies just inside the Parish of Finstall, about half of the land is in Tardebigge Parish. The farm was within the Hewell Estates and it was tenanted in the 1890s and on until 1936 by the Frazier family. Thomas Frazier and his wife Elizabeth ran the farm until around 1920, assisted by their son George and Thomas's brother Herbert. In the 1890s and the early 1900s George had been the skipper of the farm's own horse-drawn boat "John Bull" which was used to take farm produce by canal to Droitwich and Birmingham and bring back manure. George took over the farm from his father and carried on until he and his wife and family moved, in 1936, to Sheltwood Farm.

From 1936 to 1946 Percy Tilt was the tenant farmer. Then in 1946 James Wormington from Berrow Hill Farm, Feckenham, bought and took over Patchett's Farm, and he has since been succeeded by his son James and grandson James who now farms it together with his son Ian and his brother Michael from Berrow Hill Farm.

FARMS IN THE BENTLEY AREA

UPPER BENTLEY FARM, close to Bentley Manor, was one of the four home farms of the Bentley Estate, the other three being Norgrove, Bentley House and Lower Bentley Farm. Part of the farmhouse is three or four centuries old, the east end showing its timber-framed construction. At the beginning of the twentieth century the farm, together with Norgrove, was worked under the supervision of "The Squire" with a succession of farm tenants, there being accommodation in the farmhouse for two families. From around 1935 to 1940 the farm was being run by tenant George Price. Then in 1941 Martin Gibbs and his family moved in from Buntsford Hill Farm, near Bromsgrove. In 1958 Martin's son Harry took over with his wife Diana, and in due course their two sons, Martin and Philip, became involved and in recent years have taken over the running of the farm. Harry and Diana retired to Thriftwood, Holyoake's Lane, an outpost of what has become a widespread farming business. From some 400 acres around Upper Bentley Farm in the 1940s, the area now being farmed by the business, H Gibbs & Sons UB Ltd, extends to 1300 acres, including land in

The Warwickshire Beagles at Upper Bentley Farm in November 1958. On the left, Diana Gibbs and Harry Gibbs and, on the right, Martin Gibbs wearing a cap, and Dr Anderson in hunt gear. (Diana Gibbs)

Hanbury and Westwood Park, Droitwich. Due to mechanisation and modern farming techniques, the farming enterprise is now run by only three people, Martin, Philip and one other local man.

Memories of Harry's father, Martin Gibbs, are mostly of him on his pony "Tommy", which took him everywhere in his latter years when he suffered from arthritis. Tommy could be relied upon to bring him home safely from the pub on an evening. Of those who have worked on the farm, Bill Harber and his family, who lived at Woodbine Cottage, have been outstanding. Bill began work under "The Gaffer " (Martin Gibbs) and served on the farm all his life. His wife Milly and their children, John, Donald and Christine, have, over the years, also worked on the farm and, in addition latterly, when needed and available, Donald's sons Andrew and Neal.

In the 1970s and 1980s Harry and Diana Gibbs were happy to welcome parties of school children on visits to the farm. These included children from the nursery which met at Bentley Village Hall, but it was mainly coach-loads of children from Birmingham schools who came towards the end of the summer term. Many of these inner city children had never seen farm animals and poultry. They were able to see the pigs, eggs freshly laid, cows being milked, and the milking parlour with its tank and rotating paddle designed to prevent the cream settling before the tanker came to collect it.

POUND FARM was evidently the location of the Bentley Estate pound to which stray animals were taken to be kept until claimed by their owners. From the 1930s until the 1970s this small farm was in the hands of George Tongue who died, aged 93, in 1980. Besides keeping two or three cows and growing vegetables, he used his horse and cart to do haulage work for the local council. The next resident had a metal business. Then the elegant farmhouse was bought by John Stokes in 1985 and extended in keeping with its original stylish barge-boarding and diamond-paned windows. The old black and white barn has been converted to living accommodation.

CALLOW FARM in Angel Street, of some 20 acres, was in the hands of a branch of the Tongue family, Walter Tongue before WW1, and then his son Jack and his wife Susie and their daughter Dorothy up to WW2. In recent years it has become an equestrian centre.

BENTLEY HOUSE FARM was, until around 1840, the Manor House of Bentley and the hub of the Bentley Estate. There in the fourteenth, fifteenth and sixteenth centuries had lived members of the Pauncefoot family, and then, for over 200 years from 1630 to 1838 members of the Cookes family who followed as Lords of the Manor. After Richard Hemming bought the Manor in 1838, he extended Bentley Lodge to become the new Manor House and Bentley House then became one of the home farms. Farm tenants in the late 19th century and early 20th century were Francis Drury, who died aged 88 in 1904, and his son Henry Drury.

In 1929 the Morgan family (Herbert Morgan, his wife Lucy and their three sons, Frank, Harry and Brian) moved in. In 1932, after only three years, Herbert died and Lucy then managed the farm for several years until Frank took over. Frank married Daisy in 1939 and he farmed the 200 or so acres of land with, in the 1950s and 1960s, three full-time farm labourers, until he and Daisy retired to Banks Green in 1984. Since then their son Michael and his wife and family have continued as the farm tenants, so the Morgans have been farming at Bentley House for well over seventy years.

Frank Morgan with his Hereford bull outside Bentley House Farm, formerly Bentley Manor House. (Frank Morgan)

Parts of the farmhouse and farm buildings are quite old. Attached to the farmhouse is the old two-storey granary building now converted into two flats. The ground floor was known as the millhouse, where grain was processed for animal feed. The granary above was reached by exterior stone steps which remain in situ. Below the steps is a hollow compartment with a little low entrance, and this is believed to have served as a kennel for a dog acting as a deterrent to thieves and rats. The other old building alongside the farmyard, dating back to the seventeenth century (a stone bearing the date 1649 was found when a small extension was demolished some time ago) contained stables and cowsheds, the latter being now used as stables rented by riders for their horses or ponies.

NEW HOUSE FARM, Banks Green, was formed in the mid nineteenth century by the amalgamation of three small farms located at what are now Bradley Cottage (Banks Green), Pear Tree Cottage, and Three Ways (in Angel Street, Upper Bentley). New House Farm was at one time known as Pheasant Farm, which is what the old farmhouse is still called. The new farmhouse on the other side of the farm drive is now known as Swan's Brook House, named after the nearby stream which flows under the road.

It was to New House Farm that Leslie Boffey, his wife Olive and their three young children, John, Alan and Rhona, came as tenants in 1941, after their house at the Maypole in Birmingham suffered wartime bomb damage. The previous tenant, Bob Harvey, and his father William before him, had been there about 50 years. Leslie Boffey, with the eventual help of his two sons, managed the mixed dairy and arable farm of 250 or so acres until the late 1980s when the farm was run down, the barns were converted, the land was sold off, and he retired to Malta, leaving his son Alan Boffey and his wife Wendy living at the farmhouse. In the meanwhile, in 1956, Leslie bought Cherrytrees Farm, Tardebigge, from the Green family, and he and his second wife Gwyneth moved to live there in 1958, leaving sons John and Alan at New House Farm. Then in 1960 he bought Oxleasowes Farm, off Brockhill Lane, as a place for his son John Boffey and his wife Valerie to live and work after their marriage in 1961.

JEFFRIES FARM, Coalash Lane, lies just within the parish, the lane being part of the parish boundary. It takes its name from the Jeffries family, which in the 15th and 16th centuries owned land in Bentley Pauncefoot. It was part of the Bentley Estate until purchased by the tenant Harold Fernihough in 1971/2. In the early 1900s, through WW1 and until 1936, the tenant farmer was William Albutt. He also worked at Stoke Prior Salt Works. Some of the timbers used in the construction of one of the barns were originally part of old wooden brine pipes from the works. Coalash Lane was surfaced with coal ash from the salt works, before the use of tarmac, hence its name.

For several years, including WW2 until 1944, the tenant was John Jones. When Arthur Fernihough and his wife Phyllis moved in, in 1944, from their smallholding just over the canal bridge from the Queen's Head, Stoke Pound, they had to clear away a vast number of empty drink bottles left around by their predecessor. Arthur Fernihough ran a mixed dairy and arable farm of around 65 acres, and he had a milk round bought from the Greenways nearby in Copyholt Lane. When Arthur retired and moved away in 1969, his son Harold, with his wife Pat and their three sons, who had been living in Finstall, took over the farm. Harold had been helping to run the farm, and soon after taking it over, besides purchasing it from the Bentley Estate, he also bought extra land from Hatchett's Farm. At first the three sons helped on the farm as teenagers, but they then chose other careers so that when, due to heart trouble, Harold had to give up farming in 1995, the land was let to neighbouring farmers, as it has been since, whilst he and Pat have continued to live in the farmhouse.

The present farmhouse, which was built in mock timbered style by the father of Harold Coombes around 1900, incorporates at the north end part of an older farm cottage. There used to be a timber-built barn and cowsheds beside the lane, but they were destroyed by a great fire in the hot dry summer of 1949. It took about a year for the Bentley Estate to get round to replacing the cowshed with a brick-built one. Meanwhile the cows had to be walked along the highway to be milked at Beasley Farm, the journey each way taking half-an-hour and causing great frustration to other road traffic. The cowshed building has latterly been converted into a dwelling "The Byre".

HATCHETT'S FARM has been in existence since before the 18th century. It was part of the Bentley Estate and was over 100 acres in extent until bought with just 12 acres of land by Thomas Harris, a retired research chemist, and his wife Joyce in 1968. The relatively modern farmhouse was built in 1880. Unfortunately an old listed tithe barn was blown down in 1988. Previous tenants have included Harvey Chesshire from 1893 to 1912, Joey Foster from 1914 to 1941, and William Lowe and family from 1942 to 1966. Thomas Harris kept a beef herd until his death in 2001. The land has since been farmed by Anthony Gibbs of Lower Bentley Farm, but Mrs Harris has continued to occupy the farmhouse.

It was on Chapel Meadow, part of the farm, that sandstone remains of the medieval chapel of St Stephen, together with fragments of pottery and other items were discovered around 1964 by William Lowe's daughter, Christine. In the 14th century this chapel, attached to Bentley Manor, was served by the monks of Bordesley Abbey who supplied a priest to take the services. Its subsequent history is unknown.

LOWER BENTLEY FARM, included in the Bentley Estate, was farmed by Francis Brown before and during the early 1900s. On 22 March 1909 Thomas Goulbourne of Woodrow Farm, south of Redditch, went with his father to view the farm, and on 31 March he arranged with Mr Jagger, the estate manager, to take on the tenancy. The removal of furniture, equipment and livestock took place between 26 September and 15 October.

These details we know from the Boots Scribbling Diary of 1909 in which Thomas Goulbourne recorded details of the weather and farming activities from day to day at Woodrow and then at Lower Bentley. Of his farm workers at Woodrow, two, George Kemp and George Bayliss, moved with him, being joined at Lower Bentley by Harry Hopkins and Reuben Nash. The weekly wage for adult farm workers was then 15 or 16 shillings. The mixed farming included the rearing of sheep and pigs, and the growing of wheat, beans, swedes, mangolds and hay. Farm work included ploughing, seeding, rolling, harrowing, harvesting, threshing, hedging, ditching, cartage and maintaining the farm buildings.

Thomas remained at Lower Bentley Farm until his death in 1953. After his wife Eliza's death in 1954, two of their sons, Dick and Ron, who had taken over the running of the farm at the beginning of the war, were given notice to quit by the estate manager. In 1955 there was a sale of all the livestock and farm equipment which yielded £4,215. Included in the sale were three tractors, a 1937 Model L Case, a 1943 Fordson and a 1947 Fordson, indicative of the initial replacement of horse power by motor power in the late 1930s. Of Thomas's three sons, Alfred, the eldest, farmed at Tack Farm, Foxlydiate, until his early death at the beginning of the war. Frederick (Dick) and his wife Mary went, in 1955, to live with her father, Walker Bray, at Holly Cottage, Upper Bentley, and Dick worked as heating engineer at the College and High School in Bromsgrove. He became a churchwarden at Tardebigge Church. Mary was organist for many years at Bentley Church and then at Tardebigge.

The new tenants of the farm in 1955 were John and Sheila Gibbs who stayed there forty years. When they took over Lower Bentley Farm they concentrated on dairy farming and the rearing of beef cattle, sheep and pigs. The area tended to be waterlogged, so they had the farmyard concreted over and much of the land had to be drained.

In 1990 John and Sheila Gibbs exchanged farmhouses with their son Anthony and his family who, until then, had been living at Common Barn Farm. In recent years, since his father retired, Anthony has farmed the land of both Lower Bentley and Common Barn Farms, and he and his wife Christine and their two sons have continued to occupy Lower Bentley Farmhouse. The sons are now helping to run the farm.

COMMON BARN FARM, also known as Barnhouse Farm in the early 1900s, was apparently so-called because the barn attached to the house was used to provide extra accommodation, which must make it one of the earliest barn conversions. It was a small dairy farm in the hands of Mr and Mrs Philip Tandy until 1906, then of William Drew until his death in 1916. Harry Gill and his wife Marion were there from the 1930s until 1961 when Harry died. Mrs Gill was a daughter of the Tandys of Tyrell's Farm. After that, Mr and Mrs Hughes lived at the farmhouse, but the land was used by John Gibbs of Lower Bentley Farm. Following the Hughes family, John's son Anthony and his family moved into Common Barn Farmhouse.

In 1990, as already mentioned, there was an exchange of farmhouses. Anthony and his family moved into Lower Bentley Farmhouse and his parents John and Sheila Gibbs came to live at Common Barn Farm. John retired from farming, and since his death in 2003 Sheila has continued to be busy, looking after horses which have been stabled and kept for members of the riding community, pursuing her interest in equestrian events, and also being greatly involved with church affairs and events, including the annual church fair and show, the plant sale held at the beginning of May in recent years, and the Evergreens.

PERRY MILL FARM was, in days gone by, the source of perry and cider for the Bentley Estate. Fruit from its pear and apple orchards was crushed between mill stones, the upper one being rotated by means of a horse which plodded round and round the press. One of the original millstones now lies outside a corner of the farmhouse. A fragment of another forms part of a mounting block beside the driveway to the farm.

The farmhouse is an early 17th century grade 2 listed building. It is heavily timber-framed throughout, except on the south side, and there have been few alterations. It lies in the midst of 90 acres of ground, eastwards towards the Thrift and to the north below Hatchetts Farm.

Tenant farmers in the twentieth century have been William Sheppard until his death in 1919, Alfred Goulbourne, Sidney Harris and Mrs Nora Morris, followed, in 1956/7 by Stewart Mitchell. Stewart's neighbour in "Grasmere" from 1960 to 1965 was Mary Moule. She joined Stewart following their marriage in 1965, and until his death in 1983 helped him run Perry Mill as a dairy farm, the milk being collected in churns from the

The timber-framed rear end of Perry Mill Farmhouse and, lying at the corner, one of the old mill stones. (AW)

end of the lane until tankers began to collect it from the farm. Since 1983 Mary has managed the farm, keeping sheep and beef cattle. Because little St Mary's Church is now surrounded by her land she has kept its churchyard hedges trimmed.

TARDEBIGGE FARM, known in earlier years as Webb's Farm, is situated just inside the boundary of the parish, in Copyholt Lane. The farmhouse, a spectacular black and white timbered building, is believed to date back to 1562. It has much exposed timberwork, wattle and daub walls, flagstone floors, fine fireplaces and a period staircase, and it is believed to have been built for John Nash, a Birmingham merchant. The Nash family certainly owned the farm until well into the 1800s. They were connected with Tardebigge Church. Thomas Nash was married there in 1698, and Goodwin Nash was churchwarden in 1746, his name being on one of the church bells.

William Albutt, farmer and carpenter, was the tenant around 1900, soon to be followed by Samuel Leedham and then Bert Leedham until around 1950. It was a mixed farm and Bert Leedham had a local milk round. The

The front of Tardebigge Farm, Copyholt Lane. (Bromsgrove Advertiser/Messenger)

Leedham family were Quakers and meetings of The Society of Friends were held in the farmhouse.

Around 1950 Robert Dunstall and his wife Monica bought the farm and continued to run it for a time before renting out the land. Monica was, for many years, organist at both St Peter's RC Church in Bromsgrove and Hanbury Church. She and her husband lived in the farmhouse until 1983 when they moved into the adjacent barn conversion. The farmhouse was then purchased by David and Sue Huband, both of whom were very active supporters of Tardebigge and Bentley churches.

BRITANNIA HOUSE was a Bentley Estate farm of 41 acres when Cecil and Molly Rogers took over in 1927 after the previous tenant, William Burford, had moved to Leasowes Farm. Cecil Rogers was the son of the village blacksmith at Himbleton. He and his wife had two daughters, Molly and Olga. Olga, who was born in 1929, has happy memories of her younger days living in Bentley until her marriage in 1948. She attended Bentley School under the headship of Morton Rowles, walking there and back along footpaths skirting the Thrift and leading up to the school. Then, from age 11 to 15, she attended Tardebigge School under Mr Knight. Her parents concentrated on the keeping of livestock, a dairy herd, beef cattle, sheep and, for domestic use, poultry and two pigs. The meadows (no spraying then) were lush and colourful with an abundance of vetch and other wild flowers.

In the fields behind Britannia House, about 50 yards from High Elms Lane, there used to be an old dwelling "Rose Cottage". It was demolished in 1938 by estate workmen and, as the thatch was removed, Olga remembers seeing the bats all flying out. Her other memories include that of Mr and Mrs Baseley, the parents of Godfrey Baseley of "The Archers" radio soap, who lived before the war at "Grasmere" nearby, and of a bomb dropped during the war on a field across the road from Common Barn Farm, which created a huge hole in the ground but no casualties.

Following the death of Cecil Rogers in 1968, Mrs Rogers moved out in 1969, and Britannia House was then purchased from the Bentley Estates by Mr and Mrs Dyson, who have lived there since. Apart from 3 acres retained by them, the remaining land has been farmed by the Mitchells of Perry Mill Farm.

THE LEASOWES FARM, to which William Burford moved in 1927, was farmed by him until he died around 1950. Since then the farmhouse has been occupied by George Lewis, but the land has been farmed by Andrew Baldwin of Berrow Hill Farm. The original black and white timbered farmhouse is believed to date from around 1660. It has a spacious entrance hall, a lounge with wooden panelling, and impressive wide and shallow-stepped staircases, one down to the cellars, the other up to the bedrooms.

KEYS FARM, with its black and white timbered farmhouse, was probably established for a well-to-do family in the Forest of Feckenham in the seventeenth century. The farmhouse has a spiral staircase which encircles the three great tudor chimneys clustered together in the centre of the building. It has timbered ceilings, walls of wattle and daub, and heavy oak doors with locks. In one of the bedrooms four large cupboards of thick oak, with heavy engraved oak doors with locks, are believed to be safes for the valuables of visitors staying there. There are four attic rooms, two with windows and two without, the latter having hard plaster floors, used probably for the storage of cheese. One of the dark attics has a trap door in the floor, giving access to a deep cavity which has a base floor some five feet above the ground floor level. Within this cavity there have been found clay pipes, old dipped matches, an old hand-made boot and much else, suggesting that it may have been used as a catholic priest's hiding place.

Keys Farmhouse with its cluster of three chimneys and lovely black and white timbered aspect. (Eileen Beale)

From around 1910 until 1937 the tenant farmer was William Walker. He was followed by Len Goode and his wife until 1965. Len was a farmer's son and came from Lickey End, Bromsgrove. He had a milking herd and a milk round, by van, in the Barnt Green area. During WW2 he had the assistance of a land girl, Miss Irene Tucker. Following Len's retirement, Noel Beale, his wife Eileen and son Adrian farmed as tenants until 2001, when Noel and Eileen retired and the farmhouse was sold by the Bentley Estates to new occupants. The house has since been modernised and its old draughty windows replaced. There have been two barn conversions, one large and one of moderate size.

HIGH ELMS FARM, adjacent to Keys Farm, has been owned by the Bentley Estates since the uninsured farmhouse was destroyed by fire around 1900 and had to be rebuilt. From about 1912 to 1936 it was farmed by James Wormington whose daughter Nellie looked after the Sunday School held in Bentley School. She also played the organ at St Mary's Church, Lower Bentley, in the times of the Revd Scott Warren and the Revd Reginald Underhill.

After James Wormington the new tenant for some thirty years from 1936 was Billy Heath. Under his not very efficient regime the farm by 1971 was run down, Billy and his wife and dwarf son-in-law Cyril continued to occupy the farmhouse, but the outbuildings and farm land were now put to use by Noel Beale and his son Adrian of Keys Farm. In 1984 Adrian was able to move into the farmhouse and he and his family have lived there since. He has gradually taken over the farming of the whole 200 acres of both Keys and High Elms Farms. Both, apart from Keys farmhouse, are still rented from the Bentley Estate and used mainly for the grazing of dairy cattle, but also for the keeping of sheep and poultry.

TYRELLS FARM, of some 70 acres and still belonging to the Bentley Estates, was farmed by Philip Tandy from the early 1900s until his death in 1931. His widow Elisabeth (Lizzie) continued to run the farm with the help of their son Jack who eventually took over until he and his wife moved, in 1949, to "The Nook", the black and white timbered poultry farm cottage just along the road nearby. In 1955 the new tenant was Ken Thompson, one of the three sons of Tommy Thompson who was the licensee of The Halfway House beside the Canal at Upper Gambolds. He has managed Tyrells farm with the assistance of his son Michael. Like many other farmers, Ken latterly gave up dairy farming and now concentrates on pigs and beef cattle.

In his 70s Ken suffered with burst varicose veins, many of which had to be removed from his legs. Eventually he was taken to the Alexandra Hospital in Redditch with bleeding from his mouth, and was given only two hours more to live. Given the option of taking an untested drug, he agreed, and soon made a remarkable recovery, and he has actively survived well into his eighties.

One memorable occasion in the annals of Tyrells Farm was the arrival, by helicopter, of Sir David Attenborough, the famous zoologist, on one of the farm fields. It was in May 1993, and he had come to see and promote Eades Meadow which had previously been purchased and donated to the Worcester Nature Conservation Trust by Christopher Cadbury. In May 1994 the Meadow and surrounding fields of Fosters Green Farm were ceremonially designated a "National Nature Reserve" by Lord Cranbrook, Chairman of English Nature, in the presence of Christopher Cadbury and many local people. The ancient unploughed pastureland, with its profusion of wild flowers and butterflies is now a well-visited attraction.

Foster's Green Farmhouse. (AW)

FOSTER'S GREEN FARM, with its picturesque black and white timbered farmhouse was, it is believed, once known as Pauncefoot Farm. Before WW1 the occupier was Mrs Butler, and between the wars the farmers were Sydney and Henry Wheelton. In the area around the farm there is a profusion of damson and other fruit trees, and it is said that many of the damsons were used, at one time, in the dyeing industry.

CHAPTER 11

Memories

KEN CLARKE

I was born in Birmingham in 1920. We lived in Sparkhill. During the first World War my father, William James Clarke, was a prisoner-of-war and he was gassed. After the war he went to work in a tyre factory, and he was advised, because of his ill health, to go and live in the country, and he came to work for T & M Dixon. My grandfather, George Knight, who was a foreman for Dixons, found him a job and he came to work on the fruit farm, and we lived in a little cottage at the Old Wharf which is now the hire-boat office. That would be about 1920/21, and we lived there about four years. From there we moved to a cottage in Dusthouse Lane, and it was from there that I used to walk in all weathers to Tardebigge School.

My father worked on the fruit farm, grafting and pruning. He was a good gardener. My mother's maiden name was Gertrude Elizabeth Knight, and in her early years she lived at Horns Hall (now Robin Hill Farm). She and my auntie Ethel were born there. My father must have met her some time whilst he was in the forces.

I was the eldest of their seven children, all boys, myself, Maurice, Dennis, Peter, Stanley, John and Bob. The cottage in Dusthouse Lane had two bedrooms and a box room. We hadn't much space and we had to sleep together, head to toe.

Ken Clarke. (AW)

Whilst I was at Tardebigge School the Head Teacher was Arthur Charles Dilks. He was a brilliant teacher and an engineer as well. He had one of the first cars in the area; I remember its number, UY46, and it was a Wolseley. I can see him now. There was a division across the room, and he used to stand in between and read stories to us. I don't think we appreciated him as we should have done. His wife was not a proper teacher but she taught the infants. Then we had Miss Worgen who used to collect children on her way to school from Aston Fields, some from Finstall, others from Tutnall. She used to wear a long skirt and high boots. We also had Mrs Badger who lived at the Paper Mills, Miss Garnham who lived at Plymouth House and, of course, Mrs Eades.

About 1931/2 Mr Dilks retired and we had a new Head Teacher, Mr Arthur Knight. He came from Martley, and he had one son, a nice lad, who was in the Air Force. He changed things round, including the way we used to write, and we got a bit confused. They say he was a good teacher, but I didn't get on with him for some reason, I don't know why. He kept good discipline, as did Mr Dilks, and you knew where you stood with him.

The Vicar then was the Revd. Percival Scott Warren. I was a server until I went into the forces, I sang in the choir, and I often pumped the organ. The organist was Mr Liddell. He lived up the Stourbridge Road, Bromsgrove, and he used to walk all the way to church for morning and evening services, always in sandals. With me in the choir were, from the New Wharf, Harold and Len Colledge and John Hawkins. In the morning the Plymouth family came to church and also Mrs Ellis, who sat in the Bentley box pew near the pulpit, sometimes with Leslie Gray-Cheape.

In April 1939 I joined the Territorials, in the 267 Field Battery which met in the drill hall in Easemore Road in Redditch. At the time I was serving my apprenticeship at the Austin Motor Company, and it was given out on the radio on Friday night, 1 September, that all Territorials should report to their barracks, and that was my last day at work. Because there was no place for us to sleep in Redditch, we went to Bentley Manor and were billeted in the stables, the cow shed and also part of the house. Mrs Ellis was still living there. We had the out-buildings and used the courtyard. We spent the bad winter of 1939/40 there. The guns we had originally were 4.5 Howitzers, but we didn't have enough guns because in the regiment we had three companies, A, B and C. So we were given some French 75s from somewhere. After about a year there we moved over to Hewell Grange, being the first troops there. We used rooms in the Grange, but not the great hall, and we exercised in the grounds. Whilst there we swam in the lake.

They were going to send us overseas, so we went down to Weymouth and I was billeted at the end of the pier. We were due to go to France, but we never went. Mind you, it was a good job we didn't go, we weren't really ready for it. It was the time of the retreat from Dunkirk and we went by train all the way up to Bella Houston Park in Glasgow, and from there to Ireland, to Londonderry. After a while I was posted to Warminster, and that was the last time I saw Peter Dixon, on the station at Warminster. From there I went by sea to India, round the Cape, with a six weeks stop in Durban where we were made very welcome. Then via Bombay, Poona and Calcutta to Chittagong and service in Burma.

Following demobilisation, I went back to Austins. I stuck it for 5 or 6 weeks, but it was different and there was not the comradeship as before. So I left and worked for myself doing electrical work, wiring houses in Redditch. Then I started at Garringtons and got up to manager/engineer. Then I went to South Africa for them, to give advice on how to do a certain job. When I returned, they asked me to go back and do the job myself, and my wife agreed. Then they asked me to stay there and we spent ten years in South Africa. That was my working life.

Looking back I remember, whilst still at school, getting up early, as soon as it was light, to go fruit picking for Dixons. It was to get extra money to help feed the family. Strawberries went into 4 lb baskets, raspberries into 2 lb punnets. You received tokens which you exchanged for money at the offices at Broad Green, 2d to 4d for a basket and 2d a punnet. Often we came home with our shoes soaking wet, and we had to go to school in them after breakfast because they were the only ones we had. We earned about 2 shillings a morning. It all went into the housekeeping. In the school summer holidays we also went fruit picking when the plum crop was ready.

Also during the soft-fruit picking season people came from the Black Country to work on the farms. Dixons used to fetch them and the vehicle they used was a big Sentinel steam lorry. It used to come steaming up the road with a trailer on, carrying luggage, trunks and other belongings, and families, mostly women and children, for most of the men would be working back home. They used to stay in the barns, stables and a loft at Dusthouse Farm, and also later in a massive shed at Horns Hall. At Dusthouse Farm a Mr Langston from Webheath stores had part of a barn for a lock-up shop, with a flap he could drop down to make a counter. He would come every day with a horse and cart, bringing provisions including bread, butter and big bread puddings. The Black Country folk would stay for the season, about six weeks. It was a country holiday for them.

In the cottage next to ours in Dusthouse Lane lived Dixons' gamekeeper, Bill Marshall, his wife and family. At the back of his cottage he had an aviary and he used to breed pheasants. When, on a Saturday, Dixons organised a shoot for themselves and their farming friends, Mr Marshall would let pheasants loose into the spinney in London Lane and into Dusthouse Quarry which at the time was a large area with a pretty dense tree cover. I was often engaged as a stop or beater. Our job was to stop the pheasants going onto other people's land and, by beating, to cause the birds to rise. We would stay for 6 to 8 hours in one place, and we were paid half-a crown (2s/6d). In those days that was quite a lot of money. During the day a Mr Attwood used to bring round cocoa in a big churn, and some bread and cheese, and the bread and cheese was about three inches thick.

At the Village Hall, for people like us who had no bathroom, you could go and get, from Mr Scudder who was the caretaker, soap and a towel for 2d and have a hot bath. This was on Friday or Saturday. There was only one bath in the bathroom which was next to the library or reading room. Otherwise the only place we had a bath was in the canal. We learnt to swim in the canal, and in fine weather we used to swim in it on our way home from school, just three or four of us lads, by the bridge below the top lock, out of sight. Our parents didn't know of course. We even jumped across the width of the top lock when it was full of water. I only did it once, but my brother Dennis was more of a dare-devil and he did it many times.

KATE EADES

Kate was one of the eight children of John Thomas Wilson who came to Tardebigge in the 1880s as electrician to Hewell Grange. Before the advent of mains electricity, the Grange had its own electricity generator and lighting system and John Wilson was in charge of it. He and his family came to live at Bentley, which is where Kate grew up. After her marriage in 1928, she and her husband Austin Eades rented Banks Green Farm, Copyholt Lane, from the Hewell Estates. It was a small holding of some 10 to 15 acres, and they bought it when the Estates were sold in 1946.

In 1992 Kate, in two interviews when she was in hospital, recorded her memories:-

I was born in Bentley in 1898. In the 1880s my father, John Thomas Wilson, left the navy and came to live at Hewell, and then at Bentley. He had a family of eight, four sons and four daughters and I was in the middle. In those days we walked to Tardebigge School which was nearly two miles. We also went to Bentley Church, where the old Vicar, Canon Dickins, used to arrive by pony and trap, sitting in a basket chair. The service was in the afternoon. The stained glass windows had not yet been done. Alfred Pike did those windows, assisted by Wally Hughes. Alfred was single, an interesting man, fond of the ladies. He had a lady friend Jeanette; she was rather sexy and quite a character. The music master, Morton Rowles, at Tardebigge School tried to get Jeanette and my sister Alice to sing duets; they both had good voices, but he gave it up in despair. He said "It's no use, you really dislike one another and you'll never be able to sing in harmony."

The headmaster of the school was Mr Dilks. He had a model railway. We used to think it was a great privilege if we could look over the wall and see his model railway. He used almost the whole of his garden for his railway. It really was quite wonderful. He made the engines, the whole lot. He

Kate Eades with her carer friend, Eileen Lewis.
(Eileen Lewis)

loved his cricket and his engines and he loved English. I must thank him for my love of the English language, because he started to teach us and then he would ramble on telling some story, and that was the end of the lesson. But he had given me an absolute love of the English language.

In those days they chose intelligent 13-year olds and they let them stay on as pupil teachers. My elder sister was to have been one, but she wasn't allowed to continue because of the family; she had to look after the younger ones, and that was always a bit of a grievance; and it wasn't until she married that she was able to become a teacher. Also teaching at Tardebigge we had Harriet Badger and Gertrude Allbut.

Our teacher Morton Rowles said he would rather be driving the plough than teaching us blockheads. Eventually he became the headmaster of Bentley School, but that was a very easy-going school. Mrs Cheape was the patron, and she had a pack of beagles, and if they went beagling the children left their lessons and went; hunting came first. Miss Phipps who taught there would get off the 9 o'clock bus which arrived 20 past at Hewell, have a cup of coffee at Miss Van Bylevelts at the dairy, cycle to Bentley, then they started school. So the school must have been very late starting. But one day an inspector, I believe it was a scripture inspector, arrived, and he was greeted by the headmaster from an upstairs window of the school house, and I think that rather put an end to Bentley School. When it closed down Miss Phipps had my job at Tardebigge as I retired at the age of sixty in 1958.

As a pupil I left Tardebigge School at the age of thirteen, having achieved that marvellous thing, a scholarship to the County High School. I took my School Certificate and with a correspondence course I became a qualified teacher in 1922. I taught for some years at Bridge Street School in Redditch, then I taught for one year at Great Witley. In the meanwhile I was married and when I told my husband that I had a good mind to apply for a job back at Tardebigge, he said "don't be silly you don't stand an earthly". But that was a challenge, and I got the job. Mr Dilks soon retired and Mr Knight was headmaster. I taught infants, and was still known to many as Miss Wilson.

In 1927 my brother was killed in a motor accident. We were to have been married that year, but we put it off to the next year. I carried on teaching, the second one in Redditch to do so. At that time people were quite shocked that you should go on working after getting married; your husband was expected to keep you.

I remember Foxlydiate House. Lady Isabel Margesson was keen on Shakespeare and meetings were held at the big house often attended by Shakespearean expert Frank Benson. They also did country dancing barefoot on the lawn under a great Cedar tree. My father was very cross when my elder sister and I went there. Lady Margesson was a suffragette, and that to many, including my father, was a terrible crime.

Eventually the timber badminton court building at Foxlydiate House was moved to the rear of the Tardebigge Village Hall and it became the weaving shed where Mrs Warner and the women did such marvellous weaving.

When my father came to the Grange, it had just been built and electricity was in its infancy. My father helped to wire the place. Jack, my eldest brother, had helped with the wiring, and when, many years later, there was a problem with the wiring, he was able to give advice. For many years they created their own electricity. They had an engine house situated just by the dairy with two steam engines and dynamos. It had a blue and white tiled floor, kept spotlessly clean. It was exciting with the dynamos creating, usually only one at a time. I can see the governors going round. Something to remember!

MARY MORRIS

I was born in 1918 in Camp Hill, Birmingham, and grew up there. I went to school in Kings Norton and on leaving school I went to Cadburys and worked in the planning office. When the war started women in unessential work could carry on until the age of 25, when they were expected to do something for the war effort. In 1942 six of us from Cadburys went to Worcester to join the Women's Land Army. They sorted us out and I was sent to work at Tack farm, Tardebigge. Mrs Goulbourne there had just lost her husband Alfred, so she was allowed to have three land girls. The other two with me were Peggy and Angela, and we lived at the farm.

On my first day in the Land Army at Tack Farm they said "You can take the horse to the blacksmiths, he wants shoeing. His name is Charlie, he's a good horse. You don't need to worry, Charlie knows the way." I'd never been on a horse in my life. I didn't know what to do. He was a great big cart horse and I managed to ride him, and he took me all the way down Hewell Lane to Broad Green to the blacksmith, Mr Tustin. He was only a little chap and when I saw him I thought "How am I going to get back onto the horse?" However he brought some steps and I climbed up onto the horse's back and rode him all the way back.

Tack Farm was quite extensive, then not divided by the later dual-carriageway. It was part dairy, part arable. We were up at 6.30 am to start the milking by hand. There were about 40 milking cows. We then came in for breakfast. Then we had to work in the fields, weeding and digging, haymaking and harvesting vegetables, potatoes, wheat and oats. We wore Land Army uniform, breeches and blouse. It was a good life. I had wanted to join the Wrens, but in the Land Army I was able to get home to Acocks Green every other weekend, and when the weather was good I used to cycle home for an hour and cycle back.

When Mary Goulbourne finished and Dr Houfton took over the farm I went to work for Mr Ted Hughes at Foxlydiate Farm. Whilst there I lodged at one of the cottages along the road from the farm. After a few months I left and went to work at Boxnot Farm for Mr Arthur Partridge until I got married in 1945. My family name was Lyddan. My husband was Edwin Morris. He came from Shropshire, and before the war he was gamekeeper for the Earl of Plymouth, and he lived at no.3 Park Cottages. Mrs Goulbourne had got him to come and work for her at the farm. That is how I got to know him.

After the war, when Hewell Grange became a Borstal, Edwin obtained a post on the staff there as a gardening instructor, and we went to live in one of the houses up Hewell Lane belonging to the prison service. When

Mary Morris. (AW)

he died suddenly in 1966, only 57 years old, I had to find somewhere else to live. The governor of Brockhill women's prison rang me and said that if I could get somewhere to live round here I could have a job there. I did a lot of looking round and then my friend Gwen Such, who lived with her family at no.4 Park Cottages, heard that no.2 was going vacant. It belonged to Mr Beckett, so I kept on going to see him and in the end he let me have it. So I got the job at the prison then in 1967.

My job as a discipline officer was to keep the women in order. I went in at 8 am. They let me work in the hospital part because my son Peter, who was just sixteen at the time, was shattered at his father's death and he wouldn't stop in the house by himself. Other staff had to work nights, but working in the hospital I could leave at 5 pm and get home. It was an interesting job. There were quite a few prostitutes in the prison and one or two murderers on remand. You could talk to the women and you learnt a lot about the seamy side of life.

After I retired in 1980, I met the Vicar, Mr Copley, one day and he said "You'll have plenty of time on your hands now, you can deliver the parish magazines round here." I did that for about 20 years until I got that I couldn't walk around. I went to church at Tardebigge and I belonged to the Mothers Union and the W.I. I was at the first meeting of the Evergreens, started by the Revd. Peter Frowley for the older people, and I still belong. My two boys, David and Peter, went to Tardebigge School and then on to Ridgeway.

AUDREY STUBBINGS

I was born in Ayrshire, Scotland, in 1921, but when I was five years old my parents, Sidney and Elsie Bowen, returned to their childhood home of Upper Bentley. There Elsie's father, Tom Morris, worked as the head carpenter for the Bentley Estate and lived in the large house on the right hand side at the end of the timberyard. Mr Arthur Farmer, the head gardener, lived next door in the house on the left hand side (he later married the district nurse). The Harding family, who looked after the hounds, lived at the Kennels; one of their daughters later became ladies maid for Lady Louise Mountbatten. The estate manager, Mr Coombes, followed by his son Harold, lived in the lovely black and white house called Nursery Cottage at the top of what we knew as Hell Lane (now Hill Lane).

My mother, Elsie, was one of six children – three sons and three daughters. Her elder brother, Jim Morris, was the blacksmith at Hewell in the 1920s and 1930s. Her younger brother, Ernest Morris, who was huntsman for the "Squire", was taken prisoner of war by the Turks in WW1 and died out there. My father's brother Harold Morgan Bowen was wounded in WW1 and died in hospital in the UK. Both their names are on the War Memorial in Bentley Village Hall.

I spent a very happy childhood in Upper Bentley. I lived first at Gothic Cottage (now Seven Acres in Angel Street) and then at my father's childhood home, Rose cottage (now Lychgates), in Angel Street. My mother had a shop at Rose cottage. Woodbine cigarettes were 5 for 2d, and Player's were 20 for 11 1/2 d. I remember that money was short and the men often had to pay for their cigarettes at the end of the week, when they were paid. My mother also sold expensive chocolates which I used to sneak when no one was looking!

Next door to us lived Mary Bray who married Dick Goulbourne. He became a churchwarden at Tardebigge Church and Mary became the organist there. Her father and my mother were related. Many of the occupants of the houses around the common were my father's cousins – called Tongues. My father's sister, Hettie, also returned to the common when she later married Henry Pugh.

Audrey Stubbings. (AW)

I attended Bentley School where Mr Morton Rowles was the Head Master. If children talked in class or misbehaved they were put in the store cupboard or they had to "sarlam", that is kneel down for a time with their forehead on the ground. I talked – and suffered!

I remember the long distances some children had to walk to school, from Lower Bentley, Callow Hill, Cruise Hill and Webheath. The assistant teachers whilst I was there were Miss Phipps, who boarded with Mrs William Hewlett in Angel Street, and Miss Bertha Thompson, who boarded with Mr Price at Upper Bentley Farm.

Bentley Manor was a lovely huge place at the end of two drives; one was the main drive to the front entrance and the other was the drive to the rear. In my time Mrs Maude Ellis and her three children – Lindsey, Sheila and Patsy – lived there. Mrs Ellis was kind to the local schoolchildren; and to those of poorer families she distributed clothes bought from the Salvation Army in Redditch. At Christmas all the children were invited to the Manor for a party and each was given a large red handkerchief, with white spots on, full of goodies. In the woodland, close to the Manor, there were the little graves of the hounds, with their names on.

It was from Rose cottage that I was married to Kingsley Stubbings at Tardebigge Church in 1940. The Revd Scott Warren took the service and Mrs Ellis was a guest. Her wedding gift to us was a wooden tea trolley, and my daughter still uses it today. Following our marriage Kingsley and I shared Gothic Cottage with my parents (my mother ran it as a smallholding), until we moved to our own home in the Meadway, Headless Cross.

An incident I have never forgotten was the death of Mr Impey. He was the farmer at the Home Farm of the Manor, Norgrove Court. He had an untimely death caused by dropping a lighted match when blasting holes in the ground with explosives for the planting of fruit trees at Norgrove.

ROY HIMS

Roy was one of the fifteen children (two of whom died in infancy) of Claude and Norah Hims who lived in the last property along Crumpfields Lane, Webheath. He went to Bentley School from 1936 to 1942 then to Tardebigge School until 1945, when he left at the age of fourteen to join his

Roy Hims. (AW)

father in his garage business at the far end of Crumpfields Lane. Latterly he and his wife Doreen have been regular church members at Tardebigge. His written memories of life as a youngster living in Webheath include the names of, and information about, many of his fellow school friends and acquaintances, and the following:-

My dad was a mechanical engineer. In the war (WW2) he made an armoured vehicle with a bren gun turret on top for the local home guard. A bullet failed to penetrate the armour at 50 feet. There were three ways to start it and you could change a wheel without getting out of the tank. The drawback was that because of the weight it was a bit slow, but we were all proud of that tank. One of my brothers, Graham, married the daughter, Beryl, of farmer Hanson over the road. My uncle Tom owned Crumpfields Lane Farm next to us, and my cousin Muriel married Lionel Tongue of Pumphouse Farm.

The Vicar of Webheath was Rev Harrison (Pop). He later moved to Inkberrow. My brother John and I were in the church choir for about 6 years.

To get to Bentley School we had to walk, usually by road via Elcocks Brook, but sometimes we would go through Norgrove Court up to Manor Road, and we would sometimes eat a raw swede or turnip from the fields if we were hungry; food wasn't very plentiful in those days.

During my time at Bentley School Mrs Ellis was at Bentley Manor. She was a lovely lady. The whole school would march down to the Manor at Christmas to have a party and receive a parcel containing an apple, orange, nuts and sweets in a large red handkerchief with white spots on it. There on the King's Coronation in 1937 we received a photograph of the King and a Coronation mug plus a silver-plated tea spoon with the crowned heads of the King and Queen at the top of the handle. There were also times when we went down to the Manor for sports day and I can remember we had ice cream.

The headmaster of Bentley School was Mr Morton Rowles, and he was a real stickler for obedience. Girls or boys, it made no difference, if you misbehaved, the cane, six of the best on your palms. If you could get to the sink and rub soap on first, it seemed to help a little. We also had as class teachers Miss Phipps and Miss Haram.

One of the lessons that I liked was nature study, which involved, once a week in all weathers, walking from school up Manor Road, left along Blacklake Lane, and down Bentley Lane as far as the Thrift (wood), returning with what seemed like half the vegetation; and, of course, we would then set about sticking them in books and adding their names.

We didn't have central heating in school in those days. All we had was a coal-fired stove and, if we arrived really wet we had to take our socks and shoes off and put them round the stove; and if it was very cold we would keep our coats on. The toilets were non-flush and were round the back of the school, just like Siberia. Toilet paper was cut-up newspaper, threaded on string.

In those days we had to walk everywhere, which included the 3 miles between Crumpfields Lane and school, each way, come rain, snow or sunshine, and sometimes the weather was severe. I can even now see the snow; it used to drift over 10 feet high along Manor Road, and everyone, or so it seemed, would be skating on the lake at Norgrove Court, especially on a Sunday afternoon.

In 1939/40, because of war-time shortages, it was difficult to get wellington boots. However I remember there was a special one-off issue of wellingtons to all those who had to walk a long way to school in all weathers. Children were encouraged to go round and collect all sorts of things for the war effort. The sorts of things we got were metal items, newspapers and cardboard. Gloves and scarves were knitted by the girls. We picked hips and haws for medicine, and also acorns for the pig farmers. So you could say that is why our generation just cannot throw things away, they may still be useful.

Across the field (pleck) opposite the school gates, was the local tuck shop (Bowens) in Angel Street, where we could spend our pocket money.

Ours was one old penny. The things we could get for this were one liquorice shoestring or one gobstopper or, if we saved for one week we could afford a liquorice pipe or maybe sherbet; and if we saved for six weeks we could get a tin of nippets – they were so hot they would burn a hole in your tongue, but they lasted you a long time.

In 1942, at the age of eleven, I moved from Bentley School to Tardebigge School, the walk there was even longer than to Bentley. The headmaster, Mr Knight, had started school dinners two years earlier. They were prepared and cooked in the former infants school, now the Church Hall but then referred to as "The Cookhouse". The food was taken from there to the dining room which was a partitioned section of the schoolroom nearest to the church. The cook was Miss Van Bylevelt, and she was assisted each day by two boys and two girls, older pupils chosen in turn, and they had the day off from normal lessons. School dinner duties included the preparation of the vegetables, the boys worked by hand a rotating potato-peeling machine and the girls helped with the pastry and pudding making; all four took part in laying the tables in the dining room, taking the food over, serving it, then doing the clearing and washing up. Undertaking these duties was, besides being a service, also an education in domestic science, and what I learnt from them was a help when it came to the cooking of meals in later life.

GEORGE DENNING BATE

George Bate was born in 1901, one of the sons of George Herbert Bate who was foreman carpenter for the Canal Company. The family lived in one of the cottages beside the canal below Whitford bridge at Stoke Pound. On leaving Stoke Prior C of E School at the age of 13, George spent just over a year working at Stoke Prior Salt Works as a rivet warmer to a gang of salt pan smiths. Meanwhile, war was declared in August 1914 and by the end of the year George's father was working on his own in the carpenters' shop at Tardebigge New Wharf, since his mate, C W Wright, had joined the army. So he got George to leave the Salt Works and come and join him. George spent the rest of his working life as a carpenter for the Canal Company, eventually succeeding his father as foreman carpenter. Following his marriage he lived in the old brickworks cottage below the

George Bate B.E.M.

canal near Tardebigge Reservoir, just within Tardebigge parish. He continued to work part-time for the canal company after his retirement, and eventually he and his wife went to live for a few years in the cottage behind the old warehouse on the New Wharf. He died in 1977, and was buried in Tardebigge Churchyard.

During 1969 and 1970, George wrote a series of thirteen articles for the Tardebigge Parish Magazine, about the canal and his experiences. The following extracts relate to events in the Parish:-

During the war years, 1916 to 1918, we used to have wounded soldiers coming into the shop to talk to my father, and also to have rides on the tugs that towed the commercial boats through Tardebigge and Shortwood Tunnels. The canal was very busy with trade, boats passing night and day carrying coal and foodstuffs. The wounded soldiers came from the village hall (now the Tardebigge) which had been turned into a hospital.

When the war was over and the village hall returned to normal use, I became a member. I used to attend whist drives and dances, play billiards, and do some reading there. But above all I used to go on Friday nights to have a bath. Friday night was bath night and a lot of us chaps used to take advantage of this at the time as lots of houses had no bathrooms then.

Referring back to my early days prior to working at Tardebigge, I went for a walk with my father along the canal from Whitford Bridge (where we lived in the middle house of three alongside the canal) to Tardebigge. At the time the workshops were being built 1909/1910. It was a Sunday afternoon, and after we had passed the top lock and were looking over to the wharf we saw a clergyman along with a congregation of boatmen and a flock of women having an open air service. My father told me it was Canon Dickins. He used to come down from Tardebigge Church and conduct a service on some Sunday afternoons when sufficient numbers of boats had come up the lock on Saturday night and Sunday morning. There were some good voices among the boatmen and the women, as a lot of them belonged to the Salvation Army of Gloucester and district, and they took their religion seriously.

The first impression I had of Tardebigge Church was the ivy-covered walls outside and a kind of green distempered walls inside. This was in 1911. I was a juvenile member of Stoke Prior Church Choir at the time, and the choir made a visit to Tardebigge Church one Sunday evening in the summer of that year. We were transported from Stoke Prior by a four-in-hand charabanc vehicle driven by Mr Frank Whitmore, a son of Mr Alfred Whitmore of Plymouth House, Tardebigge. It was something to do with the coronation of HM King George V.

The New Wharf was well represented in the church choir when I started work at the Wharf, there being Mr Frank Rowles, Mr W Hawkins, Mr W Greaves and Mr A Whitmore of Plymouth House. Vicar Dickins was very popular with the Gloucester boat people in my grandfather's day and my father's day. He used to help them and their families when they could not work owing to the canal being frozen over so strong that boats could not move through the locks. In fact they used to turn to the parishes all along the canal lengths and be provided with food, mainly soup and bread.

In 1919 I was interested in joining Tardebigge church choir. I did go for a trial and was suitable, but at the time the choir was up to strength. I do not know why I never joined after all, but I did get a position as sidesman in 1920 or 1921. Around this time my sister Mildred was a maid at the Vicarage, assisting the cook, Mrs Ackroyd. They both lived in during Mr Ellerton's ministry. I used to do various repair jobs at the vicarage about this time, such as replacing sash cords in windows, easing doors and repairing floors for the vicar.

During the last war I was a member of the Local Defence Volunteers (LDV), later the Home Guard. Our post was Tardebigge School. Later we moved to Finstall Village Hall. I was in charge of a squad of men, usually on a Saturday night. We used to have to be on duty from 5 pm to 8 am in the winter months, and from 6 pm to 6 am in the summer months. We used to draw our rifles from the Vicarage and return them after duty. The vicar at that time was the Revd Scott Warren. We had some anxiety at times when the bombing of Birmingham was in progress and shrapnel fell from our shells when our artillery was in action against enemy aircraft.

IVY BROOMFIELD

Ivy was born in 1914, the younger of the two children of Alfred and Florence Westover, who lived at 6 Hewell Lane, Tardebigge. As mentioned in chapter 5, Alf, as a teenager, came from London in 1899 to work as a wood carver for Lord Windsor, and he stayed, married, and practised and taught carpentry and wood carving in an upper room in the village hall between the wars, having served in the army in WW1.

Ivy, like her brother who was seven years older than herself, attended Tardebigge School, and she was christened, confirmed and married (to William Broomfield) in Tardebigge Church. In her later years she compiled a hand-written autobiography from which the following memories of her school life have been taken:-

When I first started school my brother was my bodyguard, but when he left to go to Redditch Secondary School, as it was called in 1919, my mother paid a few pence a week to a neighbour's son, "Tiny" Skinner, to look after me. He was big enough, as his nick-name tells, to curb the other boys' teasing.

My first teacher was an unqualified but wonderful person, Miss Worgen. She had a small alert face, with iron-grey hair drawn severely back into a small bun in the nape of her neck. Her skirt, as was the mode of the day, was ankle length of heavy dark material and her blouse was tightly buttoned to the neck. The rims of her spectacles were steel, but her heart was of pure gold. Every morning in winter our medicine, camp coffee or other bottles containing milk, cocoa, cold tea, or whatever beverage our parents saw fit to send, were carefully placed by Miss Worgen around the fire. The corks were loosened to avoid breakages, but left in place to keep out the dust. By 10.30 am they were luke-warm instead of freezing cold!

My walk to school would probably seem a long way to children today, but in those days it was nothing, just a healthy walk. Some children walked two and a half miles or more from Bentley, Foxlydiate and Cobley Hill. Indeed my own mother walked from Foxlydiate to Tardebigge School at the tender age of three years old. She has told us many times how her father, who was a postman, carried her on his shoulders for the first half mile as far as Tack Farm which was on his round. She had to walk the rest of the way which was over two miles and, of course, all the way home again after school. Her father's round took him to the Papermills.

The head-mistress of the Infants School was a very different character from her kindly assistant, but she was also a very caring lady. Mary Garnham was a fully qualified teacher and she was the most gracious lady that I have ever met. She too wore spectacles but they were not steel rimmed, and her blouses were of pure silk, topping skirts of the finest quality material. She was cultured in every way and the welfare of her pupils was always uppermost in her mind. A most regular church-goer, she was also in charge of the Sunday school. At the end of every school day she made quite sure that each of her pupils was properly dressed and in the care of older children from the "big" school as we called the other building. I vividly remember her rapping my brother's knuckles when he tried to hurry off with me before my fingers were correctly in my gloves. When I left in 1925 to go to secondary school she gave me a copy of "Flowers of the Field" by the Revd C A Johns which I treasure to this day. Besides her duties as Headmistress of Day school and of Sunday school, Miss Garnham sometimes played the church organ for services if the regular organist, Charles Liddell, was unable to attend. Otherwise she sat in the body of the church on the right hand side, three rows from the back, where she could keep an eye on the schoolboys in case they fidgeted during the sermon. Presumably she thought the girls who sat in the back pews on the left were less mischievous.

Attendance at Sunday School was rewarded with a weekly stamp, and a full book at the end of the year merited a prize. I remember weeping copiously on the disastrous Sunday morning when my father put the clock back instead of forward for summer-time and I arrived for Sunday school when everyone was coming out of church. However, Miss Garnham, being a very just person, of great compassion, dried my tears and gave me the missing stamp. It really mattered such a lot.

My memories of primary school days are few, but I remember using a slate and I remember my dresses being protected by a white embroidered starched pinafore with frilled shoulders beautifully laundered. I remember too curtsying to Miss Garnham, and the boys saluting, as we filed past her to the cloakroom when lessons were over in the afternoon. Good manners were expected of us.

Whilst I was at Tardebigge School I was able to enjoy the annual Christmas party which was given to the entire school by the very kind Earl of Plymouth. The day before this red-letter day wicker baskets were lifted down from the very top of the school equipment cupboards, and excitement mounted as we were all kitted out with a pair of red carpet slippers. These we proudly carried, tucked under our arms, on our journey the next day, in a long file, down Church Lane, across the main road to the main gates of the park and along the driveway to Hewell Grange. Once inside the building we realised the importance of the slippers as a protection for the polished wooden floors. Having removed our winter coats and hats and put on the slippers, we were ushered into the servants' hall where the tables, glistening with sparkling white linen tablecloths, were laid out for our tea. To many of the children who seldom had cake except perhaps on Sundays, the sight of dainty jam sandwiches piled high on doyleyed plates and the profusion of cakes decorated with delicious pink and white sugar icing was a source of wonderment. The tea was preceded and followed by grace, and after we had enjoyed the sandwiches, cakes and cups of steaming hot milky tea, we were taken along the corridors to the imposing ballroom, decorated with a huge Christmas tree, where we could slide and play games to our hearts content. A while later the Earl and Countess arrived on the balcony which surrounded the ball-room. I remember the dignity of the Countess as she raised her lorgnettes, as if to fully appreciate the jollity in the room below. Then laughingly they both threw gaily coloured crackers for us to catch. Afterwards they came down to stand by a table which was loaded with presents for them to distribute. There was one for each child, carefully allotted and named to ensure that they were suitable and in turn, as our name was called, we went to the table to receive our gift and express our thanks with a curtsy or salute according to whether we were girl or boy. For some it was the only Christmas gift they would receive, a treasure beyond compare. Then it was time to go home, but there was one more surprise after we were once more warmly wrapped in our winter coats and hats. As we left, two footmen stood, one each side of the portal, and handed to each of us a white paper bag containing an apple, an orange, a quarter of best quality candies and a large sugary-topped bun.

RAY KING

Ray was born in 1932 at one of the two semi-detached cottages (the one further from the road bridge) on the west side of the Tardebigge Old Wharf. The cottages are now part of the premises of the Anglo-Welsh boat hire business. Ray's grandparents Thomas and Martha King moved from Rushock to Tardebigge to live in one of the three Stoney Lane Cottages near the canal around 1895/6, when Thomas was appointed Farm Foreman for T & M Dixon. Ray's father, Edgar King, born 1894, was one of their 10 children. He attended Tardebigge School under headmaster Mr Dilks, and, on leaving school he went to work as a farm labourer for the Dixons. During WW1 he served in the army and was wounded and gassed. Back home, because of breathing problems, he found it difficult to sleep indoors in the Stoney Lane cottage, so Dixons put up a shed along the drive for him to sleep in.

Following the war, in 1920, Edgar married Gladys Clarke who, with her parents, lived at the Turnpike Cottage at Tutnall, her father being a waggoner for Dixons. After their marriage, Edgar and Gladys went to live at the back of the Old Wharf in what, it seems, was a simple one-storey stable building converted into a three-roomed dwelling. Then, in the mid 1920s they moved across the wharf to the cottage where Ray was born. In 1937 the family moved to "The Heathers", Broad Green, one of the two bungalows built by Dixons after WW1, where Ray and his wife Shirley now live. Following his father Thomas's death in 1941 Edgar took over as foreman in charge of the fruit packing and storage side of T & M Dixon's business. Ray's memories include the following:-

When I was a child at the Old Wharf in the 1930s the canal was busy with working boats, many horse drawn, which were towed by a tug through Tardebigge and Shortwood Tunnels. Percy Hawkins and John Colledge worked the tug, and sometimes they would pick me up at the Old Wharf and take me through Shortwood Tunnel and back. I can remember when the canal was frozen over and the ice breaker was used, pulled by horses and with men holding the rail and rocking the boat.

Next door to us, Mr and Mrs Davies ran the shop and post office. They had a daughter Sheila and a son Edwin. When they left, Mr and Mrs Johnson took over the shop and post office. I was at school with their son Malcolm. In my first years at Tardebigge School I was taken there by Mrs Sumner with her children, Reg, Ron and Molly. They lived in the weighbridge house on the wharf and then in Benton's Cottage on Hewell Lane at Broad Green, round the corner from us. On one occasion, on the way to school along Hewell Lane, we met a steam roller owned by Bomford and Evershed steaming along the road by The Elbows. I remember being so frightened that Mrs Sumner had to get it to stop whilst we passed by. At school I was taught by Mrs Eades in the infants class, then by Mrs Badger, and then by Mr Knight.

In 1946 I left school on reaching the age of 14 in the summer holidays and started work straight away with the gardeners of Finstall Park School. I was there for 9 months until March 1947 when I went to work for Dixons. At Finstall Park the head gardener was Mr Avery. His son Frank worked with him and also Ernie Woodward. On some days we took produce from the gardens, vegetables, fruit and flowers, by horse and trap to shops in Bromsgrove, Wakemans opposite Lloyd's Bank, and Mrs Philips in the Strand.

I worked altogether 51 years and 5 months for Dixons and Tardebigge Orchards. At first I worked on the soft fruit side, emptying the 4 lb chip baskets of gathered fruit into wooden tubs for transport, much of it to Evesham for Beech's Jams. I then worked with my father in the tree nursery behind the Broad Green offices where the root stock was grown

Ray King. (AW)

231

and varieties of apples and pears were grafted or budded on. I was involved in the planting of fruit trees on Dusthouse Farm land, 96 to the acre. Apple trees were mainly Cox's Orange Pippins, Laxton Superb and Worcester Permain; pear trees mostly Conference Pears and William Pears. After my father died in 1953 I took over his job in charge of the packing shed, where flat-packed boxes from Bowaters were assembled, red for Class I TOR Brand apples or pears, blue for Class II, containing mostly 20 lb per box packed in two layers. There were also grey cardboard boxes for Class III domestic fruit, holding 40 lb each. As well as the packing shed behind the offices, there was a building which had housed a grain drying plant but was now in use as a cold store with six separate chambers, and another specially built cold store with eight chambers. For moving the fruit, loading and unloading the pallets holding up to 40 boxes, a Coventry Climax fork truck was used.

I was also involved in the spraying of fruit trees, working with Len Voller and Tom Jackson as one of four teams of three men. We used a KEF sprayer with three Noblox lance nozzles, connected by a long rubber pipe to a 450 gallon tank which was towed by a tractor. Trees were sprayed against aphids and apple and pear scab; tar oil winter wash was used in the winter. In the 1960s there were some 50,000 fruit trees in around 600 acres of orchards.

Following WW1, the ending of T & M Dixon's dairy business, and the gradual phasing out of much of the soft fruit and most of the poultry, livestock and arable farming in favour of the concentration on the production of apples and pears, turned out to be disastrous when the French in the late 1960s subsidised their apples which were sold in our shops more cheaply than we could produce them. In consequence, in 1970/71 contractors were engaged in destroying the orchards, grubbing out the fruit trees, the roots of which went into the disused Dusthouse Quarry. I was engaged around 1972/3 with others in the further clearing of the ground and the change to arable farming, ploughing, cultivating and seed drilling. The main crops grown were barley, wheat and linseed.

I retired in 1998, along with John Bird, when, on 2 May that year there was a dispersal sale of "Ashborough Arable" farm equipment including 3 tractors, a combine harvester, a caterpillar fork lift, and a Citroen van.

I met my wife Shirley through the Olympic Cycling Club. We were both members. She had worked part-time for Tardebigge Orchards on their fruit sales. We were married in December 1955. Our daughter Susan went to Tardebigge School.

I remember as a youngster, about the age of twelve, being invited by the Broad Green blacksmith, Harry Tustin, to pump the bellows when he had to make a lot of horse shoes. I would take some bread and cheese. He would hold a piece of red hot iron over the bread to toast it, then put cheese on it and hold the red hot iron over it again to produce cheese on toast which tasted super. Harry used to have an old iron saucepan. He boiled potatoes in it, which he mixed with poultry mash to feed his hens down Old Wharf Lane. When he wasn't looking, young George Banner (grandson of Len Banner whose family lived in Laundry Cottage nearby) and myself used to pinch a couple of the potatoes to eat.

During WW2 my father Edgar was in the Home Guard. On Broad Green there was an Anderson type air-raid shelter for use by local people. I remember acting as a casualty during a training exercise by the Red Cross at Broad Green and being taken by ambulance driven by the singer Mavis Bennett to Smallwood Hospital in Redditch.

NORMAN NEASOM

Further information about Birchensale Farm where Norman spent his childhood, is contained in chapter 10 of this book. He wrote this account in 1998:-

In 1858 my great grandfather, William Neasom, came over from Foreshaw Heath, Wythall way, where he had been farming, and took out a lease with the Dowager Countess of Plymouth for Birchensale and Lowans Hill farms, the latter being to the east of Brockhill Lane. William had one son, Thomas, who, with a partner named Percy White, formed the firm of Neasom and White, Estate Agents and Auctioneers, in Redditch. Thomas had six sons and two daughters. Arthur, the third son, my father, wished to be a farmer and joined grandpa William on the farm. Father married Ethel Palmer of Hadzor Court farm, Droitwich, and took a cottage in Brockhill Lane to be near both farms. My brother Thomas Arthur (always known as Paddy) and I were born at the Cottage, he in 1914, me in 1915. Great grandpa had died 12 months before my brother was born. Great Grandma still lived at Birchensale. When she died, aged 93, we then moved into the farmhouse, my brother and I were about 8 and 7 at this time.

In those days there were 18 men working on the two farms. There were cowsheds at both farms producing milk. Harold Crow and Alf Shakles collected the churns every morning in their milk floats. They would then deliver door to door by ladling from the open churn into the housewives' jugs. Nobody seemed to catch anything! Work on the farm was by horse and manpower, but I remember father buying an Austin tractor soon after the 1st World War, and another later which gave good service up until the 2nd World War.

Farming in those days was organic at no extra cost. It required physical activities such as hand hoeing, muck spreading, turning hay by hand with a fork, rick building at harvest time, stooking sheaves of corn cut and bound by the binder (we called it shukin), hedge brushing with a slash-hook and hedge laying with a bill-hook, to mention but a few. All now done from an air-conditioned cab while listening to Radio One!

Corn was stacked in the Dutch barn, hay ricked. The Dutch barn stood on the north side of the old barn at Birchensale. The corn would be thrashed out during the winter, when required, with the Humphries thrashing box. The old half-timbered barn is a listed building, as is the farmhouse. The oak timberwork in the barn is all Bordesley Abbey material, having been used previously. When the Windsor family of Hewell were given the manors and estates of the dissolved Bordesley Abbey by Henry VIII, they used the Abbey as a source of timber and stone to build their farms etc on their new estate, so I understand.

Norman Neasom. (Helen Bourne, daughter)

Between the wars father gave up the tenancy of Lowans Hill Farm. Birchensale was productive but with very heavy clay soil which made for hard work. When war came in 1939 it was hard work all day and civil defence duty at night. There was enormous air activity during the day (ours), and early in the war nightly visits by German aircraft on reconnaissance flights – they didn't drop anything and didn't get shot at. Later on, when the blitz started, the bombs did start to fall. We were on the flight path to Birmingham, and the City's heavy AA batteries used to fire at the approaching bombers. It was advisable to get behind something when the shrapnel shower began to fall. One night the farm had a very lucky escape when a German bomber dropped a full load of incendiary bombs all across the farm, the bomb racks landing up to the west wall of the rickyard, and the incendiaries began dropping just clear of the east side of the yard. The whole farm was bathed in white light and then came the explosions as many of the bombs had charges in their fin-ends to kill or disable fire-fighters.

Of the pools on the farm my favourite one was "Big Bakers". When we were young, we and all our friends would swim there and sail our model boats. The field Big Bakers ran along under Brockhill Wood. The Cowshed Close pit (east of the farm) had a great stock of little roach which we used to fish for. If we caught any we would take them home, clean and fry them; oh the bones! Father taught us to skate on this pool. There was a pit in the Fish Pool Meadow which ran down to Salters Lane on the east side of Birchensale garden and orchard. The pit was used as a council tip in my early days.

The Bottom Brook ran from Hewell Lake through the Osierbed Meadow, on through Batchley Meadow, past the town baths, alongside Windsor Road and on past the gas works down to the River Arrow below the Bordesley Abbey site to the mill pool at the Forge Needle Mill.

The Top Brook which ran down under Brockhill Wood round the Rickyard Hill at Birchensale was always understood to have been dug by the monks of Bordesley to supply the mill ponds which served the needle mills at the far end of Windsor Road by the railway behind the present High Duty Alloys factory opposite the gas works.

Other books
and publications

A Thousand Years in Tardebigge by Margaret Dickins, 1931, Cornish Brothers Ltd.

The Squire of Bentley (Mrs Cheape) by Maudie Ellis, 1926, William Blackwood & Sons Ltd.

Lock Keeper's Daughter by Pat Warner, 1986, Shepperton Swan Ltd, and Brewin Books.

Nine Nightingales by Pat Warner, 1997, Brewin Books.

A History of Webheath by Elizabeth Atkins, 2009, Hughes & Company.

A Worcestershire Dynasty, Dixons of Tardebigge by Alan White, 1997, Brewin Books.

Tardebigge School 1815 to 2000 by Alan White, 2000, Mike Richardson.

The Worcester and Birmingham Canal by Alan White, 2005, Brewin Books.

Life in the 1930s at Hewell Grange by Mike Johnson and Anne Bradford. (Recorded memories of Jeanette Frisby, Frank Colledge, Ethel Bennett, Ron Tongue, Sid Wall, Jack James, Rhona Cash).

Centenary 1870-1970 of St Philip the Apostle, Webheath, (booklet), 1970, Sharp Bros (Printers) Ltd.

A Short History of St Bartholomew's Church, Tardebigge by David Harris, (booklet), 1877, (several reprints).

The Windsors of Hewell by Margaret Mabey, (booklet), 1984, Lickey Hills Local History Society.

A Dozen Dreams by Catherine Drabble, 2005, Daily Mail, (about the family of Frank and Esther Green of Webheath).

The Tin House by Elizabeth Owen, 2008, Derwent Press, (Fictional, but based on the lives of her parents and their family in Webheath from the 1930s onwards).

Index

Not all names have been included